DATE DUE

DEMCO NO. 38-298

HENRY JAMES AND THE
PROBLEM OF ROBERT BROWNING

SOUTH ATLANTIC
MODERN LANGUAGE ASSOCIATION
AWARD STUDY

HENRY JAMES
AND THE
PROBLEM OF
ROBERT
BROWNING

ROSS POSNOCK

THE UNIVERSITY OF GEORGIA PRESS
ATHENS

© 1985 by the University of Georgia Press
Athens, Georgia 30602
All rights reserved

Designed by Sandra Strother Hudson
Set in Trump Medieval types
The paper in this book meets the guidelines for
permanence and durability of the Committee on
Production Guidelines for Book Longevity of the
Council on Library Resources.

Printed in the United States of America
88 87 86 85   5 4 3 2 1

Library of Congress Cataloging in Publication Data

Posnock, Ross.
Henry James and the problem of Robert Browning.

1. James, Henry, 1843–1916. 2. Browning, Robert,
1812–1889—Influence—James. 3. James, Henry, 1843–1916—
Friends and associates. 4. Browning, Robert, 1812–1889—
Friends and associates. 5. Authors, American—19th
century—Biography. I. Title.
PS2123.P58 1985   813'.4   84-2436
ISBN 0-8203-0729-7

In Memory of My Mother
and
To My Father

". . . if we were never bewildered there would never be
a story to tell about us. . . ."

The preface to *The Princess Casamassima*

✿ CONTENTS ✿

ACKNOWLEDGMENTS

 It is a pleasure to thank Avrom Fleishman, whose rigor and skepticism, encouragement and good humor, helped sustain this project from its earliest stages. He continues to provide an invaluable standard of excellence. I am grateful too for the helpful suggestions and support of William Cain and Michael Gilmore. William Veeder gave generously of his time to a scholar unknown to him, and I thank him again for his incisive reading of portions of the manuscript. Kimberly Sands and Sherry Laing were most patient and skillful typists. I owe special thanks to Robert Casillo. From first to last his energy and erudition were, and remain, inspiring. I am thankful for Debra Ratner's keen critical eye but, more important, for her friendship over many years.

I was extremely fortunate to study Henry James with the late Laurence B. Holland, and to him I owe my greatest debt. I join a number of others in saying that *The Expense of Vision* is the indispensable book on James and one of the few essential works on American literature. It is difficult to speak of an influence so pervasive, so I will simply record here my gratitude for his legacy and my fondness for his memory.

HENRY JAMES AND THE
PROBLEM OF ROBERT BROWNING

A WIDENING, NOT A NARROWING CIRCLE

 Robert Lowell, writing not long before his death in 1977, reflected on the "large poet of the nineteenth century who attracts and repels us": Robert Browning. "Who couldn't he use?" Lowell admiringly wonders. "Napoleon III, St. John, Cardinal Manning, Caliban? He set them in a thousand meters. . . . And yet Browning's idiosyncratic robustness scratches us . . . one wishes one could more often see him plain, or as he might have been rewritten by some master novelist."[1]

Almost exactly a century before, Henry James was making many of the same observations concerning his difficult, disturbing, fascinating contemporary. Lowell's attraction and repulsion, his uneasiness with the poet's "idiosyncratic robustness" and frustration at never seeing the poet "plain," and finally his interest in having Browning "rewritten" by a novelist are remarkable, if unintentional, echoes of many particulars of James's relation to Browning. Although Lowell's statement encapsulates some of the issues central to this study, his ambivalences concern Browning's poetry and are stated at the comfortable distance of a century. But James was disturbed by Browning on a profoundly personal level and in intimate proximity. Across the dinner table of

London parties James encountered the aggressively hearty poet, whose handshake, it was remarked, was like an electric shock.

James found Browning's obstreperousness not only "vulgar" but inexplicable: How could the author of such subtle verse behave like any other "sane, sound" London gentleman? Browning "is no more like to Paracelsus than I to Hercules," remarks James in a letter written shortly after his initial meeting with the poet sometime in early 1877.[2] Though Edmund Gosse, a friend of both writers, was content to describe Browning blandly as "the subtlest of poets . . . the simplest of men," James found in this fact a puzzling, at times tormenting, discontinuity between Browning's public and private selves which he was to analyze and dramatize in fiction and nonfiction. Even four years before his death in 1916 James is still absorbed by the poet, as he ponders the "perpetual anomaly" of Browning's poetry, which, in its fusion of the dramatic and lyric genres, mirrors the perplexing incongruities of his personality. Consistent in James's various responses to the poet over the course of thirty years is his sense of Browning's irreducible ambiguity: both his art and his identity remain impervious to James's efforts to "tame and chain" them.

The persistence of Browning as a "mystifying" "puzzle"— a problem resisting solution—is the very source of the poet's fascination for and influence over James. Through the years James attempts a number of solutions both fictional and nonfictional. While James's efforts meet with success, his dispelling of the poet's mystery is never permanent. James's most creative solution to the poet—the rewriting of his work—provides a remarkable means of coping with Browning but, again, is not definitive since he is compelled to rewrite no less than four times.

James's interest in Browning, while occasionally noted by his critics, is more often remarked by Browning scholars.

Indeed, one recent biographer, Maisie Ward, begins her second volume by declaring: "those most involved with Browning must stand out in any study of him—and perhaps still more those who themselves wrote about him. Among these Henry James comes first." I reverse Ward's perspective by focusing on what James's personal and literary response to Browning reveals about the novelist's mind and art. Since this is the first full examination of their connection, a brief summary of the facts of James's relation to Browning may be helpful.

The poet, a literary hero of James's youth, was an acquaintance from the late 1870s until his death in 1889. James summed up his esteem for Browning in 1888 by rating him "higher" than any other English writer of their time. From 1875 to 1912 James discussed Browning in letters and a book review and on four more significant occasions: in the short story "The Private Life" (1891), which portrays the "mystery" of two Brownings; in the biography of W. W. Story; in the memorial tribute upon Browning's interment in Westminster Abbey; and in the address honoring the poet's centenary in 1912. My belief that certain of the poet's texts influenced particular James works is based on the following facts: James's avowed urge to "re-handle" other authors' worthy "subjects" according to his own lights; his confessed desire, expressed in his late homage, to redo a major work (*The Ring and the Book*) whose author's entire corpus he was proud of knowing; the patently obvious parallels in plot between a late James novel and a Browning text; and, finally, the novelist's sympathetic praise of Browning's aesthetic of "intimacy" and "magnification."

In seeking to make sense of James's relation to Browning, I have pursued from this cluster of facts some plausible implications. I contend that Browning disturbed James on a deeply personal level and that the novelist explored his unease with

3

the poet in both "The Private Life" and "The Lesson of the Master," written three years before. While the earlier tale is also a rewriting of the poet's *The Inn Album*, it is not until the creation of the late masterpieces that James's rewriting becomes most significant. More than ten years after the tales have sufficiently relieved James's anxiety about Browning, he is free to use the poet without the need to struggle with the man. Browning's portrayal of intense passion and his depiction of the theatrical self in *In a Balcony* influences *The Wings of the Dove*, as does the compressed dramatic form, plot, and characterization of Browning's play. His complex interior monologue *Fifine at the Fair* anticipates the technique and form of *The Golden Bowl*; and the representation in *Fifine at the Fair* of a Victorian Don Juan's adulterous desires has an impact upon the depiction of adult sexuality in James's last complete novel. But the use of Browning in two of the late masterpieces was not James's final engagement with him. In 1912 James produced his most remarkable nonfictional work on the poet—"The Novel in *The Ring and the Book*"—which sketches his audacious project to rewrite Browning's masterpiece as a Jamesian novel. James's tribute confirms what the juxtaposition of *The Golden Bowl* and *Fifine at the Fair* makes clear: Browning's art of process, which creates a mimesis of mental activity, helps James inaugurate the modern novel of consciousness.

To claim to have uncovered a source of influence on a writer who more than once declared his "instinct everywhere for the indirect" requires a word of explanation concerning method. James's passion for indirection informs both his fiction and those nonfictional contexts when he discusses his and other writers' work. His tendency to conceal or minimize sources, even more pronounced than in most writers, is often apparent in prefaces, essays, and addresses. Thus one must be alive to the novelist's "supersubtle" nods of admission expressed in hints and clues. To construct an argument, one should "establish speculative and imaginative connections" (borrowing James's phrase concerning his desire to "cultivate belief" in immortality) precisely in response to the Jamesian injunction to be "richly responsible." This means to be one of "those . . . who 'get most' out of all that happens to them," as James describes his ideal reflectors in the preface to *The Princess Casamassima*. To "get most," James's art and aesthetics everywhere insist, requires imaginative engagement, be it with life in general or, more pertinently, with the master's "inexhaustible sensibility," as he was fond of calling his "poor blest old Genius."

We need to keep in mind Kenneth Graham's cautionary remark, the principle of which applies with more or less force to many writers: "There is never one satisfactory analogy for James's blend [of literary sources], especially in his late work, and it is as true and as false, as helpful and as misleading, to cite late Ibsen, or Maeterlinck, or Debussy . . . or Racine, as it is to cite George Eliot, Balzac, Turgenev."[3] Thus my focus on Browning is not meant to provide a unitary, comprehensive account of the novelist's development. My argument that Browning had a significant impact on James's life and work rests, finally, on the degree of psychological and literary coherence my interpretation of the evidence may possess. Such interpretation necessarily relies upon close reading of a variety of texts—short stories, novels, verse plays and a verse novel, an interior monologue, memoirs, essays, and addresses.

Browning's influence on James's art and life makes him a special figure in James's biography. Gustave Flaubert and George Eliot leave obviously important marks on James's art, but their influence is essentially literary. And while the lessons of Balzac and Hawthorne are both artistically and personally formative, their personal effect on the novelist is secondary to their literary influence because James lacked

5

actual acquaintance with them.[4] Since James's literary response to the poet is formed by Browning's personal impact upon him, their relationship must be discussed in both a literary and psychological context; this double focus makes my study markedly different from the tide of recent books comparing the novelist to other writers. Balzac, Henry Adams, Nietzsche, Conrad, Ibsen, Hawthorne, Turgenev, Chekhov, and Flaubert have all been paired with James. While the quality and critical sophistication of these works vary, the context of all these comparisons is essentially literary.[5] But the primary aim of this study is to enlarge our understanding of the relation of James's life to his art. In exploring his reaction to the writer whom Hardy called the "literary puzzle" of the nineteenth century, we witness the novelist acknowledging and confronting a psychological problem and finally discovering an artistic solution. James's rewriting of Browning makes explicit the intimate connection between the personal and literary aspects of his awareness of Browning, for in redoing the poet's work James seeks to mitigate his personal anxiety about the older writer and pays tribute to the suggestiveness of his poetic achievement.

My concern with the interplay between the literary and the biographical is reflected in my emphasis on theatricality; the masks, roles, and conventions that express the self in its experience of social reality engage James and Browning throughout their lives and art. Theatricality's prominence is inevitable when we recall that both men, as two of the most gregarious writers of their time, were adept, if vastly different, performers on the social stage. And the fabricating of social masks was not abandoned when they came to write, but itself became a subject of their art. James and Browning share a concern with how the self represents rather than simply presents itself to others, how it playfully cultivates roles that at once disguise and communicate. Indeed, their oeuvres provide two of the nineteenth century's most searching accounts of theatricality and the intimately related impulse to aestheticize reality by reducing one's self and others to objects.

Of "social performances" James notes that "we are condemned . . . whether we will or not, to abandon and outlive, to forget and disown and hand over to desolation" most of them, as they fade into the "general mixture" of life.[6] But if social performances elude sharp scrutiny in life, in the texts of Browning and James theatrical behavior is often revealed as morally ambiguous. This ambiguity darkens in characters who are preoccupied with manipulating a social mask and imprisoning others in forms. At an extreme is the malevolent aestheticism of the Duke of Ferrara and Gilbert Osmond, who wear masks of icy connoisseurship to conceal the brutal subjugation of their wives.[7]

Both authors inherit the modern sense of theatricality, which consists of an "increased self-consciousness about the fashioning of human identity as a manipulable, artful process." Stephen Greenblatt has provided a vivid sense of the scope of theatricality: "self-fashioning . . . is linked to manners or demeanor . . . it may suggest hypocrisy or deception, an adherence to mere outward ceremony; it suggests representation of one's nature or intention in speech or actions. And with representation we return to literature, or rather we may grasp that self-fashioning derives its interest precisely from the fact that it functions without regard for a sharp distinction between literature and social life. It invariably crosses the boundaries between the creation of literary characters, the shaping of one's own identity, the experience of being molded by forces outside one's control, the attempt to fashion other selves."[8] Greenblatt's view of theatricality is deeply relevant to the present study's examination of how literature and social life interact. One reason is his stress on representation, which is a pivotal word for James, who declares in the first paragraph of his first preface that "the art

7

of representation" "bristles with questions the very terms of which are difficult to apply and appreciate."

Representation bristles, spreading in a "widening, not in a narrowing circle," because it is unstable, belonging to both artistic and social experience and implying their continuity. Throughout his fiction James dramatizes his sense of the artfulness of human behavior, a belief rarely expressed more succinctly than in his often-employed metaphor "the canvas of life." James's notion of life as an artifact counts as one of the "earliest aesthetic seeds" planted in his fertile consciousness, as is evident in *A Small Boy and Others*, where he narrates his evolving understanding of the relations of art and life. What focuses the matter for James, making it concrete and urgent, is his love of the theater. "I was with precocious passion 'at home' among the theatres"; "a sacred thrill" and "unbearable intensity" accompany his "very first sitting at a play,"[9] and his early efforts at writing are in "dramatic form" rather than narrative prose or verse, as if to recapture something of his excitement at playgoing. But James's enthusiasm for the often "infirm and inadequate theatre" wavers and at points in his life even fades before a more compelling phenomenon: "the fact that life in general, all round us, was perceptibly more theatrical."[10]

In his memoirs James recalls the precise moment when life's theatricality was impressed on him. A young cousin had been admonished for "making a scene," an expression unknown to the eleven-year-old James. "Epoch-making" was this idiom, for "it told me so much about life," principally that "we could make" scenes or not make them, "as we chose."[11] The element of choice is, for James, "the immense illumination" because choice suggests will and calculation, attributes that enable one in everyday life to impose dramatic form upon "mere actuality." The revelation that life is routinely subject to scenic arrangements, that man is a quasi artist in his manipulation of form and con-

8

vention, strikes James as momentous. "The mark had been made, the door flung open," revealing "a rich accession of possibilities": the usual relation of art to life had been permanently altered in his mind.

Browning too reorders the relation, collapsing the polarities of life and art, as one sees in the calculated self-dramatizations of the speakers of his dramatic monologues, who adroitly invent themselves. The poet summarizes his keen awareness of the interpenetration of art and life in a line from *Fifine at the Fair:* "The histrionic truth is in the natural lie."[12] This gnomically compressed set of oxymorons implies the equivalence, the interchangeability, of words conventionally opposed to each other. A chief burden of both men's art is to interrogate radically our received notions of the truth, the lie, the histrionic, and, especially, the natural. The interplay of these elements dissolves the dichotomies that organize and simplify human experience, and this challenge to conventional assumptions and expectations is central to their writing.

In conceiving the self as theatrical James and Browning subvert customary views of identity as unitary or fixed. Both writers tacitly oppose what bourgeois individualism deems "natural"—the self as an entity, a "substantial, Cartesian-like rock of stability."[13] But in resisting a unified stability, the theatrical self should not be mistaken for the deconstructed self made prominent in recent critical theory. In what has been called the deconstruction of the subject, the self is displaced as center or source of meaning and comes to appear as a locus of relations generated by cultural conventions beyond its control. The theatrical self insists on a freedom, always limited and precarious, to renovate the forms it depends on. Fredric Jameson has observed that "nowhere do the continental and the Anglo-American critical traditions diverge more dramatically than on this whole issue of the subject, or the ego, or the self, and the value and reality to be

9

accorded to it."[14] Although this critical debate cannot directly concern us here, Jameson's claim that "the rhetoric of the self . . . will no longer do" is useful precisely because a centered self could no longer do for Browning and James. The prevalence of roles and masks in their portrayal of the self marks a rejection of the Romantic (and Emersonian) cult of sincerity and its correlative notion of the self as absolute, existing in autonomous isolation.[15]

James and Browning both place in question the Romantic self's potential for unconditional subjectivity and freedom, for the theatrical self is at once creative and constrained, free to appropriate actuality and imaginatively transform it into a scene, free to fashion the self artfully, yet reliant on the impersonal codes of social form and the conventions of representation. In short, the theatrical self, at its most expressive and powerful, is neither centered nor deconstructed but is ceaselessly dialectical in that it belongs both to the world of subjects and the world of objects.

James's premise on which he bases his portrayal of the self as relational, ineluctably involved with others, is his definition of experience as "our apprehension and our measure of what happens to us as social creatures."[16] James explicitly dramatizes the question of "what shall we call our 'self' " in the famous debate between Madame Merle and Isabel Archer. His suspicion of fixity and autonomy extends to a skepticism of the possibility of experience liberated from "the whole envelope of circumstances" that Madame Merle insists on. But while James would likely concur with Madame Merle's declaration that "there's no such thing as an isolated man or woman," he honors the ideal of the unrelated self by devoting a novel to a young woman's attempt to "affront her destiny" as a social being.[17]

James's conviction that man is rooted in social reality and his concern with representation in art and life both derive in part from the particular circumstances of his life as a young man. While it may indicate his sociability, the fact that James dined out over two hundred times in one year also has significance for his fiction. As R. P. Blackmur points out, James spent so much time in the social arena that he was forced to master "the means which, because of his life . . . were almost alone at his disposal." Thus his fiction recognizes that "the artifices that in actual society do most to prevent communication and obscure situations" can be used "to promote intimacy and to clarify situations."[18]

That the theater of social life renders artifice and identity inextricable is a truth that few of James's characters know more deeply than Hyacinth Robinson in *The Princess Casamassima*. Early in the novel when the vulgar but intuitive Millicent remarks that he would "look very nice in a fancy costume" and that he deserves a "place" in the theater, Hyacinth is at first dismissive. But he checks himself with the reflection that he "was to go through life in a mask, in a borrowed mantle; he was to be every day and every hour an actor." Perhaps Hyacinth's consciousness of occupying, from birth, a "place" at the theater is one reason he is drawn to the poet of role playing. When he is alone with that other self-consciously theatrical self, the Princess, who describes her latest "pose" as one of "only trying to be natural," Hyacinth takes *Men and Women* "from his pocket" and reads aloud from Browning.

James's man and woman read *Men and Women* because they share the dramatic monologues' preoccupation: the process of representing a self responsive to the pressure of social reality. The implied auditor in most of the monologues provides, in effect, a social context, a public stage, on which the monologist performs his improvisational act of self-portrayal. The poet's adoption of various masks in his monologues defines his fictive role playing, which finds a counterpart in his own performance of the Victorian sage before an adoring public.

By the late 1880s James had ample opportunity to witness the great man in his public role, since Browning spent the last few years of his life living next door to James in DeVere Gardens, London. They had never become friends: they had always been the pleasantest of dinner companions, reports Leon Edel in his summing up of their relation. Although his bland synopsis, which has served as the standard summary of their personal connection, ignores James's often-confessed sense of unease with Browning's public performance, Edel's appraisal is mainly just, given the fact that an absence of intimacy, a carefully maintained distance, marked their relations. But when one tries to find out *why* these neighbors never became friends, one finds beneath the cordial surface of their acquaintance surprising "complications and consequences."[19]

CHAPTER I

HENRY JAMES
AND THE PROBLEM OF
ROBERT BROWNING

 Browning consistently troubles James, not simply on account of his baffling behavior in society, but because the poet defies the novelist's cherished belief that the cost of creating great art is so "ruinously expensive" that it requires asceticism of the artist. Browning's marriage to a poet embodies a harmonious balance of the literary and the sexual that sharply challenges James's dictum, exposing it as a self-serving excuse for avoiding physical relations. James's response to Browning's assault, as chapter 3 will show, is to seek "revenge" against the poet by rewriting him. James's personal conviction that artistic and sexual fulfillment are mutually exclusive is one reason for his fiction's persistent, even notorious, interest in the tension between vision and action, which often is manifested in the seeming impossibility of a "man of imagination" (as James describes Strether) enjoying physical intimacy with another. Although Browning's refusal of this opposition impels James to cling all the more strongly to his belief in the dichotomy of art and sexuality, the critic must explore their interplay, for James struggles to resolve in his fiction his vexed personal re-

sponse to Browning. This struggle begins with "The Lesson of the Master" and "The Private Life," where James dramatizes his sexual renunciation, a choice prompted, in part, by the disturbing poet.

In both tales James portrays Browning as a manipulative older writer who sexually humiliates his younger admirer. And James not only dramatizes the tension between master and disciple but is fascinated by Browning's depiction of the theme. In *The Ring and the Book* the clash between Guido the masterful sexual manipulator and Caponsacchi the celibate priest is compelling to James because it nearly repeats the conflict central to his tales about Browning and to the poet's earlier *The Inn Album:* the confrontation between an older man, elaborately masked and devious, who victimizes his youthful, naive disciple. This configuration continually recurs in James's reaction to Browning because it reflects his psychological anxiety about the poet.

If on a conscious level James manifests anxiety in his repeated puzzlement with Browning's social performance, James's fictional encounters with him reveal that his unease about the poet's social roles is symptomatic of a profounder anxiety, derived from his sense of Browning as a threat to his sexual identity. I will now examine James's psychological problem with Browning and the novelist's transformation of this source of anxiety into a rich vein of literary influence.

In joining anxiety and influence I allude of course to the work of Harold Bloom. Although I claim that James was both anxious about and influenced by Browning, my study diverges significantly on several counts from Bloom's belief that an "anxiety of influence" governs the relations of disciples to their literary masters. Bloom argues that the precursor stands as a powerful "blocking agent" or threat to the ephebe's insistence on imaginative priority; thus the young poet is compelled to defend himself by creating the illusion of priority. The ephebe's poem is less a triumph over or denial of the precursor than a creative misreading of the ancestor's poem: "every poem is a misinterpretation of a parent poem . . . [It is not] an overcoming of an anxiety, but is that anxiety."[1] My analysis of James's various attempts to minimize or conceal Browning's influence confirms Bloom's belief that in his intense struggle for creative priority the young writer relies on cunning, even devious strategies. Indeed, there are few more vivid instances of "perverse, willful revisionism" (which constitutes for Bloom "the history of fruitful poetic influence") than James's essay "The Novel in *The Ring and the Book.*" James's subtle, often deceptive and sometimes violent rhetorical encounters with Browning strikingly support Bloom's sense of the brutality of literary inheritance.

Illuminating though Bloom is, his usefulness is limited by a self-imposed stricture: "my concern is only with *the poet in a poet,*" he declares, although he concedes that even "the strongest poets are subject to influences not poetical."[2] My concern, however, is twofold: to examine both the nonpoetical influence between two writers and the impact of the nonpoetical on the formation of their literary relationship. Although James is anxious about Browning, his anxiety, unlike that experienced by Bloom's ephebe, is primarily personal and sexual. Only by rewriting Browning is James's anxiety assuaged. Thus influence becomes James's solution to his anxiety. Rather than suffering an anxiety of influence, he uses Browning's poetry and aesthetics to enrich his art. Because James's relation to Browning can only be fully revealed by tracing the entanglements of art and life, Bloom's textual model cannot explain their relationship. As Jerome McGann says, Bloom's theory "represents the poet as a citizen of a purely literary world."[3]

While I wish to avoid Bloom's compartmentalizing, his Oedipal framework is suggestive for "the father-son struggle that a man inevitably has with his own literary progenitors when he attempts to become an author" describes part of James's conflict with Browning.[4] But this Oedipal paradigm must be enlarged to include James's simultaneous effort to affirm and defend his sexual identity. Because both efforts are enacted in "The Lesson of the Master," this story is the most dramatic and compressed instance of Browning's unique force on James. Here James not only rewrites Browning's "rough notes for a poem," as the novelist described *The Inn Album*, but, under the pressure of Browning's sexual challenge, constructs a myth of celibacy to legitimize his sexual choice. I might sum up the older writer's status by borrowing a concept of Bloom's: in James's imagination Browning served as a necessary blocking agent whose threatening example helped provoke James to define himself as man and author.

Despite his strictly literary account of the relations between authors, Bloom's conviction that authentic origination is impossible is most acute and relevant. Bloom insists that even the "fresh start" that is a strong poem is actually a "starting-again." To illustrate his point that "poetry always lives under the shadow of poetry," Bloom speaks of a caveman who, in tracing "the outline of an animal upon a rock always retraced a precursor's outline."[5] Poetry's essential belatedness is, of course, the moral of the fable; retracing is the primal condition of art. Faced with such a dilemma, the ephebe's "seeking of an identity as an artist" involves "extraordinary . . . risk," "a risk that has obsessed Bloom as a form of anxiety," as Wesley Morris observes.[6] Morris, echoing Bloom, locates the source of this anxiety in the ambiguity or ambivalence of artistic creation, which is at once "mimetic (to write in the literary styles of others)" and "revolutionary (to articulate one's style)."[7]

Bloom clarifies the ambiguous nature of the ephebe's coming to poetic birth by invoking the concept of the double bind, which was invented by Gregory Bateson in his discussion of the etiology of schizophrenia. " 'Be me but not me' is the paradox of the precursor's implicit charge to the ephebe. Less intensely, his poem says to its descendant poem: 'Be like me but unlike me.' If there were no ways of subverting this double bind every ephebe would develop into a poetic version of a schizophrenic."[8] Although Bloom's use of the double bind is limited, once we liberate it from his strictly literary and Bateson's pathological contexts it will prove to be valuable in illuminating James's father-son struggle with the poet.

René Girard's conviction that the double bind structures human relationships and desires provides an escape from the impasse of intertextuality. A Girardian perspective emphasizes the interplay of psychological and literary motives in James's relation to his precursor. To move from a limited paradigm to a broader one we have only to translate Bloom's caveman fable into terms of the Girardian model. The fable can be read to mean that "the role of disciple" defines "the basic human condition." This Girardian version sets aside the myth of belatedness in favor of exploring man's status as disciple. Girard explores the caveman's motivation: What creates the disciple's desire to retrace?

The central premise of Girard's *Violence and the Sacred* is that man's inescapable position as disciple determines his desires. As readers of his *Deceit, Desire, and the Novel* are aware, Girard believes that man's desires are neither spontaneous nor his own because "desire itself is essentially mimetic, directed toward an object desired by the model." If poetry, for Bloom, "always lives under the shadow of poetry," for Girard, man's desires are created in the shadow of an Other—a third presence (in addition to subject and object) who serves as a model for the subject's desires. This third figure is an eventual rival—"some other person" who seems to possess the "being" the disciple himself lacks. The subject "thus looks to that other person to inform him of what he should desire in order to acquire that being."[9]

Girard sees mimetic desire as consisting of three elements: "identification, choice of object, rivalry" (p. 180). Identification, the "disciple's desire to *be* the model," is enacted by means of "appropriation; that is, by taking over the things that belong" to the model. Inevitably, this choice by model and disciple of the same object produces conflict—a rivalry which "transforms desire into violence" (p. 146). Because the disciple's model is also his rival and obstacle, Girard concludes that mimetic desire is a "source of continual conflict" in which the disciple is caught in a double bind. The model, who seems to say, " 'Imitate me,' immediately confronts the disciple with an inexplicable counterorder: 'Don't imitate me!' (which really means, 'Do not appropriate *my* object'). Man and his desires thus perpetually transmit contradictory signals to each other" (p. 147). The double bind, "far from being restricted to a limited number of pathological cases, . . . is so common that it might be said to form the basis of all human relationships."[10]

Girard has employed his concept of the double bind of mimetic desire in analyzing the relationships of pairs of writers, including Rimbaud and Verlaine, Holderlin and Schiller, and in particular Nietzsche and Wagner. Girard's "Strategies of Madness: Nietzsche, Wagner, Dostoevsky" examines the philosopher's obsession with the composer "in the light of the mimetic conception of desire" outlined in Girard's earlier works and is of considerable interest not only for its view of literary rivalry but because of its methodology. In elucidating Nietzsche's relation to Wagner, Girard moves easily from the life to the work to reveal in both the shaping pressure of mimetic desire. Indeed, one of his major assertions is that the "advanced case of the mimetic disease" from which Nietzsche suffered in life finds "intellectual justification" in one of his central philosophical concepts—"the will to power," which Girard redefines as the "ideology of mimetic desire."[11] Girard insists that to understand fully Nietzsche's most famous doctrine his "relationship to the will to power cannot be separated from his relationship to Wagner."[12] Unlike Bloom, Girard refuses to separate an author's life and work, believing that only by examining the ways in which they interpenetrate can relations between authors become meaningful. This implied methodological premise is expressed more directly in Girard's important summary statement: "It is misleading to define such themes as 'Dionysus' or 'the will to power' exclusively as we find them in their final state of metaphysical quintessence and frenzied abstraction. The final state is the result of a process which must be viewed in its entirety and which begins in a very different key."[13] In other words, to view such themes in their "entirety," as a process, is to see them as a result of a dialectic of imitation and rivalry.

Many of the central aspects of James's relation to Browning—his theory of the "two Brownings," the allegedly supernatural elements of "The Private Life," James's urge to "appropriate" *The Ring and the Book*—should be seen as the "result of a process which must be viewed in its entirety." Specifically, this process is the struggle of disciple and master, which is based on the double bind of mimetic desire. And the ultimate value of this perspective is its ability to go "to the heart of individual motivation in the cultural field, studiously avoided or camouflaged" by others. Girard's concept, then, permits the uncovering of the inner structure of James's problem with Browning, who presents a double bind to the novelist. That such a relation between the two men is highly likely becomes apparent when one examines the circumstances surrounding James's discovery of the poet in the summer of 1859.

James's initial exposure to Browning at the age of sixteen is more than simply another step in his literary education. As he would vividly recall years later, his discovery of Browning was one of the "sudden milestones" "on the road of so much inward . . . life."[14] One of the crucial reasons for

Browning's prestige in the development of James's inner life is indirectly revealed in *Notes of a Son and Brother*, where the dazzling presence of John La Farge suffuses the novelist's memories of the Newport summer of 1859 when La Farge introduced his younger friend to Browning's work. James's early awareness of Browning is inseparable from his veneration for La Farge, who emerged in that momentous summer as a commanding figure, one of the most influential people of James's early manhood. Although only seven years James's senior, La Farge nevertheless became "the original inspirer, the first to prod Henry to a constructive writing effort," as Edel describes the man who served as a "much needed . . . guide—the first to take James seriously as a potential writer."[15] In offering James the encouragement his family had failed to provide, La Farge showed him not only Browning but another writer destined to be of signal importance: Balzac.

But La Farge's literary sophistication accounts for only part of his stature in James's eyes; the greatest source of his "authority," James writes, is that he is a "man of the world," a "bright apparition" of cosmopolitan charm and experience. To the enthralled James, La Farge is the "embodiment of the gospel of esthetics" not only in his "wealth of cultivation" but in his role of "dandy and cavalier" (p. 290). Whether astride a "chestnut mare" or attired in an elegant "velvet jacket," La Farge's glamorous appearance and brilliant conversation made him a "figure of figures," who seemed, recalls James, to have been surrounded with the "fairly golden glow of romance" (p. 281). James was awed by this "rare original"; "a mere helpless admirer and inhaler . . . enslaved, yearningly gullible" are self-characterizations that, in their excessive humility, betray a certain envy of his idol. In his autobiography James is careful to insist that La Farge did not demand worship, and, in fact, his "personal kindness" helped to draw James out and "charmed" him "often into a degree of participation" (p. 292). "Degree" here indicates that complete "participation" did not occur, most likely because La Farge was a painter, and James soon found he had small aptitude for this art form. Thus James maintains a distance from his mentor and avoids competition. In his retrospective portrait of La Farge, James returns repeatedly to his sense of distance between the two young men.

In his emphasis on La Farge's "foreignness," which seemed great at the time "but had gained a sharper accent from a long stay made in France," James signals his recognition of the fundamental otherness of his senior, the element of the unapproachable possessed by all masters. La Farge strikes James as "personally so finished and launched," qualities which differentiate him from the obviously unfinished and unlaunched younger man who is most impressed by La Farge's remarkable "serenity." This quality of La Farge's permits him utter absorption in artistic creation, James notes; and his mentor's "imperturbable" air is also responsible for his aloofness, which James observes when he speaks of La Farge as "intensely among us but somehow not withal of us" (p. 291). We find a deeper source of La Farge's aloofness in James's definition of his "initiator's" "nature" as "essentially entire, a settled sovereign self" (p. 295). The painter seems to possess the integrated being that young James lacks. Therefore it is not surprising that James looks to La Farge "to inform him of what he should desire in order to acquire that being," as Girard has described the initial stages of mimetic desire. Girard's explanation of how the object of the disciple's desire originates with the model illuminates La Farge's pivotal role in James's discovery of Browning. "If the model, who is apparently already endowed with superior being, desires some object, that object must surely be capable of conferring an even greater plenitude of being. It is not through words, therefore, but by the example of his

own desire that the model conveys to the subject the supreme desirability of the object" (p. 146).

Such an object emerges from James's recollection of La
Farge. With the remarkable precision which attests to the
object's still potent hold, James recalls that *Men and
Women* was a book so loved by the painter that he devoted a
series of drawings to celebrating its poetic characters. But
there is another element in James's remembrance of the
volume that contributes to the book's special status. When
La Farge placed *Men and Women* in James's hands he over-
ruled the authority of James's parents, who had deemed the
book off limits to their son.

Browning's book was thought unsuitable for the young
James because of its intimate portrayal of passionate men and
women; thus James's initiation into the adult world of
Browning's poems transgresses parental authority. This association remains vivid in James's mind, as he praises his initiator La Farge at the expense of his parents. Unlike La Farge, his
parents "had not divined in us an aptitude for that author,"
James recalls more than half a century later (p. 291). Edel
remarks that James's "reproach does not appear to have been
entirely justified. There was nothing to prevent Henry James
from reading Browning and indeed once the father discovered
that his son liked the poet he gave him at least one of his
works."[16] The unreasonableness of the slight makes even
clearer James's sense that an aura of the forbidden infuses
Men and Women with the symbolic power of a sacred object.
Indeed, Browning quickly became a "God" in James's eyes, as
Thomas Sergeant Perry described the poet's stature that
Newport summer.[17] Browning's rapid ascent to this lofty
position is not solely the result of his subject matter. Even
more crucial is the imprimatur of the other Newport god, La
Farge, whose revelation of Browning exemplified for James
his mentor's power to make "the future flush and swarm"
with "prospects and possibilities" (p. 287).

The link implied here between Browning and La Farge, while never noted in print by James, is so unmistakable as to make them near mirror images of each other. In James's "enslaved" eyes the men share a common duality: they are artists *and* "men of the world." (Indeed, Browning's fame as the lover of the renowned Elizabeth Barrett exceeded, at that time, his poetic reputation.) Both men embody, in their easy balance of artistic and masculine authority, a "nature essentially entire." This double authority, which constitutes the "sovereign" self possessed by each of his Newport gods, is inaccessible to the awkward and withdrawn James, who significantly admits that La Farge was "not at all a direct model for simpler folk, as we could but then feel ourselves" (p. 290). Although the "simpler" James, in seizing his model's cherished object, hopes to acquire "a greater plenitude of being" (Girard's phrase) when he adopts Browning as a god, he discovers that the poet, like the painter, is at once an encouraging and discouraging model. James's words used to describe La Farge also apply to the poet: Browning is "among us but somehow not . . . of us," "not at all a direct model" though an indirect one. James's relation to both men is characterized by an unresolved ambiguity, which he evidently tolerates in La Farge since he enjoys a lifelong friendship with him.

But with Browning a problem develops: the ambiguity comes to preoccupy James. Because Browning is the first contemporary male British writer whom James comes to revere, the novelist feels both a more intimate identification with the poet than with the painter and a greater competitiveness. In his exposure to his fellow author Browning, James cannot maintain the distance he preserves with La Farge. The ambiguity of his response to Browning deepens into a double bind, and this structure, present but latent in his relation to La Farge, comes to define James's response to Browning. James perceives the poet, in his double mastery, as transmitting a "contradictory double imperative": "Imitate me" (as a literary model); "don't imitate me" (as a sexual model).

Unlike Nietzsche, who, according to Girard, succumbs to "an advanced case of the mimetic disease," James manages to cope with the double bind. The philosopher's ambivalence to Wagner "gives way to the nightmarish 'identity crisis' and 'megalomania' characteristic of the last stages" of the double bind, whereas James achieves what Holderlin in his relationship to Schiller desperately sought: a "state of moderate equilibrium" (p. 156). James's unconscious adjustment is remarkably akin to Girard's explanation of how an individual resolves the "contradictory double imperative": "the individual who 'adjusts' has managed to relegate the two contradictory injunctions of the double bind—to imitate and not to imitate—to two different domains of application. That is, he divides reality in such a way as to neutralize the double bind" (p. 177).

By neutralizing the contradictory injunctions implicit in his initial sense of Browning as both a model and not a model, James accomplishes a psychological resolution. Instead of passively receiving Browning's "contradictory signals" James resolves: I will imitate Browning the artist; I will not (or cannot) imitate Browning the man. Thus the psychological process of adjustment which Girard outlines is also the basis of James's *conscious* solution to the "mystery" of his "mystifying" contemporary. His theory of two Brownings is a variation upon his unconscious division of Browning into "two different domains."[18]

Although I have been stressing James's adjustment to the double bind, I must be equally emphatic that this adjustment represents "the result of a process," a "final state," that must be seen in its "entirety," to repeat Girard. Only in this light is James's resolution accurately perceived as a continually precarious, protracted, and psychologically painful struggle. In his intermittent but always telling encounters with Browning over the course of thirty years, James coped with but was not immune to the poet's power to disturb and mystify.

James, in his profound self-honesty, knew that his resolution to the double bind was tentative, to be tested anew with each confrontation; and this realization won for him a certain mastery over Browning. James's self-knowledge also gave him the authority to ridicule his own mastery and thereby confirm it, as he does in "The Private Life." Like anything of value in his fictional world, mastery is gained at considerable cost, paid by James in his acknowledgment that the poet's vigorous sexuality and literary brilliance arouse in him fear, envy, and a sense of failure. James confronts and exorcises these emotions in "The Private Life" and "The Lesson of the Master," thus enabling himself to use the lessons of Browning's art in his late fiction.

The two stories and the 1912 homage, in which he discloses his impulse to use Browning, constitute the major sites of the novelist's struggle with the poet and should be viewed as a unity, a complex of works that at times seems distorted by an excess of emotion and conflict hardly accounted for by their manifest content. We can give coherence to James's effort to cope with Browning in these works by reading them as the narration of his process of adjustment to the double bind—his division of Browning into "two different domains." The tales declare the negative assertion (I cannot imitate Browning the man), while the homage states the positive claim (I have imitated Browning the artist). James enacts his resolve to imitate Browning the artist only after discovering he cannot imitate Browning the man. This latter realization is dramatized in both short stories, as the James surrogate comes to the painful recognition of his difference from the Browning figure. But in 1912 the internationally acclaimed master of the novel successfully imitates the poet by reworking *The Ring and the Book*, as disciple and model come to mirror one another. James's brazenly public "appropriation" (both James's and Girard's word) of his model's object culminates his artistic identification with Browning. In 1912 James commemorates his use of the poet, for by that late date he had reaped the benefits of his "appropriation," which had begun nearly twenty-five years earlier with his rewriting of *The Inn Album* as "The Lesson of the Master."

Having speculated on the inner structure of James's relation to Browning, I will briefly show how his psychological sense of Browning as the embodiment of a double bind is expressed in his public response to the poet. At the start of his 1912 address James distills into a single word his perception of Browning as contradictory, ambiguous, and double: "I cling to the dear old tradition that Browning is 'difficult.' "[19] The serpentine complexity of the homage affords little direct explanation of the poet's difficulty; James's adjective remains as frustratingly opaque as Browning. But illumination comes from another source—an 1888 letter from James to Daniel Curtis, a mutual friend of the two authors. Unlike James, Curtis had evidently caught a glimmer of Browning's literary self. The novelist admits his inability to accept the fact that his chattering dinner companion was also "the author of *Men and Women*." "I am glad he has given you some glimpse of his diviner part—I have never seized the link between the two—it is a solution of continuity."[20] This response frames James's fundamental reaction to Browning: the poet is "difficult" because he embodies a discontinuity which the novelist finds impossible to bridge. But James's failure to "seize" the "solution" to the poet's identity results not from deficient insight but from a kind of negative perception which reveals that the absence of the "link" of "continuity" fragments Browning's self. In other words, James records here less a lack of perception than the

26

perception of a lack. This recognition is precisely what James dramatizes at the climax of "The Private Life," where his fictional surrogate, after perceiving the figure of Browning as, somehow, simultaneously present and absent, experiences a moment of uncanny disorientation. Although in the 1888 letter James fails to register these emotions, the cognitive difficulties he reveals here are the roots of his sense of Browning as an uncanny and disturbing figure.

The gap in James's understanding mirrors the gap in Browning's identity, which Hillis Miller has defined as "the failure to have any one definite self." Such an unstable self, relying on the mobility of role playing to defer a fully present and continuous identity, is most accurately described as theatrical. Thus, upon close examination, James's 1888 remarks suggest two of the major constituents of his image of Browning: the poet's puzzlingly discontinuous identity which, in James's fiction, will result in an uncanny moment, and the social manifestation of this discontinuity— Browning's theatricality.[21]

The double bind, the "difficult," the uncanny, the discontinuous, the theatrical—these five types of ambiguity overlap and converge in James's apprehension of his contemporary. This cluster of terms charts a movement from private to public, from the unconscious anxiety generated by Browning's contradictory double imperative to bafflement at the poet's social mask.[22] Linking the passage from private to public is the middle term—the uncanny. The next chapter will demonstrate the centrality of the uncanny now that I have (to borrow James's words about the poet) dug "to the primary soil, from which so many disparities and contradictions spring."[23]

27

CHAPTER II

THE SHARP RUPTURE
OF AN IDENTITY

"His imagination ... had faced every contingency but that Chad should not *be* Chad, and this was what it now had to face with a mere strained smile and an uncomfortable flush." Strether's "emotion of bewilderment" upon his initial confrontation with Chad's "sharp rupture of an identity" recalls James's response to the riddle of Browning in society. That Browning should not *be* Browning, that he is a "great chatterer but no" genius at all, preoccupies James when he records his first impressions of the poet in early 1877. "Robert B. I am sorry to say does not make on me a purely agreeable impression ... strange to say, his talk doesn't strike me as very good. It is altogether gossip and personality and is not very beautifully worded."[1] Although no one was more fascinated or devoted more thought to the oddity of Browning's public performance than James, the novelist was not alone in reacting "with a mere strained smile and an uncomfortable flush" to this formidable social lion of London society in the late 1860s and 1870s.

Reports of Browning's "boisterous cordiality," his sparkling eyes and booming voice, and his "dazzling white waistcoat" and "constant flow of anecdotes and social allusions" testify to the nearly overbearing impression he made on his dinner companions.[2] Indeed, to a few observers the poet's garrulous exuberance broke the bounds of propriety. Mary Gladstone complained that "he talks everybody down with his dreadful voice, and always places his person in such disagreeable proximity with yours and puffs and blows and spits in your face." Browning seemed such a permanent fixture at the leading London soirees that Hallam Tennyson remarked that he "would never be surprised if Mr. Browning expired in a white choker at a dinner party."[3]

The poet liked to explain his vigorous socializing as his way of combating the loneliness and morbidity of middle-aged widowerhood. Elizabeth had died in 1861, leaving Browning to return alone from Florence to London with their son Pen to rear. Edmund Gosse reports that because "after he had put his boy to bed, the solitude weighed intolerably upon him," Browning resolved to "accept for the future every suitable invitation which came to him. . . . In the process of time he grew to be one of the most familiar figures of the age at every dining table, concert hall, exhibition, and place of refined entertainment in London."[4] Gosse's account fails to note the fact that when Elizabeth was alive Browning was often out till four in the morning, having left his invalid wife to retire alone at eight in the evening. The next day Browning would regale her with stories of the glittering personages he had encountered the past evening. Elizabeth shrewdly understood that her husband not only enjoyed but needed social activity as an outlet for what she called Browning's "superfluity of vital energy."[5] She once confessed that she "was only too happy to have him a little amused."

Elizabeth's serenity about her husband's seemingly insatiable appetite for the gossip and small talk of dinner parties was not shared by other admirers of the poet. They were puzzled by Browning's behavior, viewing it as incongruous in an artist. After meeting Browning in society, Julian

Hawthorne wrote: "the barbered beard, the silk hat . . . staid, grave, urbane, polished; he was a rich banker, he was a perfected butler, no one would have suspected him of poetry."[6] W. H. Mallock, after an evening in the poet's company, remarked that Browning "did not, as far as I remember, make an approach to the subject of literature at all."[7] Instead, reports Mallock, Browning reduced him "to something like complete silence" by a barrage of talk "which, although not deficient in point, had more in it of jocularity than wit."[8]

James's disappointment that the literary hero of his boyhood was not as brilliant in his conversation as in his poetry did not extend to a dismay at Browning's taste for social intercourse, as James himself was hardly a recluse. What James objected to was the *style* of his performance. To the young novelist, thirty-one years Browning's junior, the older writer appeared to be a garrulous mediocrity, indistinguishable from many another "sane sound man of the London world" (James's phrase). James was distressed by Browning's apparent abdication of the social role of artist. For James was acutely aware that, as Erving Goffman has written, "a status, a position, a social place . . . is a pattern of appropriate conduct, coherent, embellished, and well articulated. Performed with ease or clumsiness, awareness or not, guile or good faith, it is nonetheless something that must be enacted and portrayed."[9]

Browning's refusal to enact and portray the role of the great artist stands in stark contrast to James's legendary brilliance as a social performer. And this difference contributed, no doubt, to James's fascination with the poet's public manner. James's exquisitely articulated conversation, his elegantly balanced sentences, prompted this typical response: "if ever there was a man that talked like a book too—that man is Henry James."[10] Ezra Pound has offered the most famous observation of the Master in society: "the massive head, the slow uplift of the hand . . . the weight of so many years of careful, incessant labor of minute observation always there to enrich the talk."[11] Clearly there was no disparity between James's social style and his artistic identity: one reflected the other. Or, more precisely, James's performance gave the impression that his private self was indistinguishable from his public self; he artfully created the illusion of seamlessness. In reality, then, James resembles Browning more than at first it might seem. Adopting opposite styles, both writers achieve the same end of keeping their creative selves private.

From their very first meetings James's perception of Browning's "sharp rupture of an identity" teased and provoked his imagination. In a letter to Alice James, James seeks to account for the poet's behavior: "evidently there are two Brownings—an esoteric and an exoteric. The former never peeps out in society, and the latter has not a ray of suggestion of *Men and Women*."[12] This "whimsical theory," as James would come to call it, was an explanation the novelist would tenaciously cling to over many years, reiterating and enlarging upon it as the context demanded. The persistence of the theory raises the question of whether James believed it, or was aware that it was a necessary fiction that alleviated his anxiety about Browning. With characteristically rigorous self-awareness, James explores this very question in "The Private Life." As we shall see later in this chapter, James believed in his theory while knowing it was a mere fancy.

James's "rank fantasy" of "the two Brownings," far from being dismissed as frivolous, has acquired considerable prestige in the world of Browning scholarship. Indeed, one recent critic says that James's view "offers a more suggestive approach to Browning's life than any of the full-scale biographies which have been published."[13] A major biography of the poet, Maisie Ward's two-volume study published in 1969, takes James's theory of Browning as the very framework of its enterprise. Ward's titles alone amply indicate James's influence: *The Public Face* and *Two Robert Brownings!*

The poet's "difficulty" consistently aroused James's "grasping imagination" into producing a flow of elaborate metaphors, images, allegorical constructs, and theoretical fancies all designed to fill the gap in his understanding of the poet. James excused this imaginative license when he said of Browning: "the lovers of a great poet are the people in the world who are most to be forgiven a little wanton fancy about him, for they have before them, in his genius and his work, an irresistible example of the application of the imaginative method to a thousand subjects."[14] A vivid example of James's "application of the imaginative method" to Browning occurs in *William Wetmore Story and His Friends* (1903). James's biography of the expatriate American sculptor is often most interesting when it focuses on Story's "friends," the most eminent among them being Robert Browning, whom James repeatedly discusses. As his title indicates James is serving, in effect, as Browning's biographer as well as Story's, and in the course of the work James efficiently performs a number of tasks required of a responsible biographer. He puts in print for the first time many of Browning's major letters to Story and provides striking portraits of several of Browning's closest friends, based on the novelist's personal recollections. (Included among these recollections is the infamous Lady Ashburton, the recipient of Browning's ill-fated marriage proposal.) Most important, James interprets Browning's personality, analyzing the poet with the help of "wanton fancy," which James resorts to after confronting a paradox in his knowledge of the poet. Although "we see him vividly during the early sixties in the letters before us; see him without mystery or attitude, with his explicit sense and his clear full masculine tone,"[15] the clarity of Browning's letters is at odds with James's personal remembrance of the poet. His memories are full of the "mystery" of Browning, and this sense prods James's fancy into elaborating on his theory first delineated in 1877.

In discussing Browning's return to London, where he enjoyed "felicities and prosperities of every sort" as he settled easily into the role of "the accomplished, sound, sane man of the London world," James reflects that "it is impossible not to believe that he had arrived somehow, for his own deep purposes, at the enjoyment of a double identity":

> It was not easy to meet him and know him without some resort to the supposition that he had literally mastered the secret of dividing the personal consciousness into a pair of independent compartments. The man of the world—the man who was good enough for the world, such as it was—walked abroad, showed himself, talked . . . and did his duty; the man of *Dramatic Lyrics*, of *Men and Women*, of *The Ring and the Book* . . . this inscrutable personage sat at home and knew as well as he might in what quarters of *that* sphere to look for suitable company. The poet and the "member of society" were, in a word, dissociated in him as they can rarely elsewhere have been; so that for the observer impressed with this oddity, the image I began by using quite of necessity completed itself: the wall that built out the idyll of his years in Italy (as we call it for convenience) of which memory and imagination were virtually composed for him stood there behind him solidly enough, but subject to his privilege of living almost equally on both sides of it. It contained an invisible door through which, working the lock at will, he could softly pass and of which he kept the golden key—carrying the same about with him even in the pocket of his dinner waistcoat, yet even in his most splendid expansions showing it, happy man, to none. Such at least was the appearance he could repeatedly conjure up to a deep and mystified observer.[16]

This passage is in large part a reworking of some of the central themes and images found in "The Private Life" published twelve years earlier. This story, which also concerns the reactions of a "mystified observer" of Browning (called Vawdrey in the story), contains in its crucial episode a door (not "invisible") being opened and entered. The tale also shares with the above passage the same "supposition" about Browning's "double identity," a theory explicitly avowed by the narrator, who is also the observer. The most significant difference between the quotation above and the story is the cooler, more reserved tone of the 1903 passage. Although James here gives only a slight hint that Browning's aloofness and refusal to unlock his artistic self implies a disdain of the "observer," "The Private Life" makes explicit the narrator's anger, resentment, and anxiety at Browning's remoteness.

Browning's well-guarded privacy, expressed in James's image of the "golden key" never shown to anyone (which recalls the absent "link" of "continuity" James had noted earlier), at once fascinates and vaguely disturbs James, for he admits that "it was not easy to meet him and know him" without being armed with a theory to explain the poet. James is forced, in effect, to create a key forged out of his imaginative fancy, as Browning shows his key to nobody. James's "key" opens up, however slightly, the door to Browning's private artistic life, although the "invisible door," "golden key," and double identity seem to belong in a fairy tale. The ambivalence that pervades James's response to Browning in the above passage is found, most obviously, in his perception of Browning as double; doubleness also informs James's rhetoric which simultaneously celebrates Browning's inviolable privacy and attempts fancifully to invade it. And James's description of himself as "mystified," a word that recurs in a number of passages revealing his reaction to Browning, suggests emotional ambivalence, a sense of awe and apprehension. James's uneasiness toward Browning is brought into sharper focus when we juxtapose two of his descriptions of reading the poet.

34

If Browning the man was "difficult" for James, his poetry was no less so. When James speaks of his experience of reading Browning one is struck by the highly personal terms in which James describes the rewards of his verse. He remarks late in the second volume of the Story biography: "for all his 'difficulty' Browning was, with his lovers, the familiar and the intimate, almost the confidential poet, fairly button-holing the reader with the intensity of his communication and the emphasis of his point."[17] This passage of 1903 is the seed of a much longer and more complex statement contained in the 1912 homage. In the middle of his tribute James pauses to reflect on the implications of Browning's familiarity and intimacy with his reader. How the poet's "intensity" alters our traditional conception of poetry and why Browning's relation to his reader seems more that of a novelist than a poet are matters James explores in the passage below:

> To express his inner self—his outward was a different affair!—
> and to express it utterly, even if no matter how, was clearly,
> for his own measure and consciousness of that inner self, to *be*
> poetic . . . [in reading *The Ring and the Book*] we feel our-
> selves . . . in the world of Expression at any cost. That, essen-
> tially, *is* the world of poetry—which in the cases known to our
> experience where it seems to us to differ from Browning's
> world does so but through this latter's having been, by the
> vigor and violence, the bold familiarity, of his grasp and pull at
> it, moved several degrees nearer to us, so to speak, than any
> other of the same general sort with which we are acquainted;
> so that, intellectually, we back away from it a little, back
> down before it, again and again, as we try to get off from a
> picture or a group or a view which is too much *upon* us and
> thereby out of focus. Browning is "upon" us, straighter upon
> us always, somehow, than anyone else of his race; and we thus
> recoil, we push our chair back, from the table he so tremen-
> dously spreads, just to see a little better what is on it. This
> makes a relation with him that is difficult to express; as if he

came up against us, each time, on the same side of the street and not on the other side, across the way where we mostly see the poets elegantly walk, and where we meet them without danger of concussion. It is on this same side, as I call it, on *our* side, on the other hand, that I rather see our encounter with the novelists taking place; we being, as it were, more mixed with them, or they at least, by their desire and necessity, more mixed with us, and our brush with them, in their minor frenzy, a comparatively muffled encounter.[18]

What first strikes one about this extraordinary description of the act of reading is James's complication of the terms in which he had described Browning's relation to his reader in the 1903 statement. The "familiar" poet is now "boldly familiar"; Browning's "buttonholing" of the reader has become "grasp and pull." "Vigor and violence" have replaced "intensity and emphasis"; the "intimate almost confidential poet" described earlier is now "too much upon us," and is therefore "out of focus." Clearly these revisions point toward the same conclusion: Browning's intimacy discomfits, even overwhelms, the novelist; his familiarity is so overbearing as to force James to "recoil."

Because Browning's aggressive, engulfing intimacy is unlike James's experience of "any other of the same general sort with which we are acquainted," "this makes a relation with him that is difficult to express." But James solves this difficulty with considerable finesse, as he constructs a kinetic image of Browning's deceptive generic position. According to his "fable," novelists walk on one side of the street, while on the opposite side poets "elegantly walk." But Browning is not where one would expect him to be; he takes James and his fellow novelists by surprise as he meets them "on the same side of the street." Browning brazenly risks the "danger of concussion" carefully avoided by the elegant poets; thus his grasping, hearty, slightly vulgar boldness is potentially threatening.

James's reaction to Browning the man and poet is consistent: Browning is at once familiar and unfamiliar, both the typical London gentleman and a writer of genius. He is described as the "familiar and the intimate" poet, but his effect is unlike that of any poet for he creates a novelistic intensity. This disconcerting ambiguity in Browning renders him "out of focus" for James, and the elaborate metaphors he constructs to put Browning in focus reveal more about James than they do about the poet. In the passage under discussion, for instance, the anxiety Browning produces in James is readily apparent. Here James's images stress the pressing *physicality* of Browning's demands: he is "straighter upon us" than any other poet, he comes "up against us" unexpectedly, confronting James "with the danger of concussion." In its expression of incipient bodily harm in a context that purports merely to be describing the relation of a reader to a poet, this last phrase is an unintended revelation of James's acute unease with Browning.

Whatever anxiety James felt about Browning can only be inferred by a close scrutiny of his metaphors. This lack of explicitness is partly owing to James's characteristic preference for indirection. But perhaps a more crucial reason for James's reticence is the context in which he made his statements. His remarks are embedded in official acts of public commemoration—the commissioned biography of Story and his friends and the Royal Society Centenary address. These essentially honorific occasions were not appropriate for the explicit expression of ambivalent feelings. Only through the mediation of fanciful metaphors, or, as we shall see below, the displacement of his ambivalence on others, could James reveal his personal response to Browning.

The third major public statement James made about Browning was his memorial tribute to the poet on the occasion of his interment in the Poet's Corner of Westminster Abbey on January 4, 1891. "Browning in Westminster Abbey," which was not delivered in the Abbey but printed in the newspaper, concerns the problem that so vexed James in the 1912 passage we have examined: the ambiguity of Browning's generic identity. Instead of confronting this puzzle directly, James displaces his discomfort with the poet on Browning's poetic "predecessors," his "new associates" in the Abbey.

> [Browning] introduces to his predecessors a kind of contemporary individualism which surely for many a year they had not been reminded of with any such force. The tradition of the poetic character as something high, detached, and simple, which may be presumed to have prevailed among them for a good while, is one that Browning has broken at every turn; so that we can imagine his new associates to stand about him, till they have got used to him, with rather a sense of failing measure. A good many oddities and a good many great writers have been entombed in the Abbey; but none of the odd ones have been so great and none of the great ones so odd. There are plenty of poets whose right to the title may be contested, but there is no poetic head of equal power . . . from which so many people would withhold the distinctive wreath. All this will give the marble phantoms at the base of the great pillars . . . something to puzzle out.[19]

The Abbey poets are remarkably like Henry James, as the novelist forces them to share his "sense of failing measure." But in projecting his sense of Browning as "something to puzzle out" on the great English poets, James finds relief from his anxiety. Indeed what is most striking about the memorial address is James's ease in confronting the poet. Doubtless what enables him to displace his anxiety is the recent fact of Browning's death. Death has defused Browning's potent mystery, and James's participation in the entombing provides him confidence and security—a feeling happily proclaimed at a number of points in his speech. In the opening section James is explicit about the effect of death: "we possess a man most when we begin to look at him through the glass plate of death." James seems nearly serene when he states: "by the quick operation of time, the mere fact of his lying there among the classified and protected makes even Robert Browning lose a portion of the bristling surface of his actuality." However, as the 1912 statement reveals, James's confidence that time would diminish Browning's power to bewilder proved unfounded. In fact, most of James's significant statements about the poet occur in the years following the Abbey address, testifying to the persistently mystifying force Browning exerted on the novelist. But in 1891, with Browning's "valued voice" being "committed to silence," the possibility seemed very strong that the poet had been "made sure of, tamed and chained as a classic," in James's revealing phrase.

James's confident sense of taming the poet allows him to dispense with the "wanton fancy" he would usually need to cope with Browning, and he is able to confront the "great mystery" of Browning's art without recourse to elaborate metaphor. He defines that "mystery" as "the imperfect conquest of the poetic form by a genius in which the poetic passion had such volume and range." The "patient critic," says James, must ask "how it was that a poet without a lyre—for that is practically Browning's deficiency: he had the scroll but not the sounding strings—was nevertheless, in his best hours, wonderfully rich in the magic of his art, a magnificent master of poetic emotion."[20] The answer to James's question depends on an understanding of his conception of poetry and the poet.

In James's view "the Poet is most the Poet when he is preponderantly lyrical" and expresses with his lyre "his own intimate, essential states and feelings."[21] But, James warns, "by the time" the poet "has begun to collect anecdotes, to tell stories, to represent scenes, to concern himself, that is, with the states and feeling of others, he is well on the way

39

not to be the Poet pure and simple." In other words, he is approaching the domain of the novelist. Obviously Browning's narrative gifts, his creation of a novel in verse, insure that he has not only left the purely poetic realm but has crossed over to the novelists' side of the street.

Seen in the context of these generic boundaries, James's praise of Browning in the Westminster address must be read in a new light. James briefly delineates Browning's greatest strengths as a writer: "an unprejudiced intellectual eagerness to put himself in other people's place, to participate in complications and consequences."[22] Although he does not explicitly say so, for James these are essentially novelistic qualities. Therefore to call Browning "a poet without a lyre" is to define him in negative terms as a kind of novelist. This phrase is one of the very few times in the address that the word poet is used. Earlier in the memorial James is quite cagey in his careful avoidance of the word. He calls Browning a "genius" blessed with "poetic passion," a master of "poetic emotion" possessed of "poetic character." Although he mentions Browning's "imperfect conquest of the poetic form," James does not probe the generic implications of his statement. In referring to the "magic of Browning's art," James avoids defining the kind of art it is.

"A poet without a lyre" defines Browning deceptively, for the phrase cancels itself out, as the final three words strip the first two of their meaning. And this seems to be the effect James sought. His phrase subverts its terms, both enacting the effect of Browning's ambiguous identity and forcing the reader to deduce that Browning is neither a poet nor a novelist strictly. His indeterminateness resists the power of language to make his identity fully present. Browning, in other words, refuses to be defined; at best his status can only be inferred. He is perennially beyond the grasp of James's language.

Within a year after helping lay him to rest in Westminster

Abbey, James confronted Browning once again, this time in the arena of fiction. The result of this encounter that occurred through an act of imaginative memory was the story "The Private Life," James's most obviously revealing response to the poet. That James was writing specifically about Browning is certain: in both his notebook and preface (the story is reprinted in volume 17 of the New York edition) he named Browning as the model for his Clare Vawdrey— the great writer of "The Private Life." In the 1908 preface James looks back on the germ of his story and recalls his puzzled fascination with Browning:

> The whole aspect and *allure* of the fresh sane man, illustrious and undistinguished—no sensitive poor gentleman he!—was mystifying; they made the question of who then had written the immortal things such a puzzle.
>
> So at least one could but take the case—though one's need for relief depended, no doubt, on what one (so to speak) suffered. The writer of these lines, at any rate, suffered so much— I mean of course but by the unanswered question—that light *had* at last to break under pressure of the whimsical theory of two distinct and alternate presences, the assertion of either of which on any occasion directly involved the entire extinction of the other. This explained to the imagination the mystery.[23]

James's conclusion, as stated in his preface, that the secret of Browning's mystery is "that our delightful inconceivable celebrity was double" looks back, of course, to the double theory James invented as early as 1877 in his letter to Alice. Therefore, to follow James's logic and vocabulary, his "suffering" should have been relieved earlier. The fact that fifteen years after pronouncing his theory James would still need "relief" is proof that the nagging "unanswered question" of Browning remained troublesome. "The Private Life," then, amounts to another effort at an answer, an attempt at a solution in a context far different from a mere letter or a memorial address. The realm of fiction seems to afford James a freedom from the restraining decorum of public commemoration and grants him, as it were, privacy to explore fully his tangled emotions toward Browning.

So close is James's personal involvement with this story that his prefatory remarks recounting his fascination with Browning sketch the very subject matter dramatized in "The Private Life." Rather than serving as mere background material, the preface presents the dilemma of "The Private Life." For the story is about a "deep and mystified observer" (as James describes himself in the quotation from the Story biography) who is bewildered and disappointed by a brilliant writer's mediocre social self. The narrator, a young writer who is called an "observer," resorts to a theory that two Vawdreys exist. If "The Private Life" is an intended answer to the puzzle of Browning, at the same time it is a confession of failure to solve the riddle. The narrator's anxiety about Vawdrey is never fully allayed; the small comfort he does obtain is purchased at the price of delusion and myopia. Deception and unabashed trickery pervade the story, and its most memorable scene depicts a moment of startling disorientation.

The tale's first-person narrator, who is on a holiday in Switzerland, introduces the main characters: Lord and Lady Mellifont, Blanche Adney, and Clare Vawdrey. The last two are London's leading comic actress and "literary glory," respectively.[24] Lord Mellifont is a society painter and a glittering social performer, thus the very opposite of Vawdrey. In his preface James explained that Mellifont (modeled on Frederick Leighton) provided "the precious element of contrast and antithesis." Whereas Vawdrey enjoys a vital private life of artistic creativity, Mellifont is too empty to have anything but a social existence. But Vawdrey's divided self, not Mellifont's, fascinates the narrator. Early in the story the narrator states: "when Vawdrey talked we should be silent. . . . I had been at no pains to hold my tongue, absorbed as I inveterately was in a study of the question which

42

always rose before me. . . . This question was all the more tormenting that he never suspected himself (I am sure) of imposing it" (p. 219).

The "question" that "absorbs" and "torments" the narrator is: how can this great writer be so damnably bland in public? "He was exempt from variations . . . and struck me as having neither moods nor sensibilities nor preferences. He might have always been in the same company, so far as he recognized any influence from age or condition or sex: he addressed himself to women exactly as he addressed himself to men. . . . I used to feel a despair at his way of liking one subject—so far as I could tell—precisely as much as another. . . . I never found him anything but loud and liberal and cheerful, and I never heard him utter a paradox or express a shade or play with an idea" (p. 220).

The narrator's diction—"absorbed," "tormenting," and "despair"—suggests his intense interest in Vawdrey, but why Vawdrey seems to exert such a hold is never probed. What is clear is the younger man's resentment: "I envied him his magnificent health." The narrator's fascination, tinged with envy, is not confined to Vawdrey; he is also curious about Blanche Adney and Lord Mellifont. The first moment that he is alone with Blanche he plans, as he says, to "satisfy" his "just curiosity. What had happened before dinner, while she was on the hills with Lord Mellifont?" "Did he make love to you on the glacier?" he bluntly asks Blanche. She avoids an answer: "She stared; then broke into the graduated ecstasy of her laugh" (p. 234). Later, in response to another pointed question from the narrator, Blanche will again stare and laugh. While her stare seems to signify that the narrator has hit upon a truth she wishes to remain private, her theatrical burst of laughter attempts to divert him. Her strategy succeeds, for the narrator fails to gain an admission from her.

But the real interest of this scene is elsewhere, contained

almost in passing. Into the middle of the narrator's confrontation with the evasive Blanche, James weaves a brief but crucial exchange. "How do you know anything happened?" Blanche asks the narrator.

> "I saw it in your face when you came back."
> "And they call me an actress!" cried Mrs. Adney.
> "What do they call *me*?" I asked.
> "You're a searcher of hearts—that frivolous thing an observer."
> "I wish you'd let an observer write you a play!" I broke out.
> "People don't care for what you write."
>
> (p. 234)

Blanche's indictment of the narrator is prompted by his own abrupt demand to know how others perceive him. She relegates him to a minor status—a "frivolous" "observer" who writes plays no one cares about. Implicit in her condemnation is a comparison with the great Vawdrey, who is supposedly at work on a play for Blanche that she eagerly anticipates will be the "great part" of her career. Vawdrey has agreed to read from this work in progress, and Blanche bids the narrator "go and look" in Vawdrey's room for the manuscript. "I go for it, but don't tell me I can't write a play," says the narrator, evidently still smarting from Blanche's harsh dismissal. He is to pick up the play and bring it to Vawdrey who will read to the guests in the drawing room.

The narrator's exchange with Blanche reveals his need for a response from others that will define his identity. In this light his fascination with Vawdrey can be explained: the narrator demands a defining response from a fellow playwright, *the* playwright of his time, and a figure of immense authority. Vawdrey's blandness is so infuriating precisely because he seems to refuse the narrator any sign of confirmation, the nod of recognition that will bolster the young writer's precarious sense of himself as a man and artist.

As the narrator heads for Vawdrey's room in search of the manuscript, "the sound of voices outside" comes to him. He looks forward to the prospect of Vawdrey reading his scene; it "would be an episode intensely memorable. I would bring down his manuscript and meet the two with it as they came in." I quote James's description of the events that next occur:

I had been in his room and knew it was on the second floor. . . . A minute later my hand was on the knob of the door, which I naturally pushed open without knocking. It was equally natural that in the absence of its occupant the room should be dark; the more so as, the end of the corridor being at the hour unlighted, the obscurity was not immediately diminished by the opening of the door. I was only aware at first that I had made no mistake. . . . Suddenly I . . . utter[ed] an ejaculation, an apology. I had entered the wrong room; a glance prolonged for three seconds showed me a figure seated at a table near one of the windows—a figure I had first taken for a travelling-rug thrown over a chair. I retreated, with a sense of intrusion; but as I did so I took in, more rapidly than it takes me to express it, in the first place that this was Vawdrey's room and in second that, surprisingly, Vawdrey himself sat before me. Checking myself on the threshold I was briefly bewildered, but before I knew it I had exclaimed: "Hullo! is that you Vawdrey?"

He neither turned nor answered me. . . . I definitely recognized the man whom an instant before, I had to the best of my belief left below in conversation with Mrs. Adney. His back was half turned to me, and he bent over the table in the attitude of writing, but I took in at every pore his identity. "I beg your pardon—I thought you were downstairs," I said; and as the person before me gave no sign of hearing me I added: "If you're busy I won't disturb you." I backed out, closing the door—I had been in the place, I suppose, less than a minute. I had a sense of mystification, which however deepened infinitely the next instant. I stood there with my hand still on the knob of the door, overtaken by the oddest impression of my life. Vawdrey was at his table, writing, and it was a very natural place for him; but why was he writing in the dark and why hadn't he answered me? I waited a few seconds for the sound of some movement, to see if he wouldn't rouse himself from his abstraction—a fit conceivable in a great writer—and call out; "Oh, my dear fellow, is it you?" But I heard only the stillness, I felt only the starlighted dusk of the room, with the unexpected presence it enclosed. I turned away, slowly retracing my steps, and came confusedly downstairs . . . the room was empty. . . . Empty too was the terrace. Blanche Adney and the gentleman with her had apparently come in. I hung about five minutes; then I went to bed.

I slept badly, for I was agitated. . . . I was vaguely nervous—I had been sharply startled.

(pp. 237–39)

This passage is extraordinary in its minutely detailed dramatization of an experience of emotional and perceptual disorientation, as the narrator's vision fluctuates wildly between clarity and confusion, certainty and bewilderment. The shock of seeing Vawdrey at his desk when the narrator had assumed he was on the terrace precipitates an uncontrolled barrage of contradictory impressions. On pushing the door open and finding the room dark the narrator is convinced that he "had made no mistake." But seconds later he withdraws with a "start": "I had entered the wrong room." This realization is soon revised, as he states that "this was Vawdrey's room. . . . Vawdrey himself sat before me." Nevertheless this certainty affords the narrator no comfort, as a momentary feeling of bewilderment engulfs him. His feeling of perceptual confusion is finally relieved, as the narrator states with conviction: "I definitely recognized the man. . . . I took in at every pore his identity." Despite his achievement of cognitive accuracy, at this point the narrator experiences considerable anxiety. Because Vawdrey's utter absorption in writing has made him oblivious to the nar-

46

rator's presence, the young writer is "overtaken by the oddest impression" of his "life": Vawdrey writing in the dark and ignoring his unexpected visitor. "Why hadn't he answered me?" wonders the narrator as he faces another "tormenting" question. On a literal level Vawdrey has refused to grant the narrator recognition; his "half turned" back "bent over the table" remains "in the attitude of writing." The narrator waits in vain for a greeting; hearing only the stillness, he walks away disconsolate.

The psychologically bruising experience James dramatizes is an uncanny moment in the Freudian sense of the term. The uncanny, which is bound up with anxiety, "is not, as might be supposed, something entirely unknown or unfamiliar" but rather simultaneously familiar and unfamiliar.[25] The narrator confronts this disturbing doubleness, and his perception of Vawdrey as both familiar and unfamiliar creates anxiety and a sense of helplessness typical of an uncanny experience. When the narrator comes upon Vawdrey he does not recognize his friend; he perceives a "figure" that he "had at first taken for a travelling-rug thrown over a chair." Furthermore Vawdrey is not his "familiar" (James's description in the Westminster address) chattering self; he is silent, immersed in writing. To compound the narrator's bewilderment, his friend is unaware of the narrator's presence—he offers no greeting in response to the young man's apologies. Vawdrey's ambiguous identity creates an unresolved tension that is at the center of the narrator's uncanny experience and the source of his anxiety. The undecidability of Vawdrey's identity—it is Vawdrey and yet it is not the Vawdrey the narrator knows—reduces the narrator to a nearly helpless, dazed confusion: "I turned away, slowly retracing my steps, and came confusedly downstairs." He leaves Vawdrey alone in the stillness of the darkened room.

Samuel Weber's revisionist reading of Freud on the uncanny, which specifically links problems of perception and

47

identity with the uncanny, can illuminate this scene. Late in his essay "The Sideshow, Or: Remarks on a Canny Moment" Weber summarizes his conclusions:

> What should have remained concealed and what has nonetheless, in a certain manner, emerged engenders the uncanny because its very appearance eludes perception, its being is not to be had, because it side-steps and side-tracks . . . by repeating, doubling, splitting and reflecting. The uncanny is thus bound up with a *crisis* of perception and of phenomenality, but concomitantly with a mortal danger to the subject, to the "integrity" of its body and thus to its very identity. . . .
>
> The uncanny is thus bound up with subjective emotions, and upon an affective scale it can even be situated with some precision: it is not simply a form of anxiety but is located between dread, terror and panic on the one side, and uneasiness and anticipation on the other.[26]

Weber's location of the uncanny on an "affective scale" accords with James's descriptions of the narrator as mystified, bewildered, confused, agitated, and startled when he encounters Vawdrey.

Weber's assertion (borrowed from Schelling by way of Freud) that "what should have remained concealed" but nonetheless emerges points to the unexpected, shocking nature of the uncanny; its sudden appearance makes a face-to-face encounter with it impossible. The uncanny is always "off to the side," its "being is not to be had,"[27] for it "can never be made sure of," to use a phrase from James's Westminster Abbey address. Vawdrey "eludes perception," as his "half-turned back" "bent over the table in the attitude of writing" makes him difficult for the narrator to see clearly. The older writer "should have remained concealed" for he seems to have been drained of human qualities in his effort at writing. He is a figure seemingly without human shape (a "travelling-rug"), voice or face, deaf to all solicitations, as if absorbed into the darkness that surrounds him. Vawdrey's immersion in the creative act has transported him beyond the claims of any social context; the narrator's attempt to converse with him is ignored.[28]

The narrator's "crisis of perception" is created by his sudden encounter with a scene of writing that bears interesting symbolic analogies with the primal scene as described by Freud and Weber. Weber locates the origin of the crisis of the uncanny in a primal moment of discovery: the male child perceives the absence of the mother's phallus as a "kind of negative perception."[29] This discovery engenders castration anxiety in the child, for he had anticipated seeing his mother's phallus; his recognition of this loss gives rise to the possibility of a similar loss to himself. The child's narcissism is assaulted by this encounter with the Other; his body and identity feel threatened. The narrator's observance of a figure of authority in the act of writing is not without sexual overtones, which James suggests by emphasizing the narrator's sense of trespass as he suddenly opens the door to the darkened room. On entering, the narrator acts *as if* he has come upon people in the dark, for his description of his emotions repeatedly centers on his sense of having inadvertently invaded someone's privacy. "I withdrew it [his hand] uttering an ejaculation, an apology. . . . I retreated, with a sense of intrusion." James's stress on the narrator's feeling of having violated privacy suggests that a scene of intimacy is hidden in the room's "obscurity"; and this sense of sexuality persists not despite but because of a lack of direct textual evidence. This moment instances what Leo Bersani has observed as James's tendency for "fluttering verbal evasiveness" which "increases the power of traumatic scenes."[30]

The narrator gains his bearings only to be bewildered by a "kind of negative perception"—the discovery of absence. The Vawdrey he has known is absent, replaced by an unfamiliar, "unexpected presence" in the dark. Instead of hearing Vawdrey's expected cry of recognition—"Oh my dear fellow is it you?"—the stillness of the room fills the narrator with confusion. As he descends the stairs the shock of absence seems to engulf his very surroundings: ". . . the room was empty. . . . Empty too was the terrace."

The uncanny nonrecognition scene between the narrator and Vawdrey implicitly threatens the young writer's identity as an artist. Inadvertently he has stumbled into the private world of a great writer, and finds himself ignored rather than welcomed as a fellow playwright. His artistic identity, assaulted earlier by Blanche, is further undermined by Vawdrey's indifference. Perhaps the narrator's deep anxiety in this scene stems partly from his experience of the writer at work as a wholly alien Other who refuses entry to the young playwright, implicitly declaring his private domain of creation off limits. After this encounter with Vawdrey the narrator's perception of him is permanently altered—he views Vawdrey as split into a private and public self. This restructuring of the narrator's vision is analogous to the effect of "ocular anxiety," which is produced, says Weber, by the primal scene of castration. "The subject" is confronted "with the fact that it will never again be able to believe its eyes since what they have seen is neither simply visible nor wholly invisible." What results is a "restructuring of experience . . . in which the narcissistic categories of identity and presence are riven by a difference they can no longer subdue or command."[31] Because Vawdrey is now "neither simply" familiar "nor wholly" unfamiliar, the narrator perceives him as a person without a stable identity, a presence whose wholeness is continually deferred. Neither the public nor the private Vawdrey is ever again a unified, fully present self.

The narrator is convinced that two Vawdreys actually exist. The night after his uncanny experience he excitedly reports his conclusion to Blanche: "There are two of them. . . . One goes out, the other stays at home. One is the genius, the other's the bourgeois, and it's only the bourgeois whom we personally know" (p. 244). Earlier in the same conversation, the narrator asked Blanche whom she was talking with on the terrace last night:

> "Last night?"
> "You came here with a gentleman; you talked about the stars."
> She stared a moment; then she gave her laugh.
> "Are you jealous of dear Vawdrey?"
> "Then it was he?"
> "Certainly it was."
>
> (p. 241)

Blanche is careful to answer the narrator's question with her own question—"Are you jealous" of Vawdrey?—and thereby avoids being trapped in a lie. As soon as she ascertains that the narrator thinks Vawdrey was with her on the terrace she confirms his suspicion: "certainly it was." The pattern noted before in Blanche's behavior—a stare and then a burst of laughter—recurs in this scene, again indicating that she is uncomfortable and seeks to evade the narrator's probing questions.

In his eagerness to spin his theory of two Vawdreys the narrator is blind to the possibility that Blanche might be lying. When he confronts her with the fact that Vawdrey was in his room writing at the same time he was allegedly out on the terrace with Blanche, the actress seems trapped and startled: "She stopped short at this . . . she wanted to know if I challenged her veracity; and I replied that, on the contrary, I backed it up—it made the case so interesting" (p. 242). Here the narrator is revealed in all his obtuseness— he is concerned with an "interesting" theory rather than the realities of the situation. Instead of realizing that he has caught Blanche in a lie, he seeks only her corroboration of his notion about Vawdrey.

The reality of the situation, which is never made explicit but can be inferred from Blanche's behavior, is that the actress is conducting an illicit affair with Lord Mellifont. Although this possibility had been raised by the narrator early in the story, his fascination with Vawdrey has diverted him from pursuing his suspicions. Blanche is only too happy to support the narrator's supposition, for it provides the means of keeping him occupied. To delude the narrator further and keep him on the wrong track, Blanche constructs a complementary theory: "my idea is almost as droll as yours," she tells the narrator. "If Clare Vawdrey is double," Lord Mellifont "has the opposite complaint: he isn't even whole." The narrator is taken with this theory and its snug symmetry; he elaborates on it in his mind: "He [Mellifont] was all public and had no corresponding private life, just as Clare Vawdrey was all private and had no corresponding public one" (p. 246). Blanche's calculated enthusiasm for the narrator's notions captivates the young writer and places him firmly under Blanche's control. "She glanced at me like a lovely conspirator. . . . I was elated by the way our mystery opened out." Musing to himself, he compares his "discovery" about Vawdrey to Blanche's "secret" about Mellifont: "my own was, of the two mysteries, the more glorious for the personage involved." But the narrator promises that he will not violate Blanche's secret. Speaking of Mellifont, he says: "Oh, he was safe with me, and I felt moreover rich and enlightened, as if I had suddenly put the universe into my pocket." The irony is pointed here: Mellifont is indeed "safe" thanks to the narrator's myopia; the latter will never gain insight into the actual state of affairs.

Blanche's strategy of feigning interest in the narrator's theory of Vawdrey grows into a "love" of the great writer. When she declares, "I'm in love with him," she prepares the ground for her boldest move. She asks the narrator to "keep . . . out" the public Vawdrey, so that she can visit the private Vawdrey alone in his room. Blanche decides to do this only after making sure that Lord Mellifont is alone at the "window of his sitting room," for her actual intent is to tryst with him while Vawdrey and the narrator wander the countryside. So duped is the narrator by his own theories, despite their implausibility and fantastic nature, that he never doubts Blanche; in fact, he is thrilled with her scheme to visit Vawdrey alone, for he is eager to know the details of the private Vawdrey's mysterious life. "I'll keep Vawdrey for ever! I called after her. . . . Her audacity was communicable, and I stood there in a glow of excitement" (p. 259). Blanche is indeed audacious, but not for any reason the narrator can fathom. She shamelessly manipulates the young writer and gains the freedom to be with her lover.

When the narrator overtakes Vawdrey, who has been out strolling, a storm suddenly breaks and the two men seek refuge in an empty cabin. As the "grand rage of nature" explodes in thunder and lightning the narrator's mood also is stormy. He grows angry and uncontrolled, feeling the rare moments he is spending alone with the great Vawdrey dissolve in the loquacious gossiping of the playwright. The closest approach to literary matters Vawdrey makes is to attack a notorious reviewer. "It broke my heart to hear a man like Vawdrey talk of reviewers," comments the narrator, distressed at the playwright's immersion in the trivial (p. 261).

The tempestuous weather not only mirrors the narrator's mood; it also helps him clarify his thoughts about Vawdrey. At long last he attempts to confront his feelings concerning the playwright:

The lightning projected a hard clearness upon the truth, familiar to me for years, to which the last day or two had added transcendent support—the irritating certitude that for personal relations this admirable genius thought his second best

53

good enough. It *was*, no doubt, how society was made, but there was a contempt in the distinction which could not fail to be galling to an admirer. The world was vulgar and stupid, and the real man would have been a fool to come out for it when he could gossip and dine by deputy. None the less my heart sank as I felt my companion practice this economy. I don't know exactly what I wanted; I suppose I wanted him to make an exception for *me*.

(p. 263)

What exacerbates the narrator's feeling of neglect is his assumption that Blanche is in touch at that very moment with the real Vawdrey: "at such an hour his chair at home was not empty: *there* was the Manfred attitude, *there* were the responsive flashes. I could only envy Mrs. Adney her presumable enjoyment of them" (p. 264).

The narrator's vocabulary—Blanche's "enjoyment" of Vawdrey's "responsive flashes"—seems to betray his unconscious awareness of a romantic dimension to their private meeting. Ironically, Blanche is doubtless enjoying "at such an hour" the pleasures of Mellifont's intimacy, not Vawdrey's. At this point in the narrator's thoughts the private life acquires a crucial, if not explicit, significance: the private life is no longer simply the domain of artistic creation but is also the realm of sexuality. The sexual overtones in the narrator's uncanny experience on entering Vawdrey's darkened room become more apparent here as the private life is redefined. It is where Vawdrey can be his creative self and where Blanche has the enviable privilege of privately enjoying the playwright. And the narrator, of course, is excluded from both aspects of the private life—he is not granted the nod of recognition from his idol and can only envy Blanche's apparently easy access to Vawdrey.

When the storm abates and the narrator escorts Vawdrey back to the inn, they encounter Blanche. As Vawdrey comes toward her she shrinks from him; "with a movement that I

54

measured as almost one of coldness she turned her back on him and went quickly into the salon" (p. 204). As the narrator approaches her, eager to learn the details of her visit with the private Vawdrey, he remarks that "she had never been so beautiful." "He was there—you saw him?" asks the narrator. "He saw *me*. It was the hour of my life!" Blanche replies (p. 264). "It must have been the hour of his, if you were half as lovely as you are at this moment," says the narrator, giving evidence here of a conscious awareness of the sexual dimension of her session with "Vawdrey." Blanche's elaborate performance—"she flung round the room with the joy of a girl"—is designed to convince the narrator that her meeting with Vawdrey has resulted in her winning a great part. Lost on the narrator is the fact that she avoids the actual Vawdrey because he is the one person who knows that she was not with him alone in his rooms. When Vawdrey and the narrator leave the inn together for the journey back to England, the older man asks, "What was the matter with her?" The narrator smugly tries to "comfort" the public Vawdrey, for he feels sorry that the public man has been spurned by Blanche. The narrator remains hopelessly deluded to the very end of "The Private Life"; the last lines of the tale, which project into the future, reinforce our sense of the narrator's lonely isolation: "She [Blanche] is still, nevertheless, in want of the great part. I have a beautiful one in my head, but she doesn't come to see me to stir me up about it."

In his obsessional interest in the lives of others the nameless narrator of "The Private Life" has certain affinities with the nameless narrator of *The Sacred Fount* (1901). Both men are loners, surveying at a distance the private lives of people that fascinate them and creating theories to explain the mystifying behavior of the men and women around them. The "house of cards," as the narrator of *The Sacred Fount* calls the theoretical construct he has erected, finally collapses at the conclusion of that novel when Grace Brissenden scornfully attacks its purely suppositious foundation. But the narrator is able to reconstruct in memory his edifice of imaginative speculation only because he never loses sight of the fact that his theories are at best tenuous. In contrast, the narrator of "The Private Life" mindlessly mistakes his theory for fact and tempts the reader to remark of him, as Mrs. Briss does of the narrator at the end of *The Sacred Fount*, that he is "crazy." The narrator of "The Private Life" has his "house of cards" containing his theory of the two Vawdreys still standing at the end of the tale, but only at considerable cost.

The price the narrator pays, albeit unknowingly, is to be the dupe of Blanche Adney. James grants the narrator peace of mind by making him a fool whose solution to the riddle of Vawdrey is a mockery of insight. Yet what is most memorable about the tale is not the narrator's dearly bought equanimity, but rather his emotional torment provoked by the inscrutable Vawdrey. The two most intense moments in the story occur when the narrator is overwhelmed by anxiety at the inexplicable mystery of the great writer: as he stumbles upon Vawdrey in the dark and as he bitterly endures Vawdrey's chatter in the cabin.

What is striking about the narrator's fascination with Vawdrey is that his emotion, like Hamlet's according to T. S. Eliot, is in "excess of the facts as they appear."[32] Because James does not dramatize the relation between the two men the reader is never given any reason why Vawdrey is such a compelling figure in the narrator's eyes. Their two scenes together serve to emphasize the very absence of relationship. Eliot's phrase used above is part of his essay on *Hamlet,* which is notoriously perverse concerning Shakespeare's play and dubious as a theory of literary expression. Yet his comments are helpful in illuminating works such as "The Private Life," where the author is too close to his subject. Eliot's contention that the prince's disgust is "occasioned by his mother but his mother is not an adequate equivalent for it" because "his disgust envelops and exceeds her"[33] describes the depth of the narrator's response to Vawdrey. From the outset of the tale an extremity of emotion marks his reaction, as his fascination turns into anxiety and then into anger and envy. Vawdrey "is not an adequate equivalent" for these emotions; the narrator's torment "envelops and exceeds" him. This excess occurs, I think, because the emotions are too much Henry James's and too little the narrator's, and they are provoked not by Vawdrey but by Robert Browning. James fails to transform his relation to the poet into fully dramatized fictional form and thereby gain the aesthetic distance necessary to create an adequate "objective correlative." Consequently, James's main characters—the narrator and Vawdrey—are not dramatically realized, despite (or because of) the fact that James invests them with deeply personal emotion.

Perhaps another way of describing James's intimate relation to "The Private Life" is to say that the narrator is James's double and Vawdrey is Browning's double. These pairs of doubles testify to the tale's profound connection, an artistically hazardous one, to life. The doubles in "The Private Life," then, have nothing to do with the supernatural. But critics of the tale, as if taken in by the narrator's theories as completely as the narrator himself, have assumed that the tale is a ghost story with two Clare Vawdreys on the loose. Indeed, Edel has collected "The Private Life" in his volume of James's ghostly tales. One reason critics have failed to cast a skeptical eye on the narrator's notion of two Vawdreys is James's use of the phrase "rank fantasy" when he discusses the story in his notebook. F. O. Matthiessen and Kenneth Murdock in their annotation on James's entry conclude, on the basis of the phrase, that "James' treatment . . . [of public and private personages] in terms of 'alternate identities' links the method of his fantasy . . . with that of his ghost stories."[34] Following this conclusion, Edel writes that James "noted that the story was 'of course a rank fantasy.' "[35]

These critics focus on the words "rank fantasy" without attending to the sentence in which the phrase occurs. When one examines the context of James's remark one sees that he is saying something quite different than the above critics suggest. James writes: "the idea of rolling into one story the little conceit of the private identity of a personage suggested by F.L. and that of a personage suggested by R.B., is of course a rank fantasy."[36] Here James is not saying that his story will be a "rank fantasy"; rather he calls his "idea" of combining into one tale the two conceits about Leighton and Browning a "rank fantasy." His "idea" strikes him this way perhaps because he feels that his intention to incorporate two of the best-known figures of the London world into one short story is audacious. Significantly, in his prefatory remarks on "The Private Life," where James recounts in some detail the story's genesis, he makes no mention of fantasy or supernatural aspects of the tale. He labels it a "small experiment" and a "piece of ingenuity."

Nevertheless, most critics view the tale as a fantasy; discussions of the story take as a premise that it is not strictly realistic. Edel describes "The Private Life" as a "cheerful fable,"[37] and Blackmur, in his well-known essay "In the Country of the Blue," briefly remarks: "of this little piece what does one say but that the ghost story is the most plausible form of the fairy tale. . . . 'The Private Life' is a fantastic statement."[38] Recently Todorov has placed the tale in the context of his generic theory of the Fantastic. Like all critics before him, Todorov assumes the story is a ghost story, but he goes on to refine this designation when he calls the tale "closer to pure allegory" in form and rhetorical effect.[39] Although he gives no clue as to the content of this allegory,

Todorov claims that as allegory "The Private Life" is a "threat" to the Fantastic, which depends on the reader's hesitation, his uncertainty, as to whether he is reading a supernatural tale or a mimetic work. In James's story, says Todorov, "the allegory is so obvious that the hesitation is once again reduced to zero." Although my insistence on reading the story as a realistic narrative containing an uncanny episode disputes Todorov's interpretation, what is of most generic significance is that the tale is so designed as to permit a mimetic and a nonmimetic reading. This doubleness makes the tale a "piece of ingenuity" as James called it.

Why did James devise a story capable of being read simply as a ghost story? I think this strategy was a defensive maneuver designed to divert readers from the real interest and drama of the tale—his personal and therefore vulnerable response to Browning. James's relation to "The Private Life" is deeply paradoxical; he attempts to conceal his thoughts about Browning in the very act of confronting them. Evidently his response to the poet was too unsettled and problematic to be made the direct center of his story; instead he placed it off to the side, hidden by a plot that can be read as a ghostly tale. By creating a tale that allows (even encourages) the reader to mistake it for a ghost story, James resembles the manipulative Blanche misleading the narrator and critics into believing in supernatural explanations. Thus not only is the narrator duped, but so are those readers taken in by Blanche's scheme. James, then, has affinities with both the befuddled narrator and the duplicitous Blanche. A mimetic interpretation cannot be privileged either, for such a reading, which relies on only hints offered in the text, is ultimately as unverifiable as the ghostly interpretation of "The Private Life." But only a mimetic interpretation can uncover what Blanche and James wish to keep hidden: private, personal relations—Blanche with Mellifont, James with Browning.

James implies in his preface that "The Private Life" represents an attempt at "relief" from the "suffering" caused by the "unanswered question" of Browning, but the "relief" he gains is a peculiar kind that demands scrutiny. It is a "relief" that seems to depend explicitly on a willful decision to delude oneself with the convenient fiction of a "whimsical theory." In the preface James happily concludes that "our delightful inconceivable celebrity was double": "this explained to the imagination the mystery." This "whimsical theory" and its proponent, James, are subjected to severely ironic parody in "The Private Life." In depicting the fatuous narrator blinded by his obsession with a theory he thinks is truth, James, in effect, turns on the " 'searchlight of irony' as an instrument of self-scrutiny."[40] The tale's ironic portrait of the young writer is created at James's own expense as he parodies his own efforts (first begun in 1877 with his letter to Alice) to solve the "puzzle" of Browning. Thus "The Private Life" is a confession of James's inability to confront Browning unaided by the mediation of theory. But in this very confession is an implicit self-awareness that constitutes the true "relief" James gained from writing the tale. His ability to parody himself becomes an act of creative authority that wins for James an increment of self-knowledge which finally severs him from his hapless narrator. The knowledge that James gains is a realization that Browning is a source of anxiety.

Although "The Private Life" makes explicit the anxiety that could only be inferred in James's nonfictional remarks, the continuity between the two contexts is evident. The connections are particularly vivid when we juxtapose James's image in the centenary essay of Browning as a poet who walks on the novelists' side of the street and the narrator's reaction to Vawdrey as he sees him writing in the dark. In both scenes Vawdrey-Browning surprises the narrator-

James by appearing unexpectedly; as a result he is not fully perceived. Instead of being confronted face to face, all the narrator glimpses is Vawdrey's "half-turned back." Similarly, Browning suddenly brushes up against James, just when the novelist thought he would be walking on the poet's side of the street. In both passages Browning is, so to speak, off to the side in the realm of the uncanny.

Eliot concludes his essay on *Hamlet* saying "we must simply admit that here Shakespeare tackled a problem which proved too much for him." "The Private Life" and the nonfictional statements indicate that Browning remained a "problem" that "proved too much for" James. The novelist nearly admits as much when he says in the centenary essay: Browning is "too much upon us"; "this makes a relation with him that it is difficult to express." James's construction of a "whimsical theory," the intricate metaphorical fables that express his sense of mystification, and the complex even contradictory strategies that we have examined in "The Private Life," all attest to James's strenuous imaginative efforts to reduce the poet's difficulty.

When James read Browning in 1859 the poet had been well known in America for about ten years, not as a writer but as the husband of Elizabeth Barrett, the internationally famous author. That summer in Newport James read with some amusement an encyclopedia entry for Browning which identified him primarily as the husband of the great poetess. Browning's elopement with Elizabeth in 1846 had quickly become romantic legend both in England and America, and "personal interest in Browning" was "to play an important part in the making of the poet's American reputation."[41] A study of Browning's reputation reports that, "as the romantic details of the marriage and subsequent flight to Italy became known, Browning was invested with some of the glamour of a figure of romance and came to be thought of as a sort of Prince Charming who had . . . carried a beautiful princess off to live happily ever after in an old Italian palace."⁴² This aura of romance that surrounded Browning helped to make him particularly popular with the young in America—among them not only Henry James but also William James and Thomas Sergeant Perry. These three, along with John La Farge, "composed a remarkable group of Browning readers at Newport."⁴³

Browning's subject matter of adult intimacy, which had caused James's parents to deem the poet sole property of the adult world, made Browning a poetic authority on sexual passion, James believed. Providing further authenticity to the poet's "complete and splendid picture of the matter" was that it directly derived from his own life, as the novelist noted years later: "Browning has thrown his most living weight" on the "great human passion" because "it remains the thing of which his own rich experience most convincingly spoke to him."⁴⁴ *Men and Women* was the product of this "rich experience" that must have seemed so remote to the sixteen-year-old James.

The associations that cluster around James's introduction to Browning are rich in implication. Browning's fame as a lover, his adult poetry, tacit parental disapproval of the poet's fitness for youths, and La Farge, the compelling man of the world, who reveals the poet to James—all these factors point to an inescapable conclusion: James's first reading of Browning was not merely a literary encounter but an initiation into a new realm of experience—one whose essence is caught in the title of the book that served as James's guide into this adult world: *Men and Women.*

Among the poems in *Men and Women,* I think one in particular was crucial in influencing James's later response to Browning. "One Word More" is the eloquent coda to the volume; in it Browning addresses his wife *in propria persona:*

14

Love you saw me gather men and women,
Live or dead or fashioned by my fancy,
Enter each and all, and use their service,
Speak from every mouth—the speech, a poem.
Hardly shall I tell my joys and sorrows,
Hopes and fears, belief and disbelieving:
I am mine and yours—the rest be all men's,
Karshish, Cleon, Norbert and the fifty.
Let me speak this once in my true person,
Not as Lippo, Roland, or Andrea
Though the fruit of speech be just this sentence:
Pray you, look on these my men and women,
Take and keep my fifty poems finished.
. . . .

17
. . . .
God be thanked, the meanest of his creatures
Boasts two soul-sides, one to face the world with,
One to show a woman when he loves her!

18
This I say of me, but think of you, Love!
This to you—yourself my moon of poets!
Ah, but that's the world's side, there's the wonder,
Thus, they see you, praise you, think they know you!
There, in turn I stand with them and praise you—
Out of my own self, I dare to phrase it.
But the best is when I glide from out them,
Cross a step or two of dubious twilight,
Come out on the other side, the novel
Silent silver lights and darks undreamed of,
Where I hush and bless myself with silence.

The "two soul-sides" Browning reveals in "One Word More" are very probably the seed of James's "whimsical

63

theory" of the poet as double. James, a great lover of *Men and Women*, would doubtless have read "One Word More" as early as 1859 in Newport. What emerges as most significant when we compare the two depictions of Browning's doubleness are the changes James makes in the poet's original conception. Only in its broadest outline—the division of the self into public and private—does James's theory correspond to Browning's notion. Browning conceives his public self, the "one to face the world with," as including his poetic self. This continuity is revealed in the poem when Browning expresses his desire to speak privately to Elizabeth in his "true person" and not as "Lippo, Roland, or Andrea"—both poetic creations and actual historical figures, therefore "all men's." Browning evidently considers that the men and women he has created in poetry are in the public domain, whereas James places artistic creation in the center of Browning's private life. Browning explicitly equates the private life with sexual love; it is the "other side" "to show a woman when he loves her." But his private life also embraces the poetic; therefore artistic creation exists in both the public and private realms for Browning. Since his private life includes the marriage of two poets, this "other side" is the realm where the sexual and creative exist in harmony. In ignoring Browning's celebration of the private life as the union of love and art, embodied in his marriage to Elizabeth, his "moon of poets," James excludes from both his theory and his narrator's theory any element of the sexual.

Although it is highly probable that James read "One Word More" and recognized its equation of the private life with sexual life, he did not employ his knowledge of the poem in creating his theory of the two Brownings. Nor did his boyhood image of Browning the romantic lover figure in James's "whimsical" construct of the poet as double. James's striking neglect of the sexual elements of Browning's identity suggests his repression of this aspect of his awareness of the poet. In "The Private Life" James's repression returns in the form of the uncanny, which, according to Freud, always involves such a return. James's repressed knowledge of Browning's sexuality reemerges to produce a moment of nearly vertiginous shock: the unexpected and unsettling discovery of Vawdrey-Browning's private life, which acutely disconcerts the narrator-James.[45] To understand why James represses his knowledge of the actual nature of Browning's private life we must delve into James's conception of the artist, a view intimately connected with sexuality.

Blackmur has succinctly described what he calls "the portrait of the artist in Henry James: the man fully an artist is the man, short of the saint, most wholly deprived."[46] Asceticism is not an abstract ideal for James, but a cherished belief he sought to exemplify personally. Indeed, for James, it justifies his life's defining decisions, such as his refusal to marry. Browning's robust sexuality and famous marriage, combined with his great stature as a poet, stood in flagrant defiance of James's conception.[47] Artists need not be deprived in order to create, Browning's example seemed to assert. To maintain intact his image of the artist, James repressed his knowledge of Browning's sexuality and thereby defused the challenge the poet presented. Now James need not face the disturbing anomaly Browning embodied: that so renowned a husband was also a great poet. James's disregard of Browning as the lover of Elizabeth allowed him to theorize on the less threatening puzzle of the superficiality of Browning's public self. The theory of two Robert Brownings relieved James's anxiety by concealing as much as it disclosed.

Because James's conception of the artist was profoundly intertwined with his own life, Browning's successful balance of the artistic and the romantic inevitably challenged his sexual identity. The discovery scene in "The Private

Life" can be read as an allegory of James's retreat from the private life of sexuality that Browning inhabits so comfortably. A feeling of inadequacy in the presence of the famed lover and poet is manifested in the overwhelming sense of emptiness the narrator-James feels as he leaves the poet's room. An early remark of the narrator's about Vawdrey—"I envied him his magnificent health"—points to the element of envy in James's response to Browning and, by extension, to La Farge's "entire" nature. Since Browning and La Farge both possess "magnificent health," a mastery unavailable to James, he can only envy them and look elsewhere for a personal model. In Girardian terms, James's response to the negative imperative of the double bind ("don't imitate me as a sexual model") is to embrace the example of the other great writer La Farge had introduced him to that crucial Newport summer—Balzac. The Frenchman provides the foundation of James's conception of the artist and is the alternative sexual model to Browning. Throughout his career James paid tribute to Balzac as both his foremost teacher of novelistic art and as the exemplary sufferer for that art.

Of Balzac's letters James writes: they are "almost exclusively the audible wail of a galley-slave chained to the oar."[48] In his 1902 essay on Balzac James asks to be "pardoned for coming back to it, for seeming unable to leave it; it enshrouds so interesting a mystery. How was so solidly systematic a literary attack on life to be conjoined with whatever workable minimum of needful intermission, of free observation, of personal experience?"[49] James concludes that "Balzac appears really never to have tasted" these "luxuries" on any "appreciable scale." Later in the essay he returns to the "question that haunts" him: "How then, thus deprived of the outer air almost as much as if he were gouging a passage for a railway through an alp, *did* he live?" "He did *not* live—save in his imagination . . . his imagination was all his experience; he had probably no time for the real thing. This brings us to the rich if simple truth that his imagination alone did the business."[50] What makes Balzac's imagination so fascinating for James is that, in the absence of personal life, it was anything but hampered. In fact Balzac's imagination had a greater range "than all the rest of us put together." "He went in for detail, circumstance, and specification. . . . The whole thing, it is impossible not to keep repeating, was what he deemed treatable."[51]

If in the 1902 essay James had stated only that Balzac "did not live—save in his imagination," three years later this same conclusion is stated in economic terms: "He collected his experience within himself; no other economy explains his achievement; this thrift alone . . . embodies the necessary miracle."[52] Balzac's "twenty years of royal intellectual spending"—James's description of Balzac's career—did not leave him bankrupt because the "original property—the high, prime genius" was "tied-up from him" in trust, and this capital had "steadily, enormously appreciated."[53] James provides a "human" explanation as to why Balzac's "spending" finally came to an end. Balzac's health had been severely strained by his creative labors; James depicts him as dying for his art: "He died at fifty—worn out with work and thought and passion; the passion, I mean, that he had put into his mighty plan and that had ridden him like an infliction of the gods."[54]

For James, Balzac's heroic asceticism had the rigor of a religious calling: "His system of cellular confinement, in the interest of the miracle, was positively that of a Benedictine monk, leading his life within the four walls of his convent and bent, the year round, over the smooth parchment on which, with wondrous illumination . . . he inscribed the glories of faith and the legends of saints. Balzac's view of himself was indeed in a manner the monkish one; he was most at ease, while he wrought, in the white gown and cowl."[55]

For James the most "essential" "lesson" the life of Balzac offers is the "lesson that there is no convincing art that is not ruinously expensive." Browning, however, never seems to have paid for his art. The poet sacrificed nothing; indeed he enjoyed the luxury of a rich personal life and a fertile creative existence. "What a wealth it constituted, what a resource for life," says the narrator about Vawdrey's "doubleness." Browning's "wealth" was manifested in the immense energy of his theatrical self, which in its mobility of role playing easily satisfied the demands of marriage, fashionable London soirees, and poetry. The poet notes his "superfluity of vital energy," as Elizabeth called it, in "One Word More": "I am mine and yours—the rest be all men's." What James called Browning's "dissociated" compartmentalized self was an inexhaustible "resource for life" and art. In sum, Browning challenges a belief that embraces but transcends the case of the artist and is the foundation of James's moral life: the necessity of renunciation. Browning rudely ignores this moral imperative over which so many of James's characters agonize. In light of the poet's example, James's cherished faith in the necessity of the artist's asceticism can be seen as an excuse for avoiding a sexual life. Browning, in effect, exposes James's version of Balzac to be an elaborate fiction that rationalized James's retreat from the demands of the "sacred relation" between men and women. Small wonder, then, that James grappled with Browning for over thirty years, attempting to explain him away, to fix him, to make him "safe," "tamed and chained as a classic."

James's personal discomfort with Browning colored his relation to the poet's texts; the novelist maintained a defensive attitude toward the poetry, a stance evident in James's avowed impulse to rewrite the poet's work. In "The Novel in *The Ring and the Book*" James reports that "far back, from my first reading of these volumes [in 1868] . . . when I was a fairly young person, the sense, almost the pang, of the novel they might have constituted sprang sharply from them."[56] He outlines how he would have transformed the "great loose and uncontrolled composition" of *The Ring and the Book* into a Jamesian novel. Although this is the one occasion in which James explicitly confesses his impulse to rewrite, his urge extends beyond *The Ring and the Book* and shall be shown to be his most characteristic response to Browning's work, the basic structure of his literary relationship to the poet.[57] In the next chapter I will discuss a particularly remarkable instance of James's use of the poet; in "The Lesson of the Master" Browning is both a literary source and a threatening presence. Not only is "The Lesson of the Master" connected to *The Inn Album*, which James redoes in the tale, but it is deeply related to "The Private Life." The earlier story presents a more artistically successful version of the hidden drama of "The Private Life": the exclusion of a younger writer from the private life of sexuality.

THE MOCKING FIEND

Perhaps the most striking aspect of the history of *The Inn Album* (1875) is the roster of distinguished names that immediately attacked it: Robert Louis Stevenson, J. A. Symonds, A. C. Bradley, William Dean Howells, and Henry James. Despite the novelist's youth—he had yet to publish *Roderick Hudson*—James began his review on a boldly condescending note: "It is growing more difficult every year for Mr. Browning's old friends to fight his battles for him, and many of them will feel that on this occasion the cause is really too hopeless."[1] James roundly condemns the work as a "decidedly irritating and displeasing performance." His haughty disdain lapses into a shrill, even hysterical tone when he writes, "there is not a line of comprehensible, consecutive statement in the two hundred eleven pages . . . it is hard to say very coherently what it is . . . his book is only barely comprehensible."[2] Hysteria and condescension achieve the same end: they distance James from the work, as indictment replaces analysis.

What is intriguing about James's review is that amid his disapproval, he asserts that a "great poem might perhaps have been made of it." This claim, so at odds with the unqualified harshness of the rest of the review, indicates why James needed to distance himself from *The Inn Album*. By dismissing the work as "barely comprehensible,"

and thereby excusing himself from having to look closely at Browning's drama, James is able to cultivate the "virus of suggestion" he has caught—his recognition of its possibilities. "The virus of suggestion," James explains in his preface to *The Spoils of Poynton*, is characterized by an "inveterate minuteness" and is best communicated to a receptive author in its most minimal form. "Anything more . . . spoils the operation."[3] Thus the deeper he might explore *The Inn Album* the less impetus his imagination would gain. Only the "single small seed" supplies the "prick" of inspiration, as James's mixed metaphor insists.

What in Browning's drama provided so precious a "germ" that James was compelled to retreat from the work so as not to lose the "particle" of suggestion? Certainly the formal properties of *The Inn Album* were of little interest to the novelist. He found Browning's hybrid form of narrative and dramatic monologue an aesthetic muddle: "it is as little dramatic as possible. It is not narrative . . . it is not lyrical. . . . We are reading neither poetry or prose." (Once again James is bothered by Browning's generic ambiguity.) Browning's style elicited equally strong disapprobation. James complained of its "want of clearness of explanation, of continuity . . . of the smooth, the easy, the agreeable . . . it is all too argumentative, too curious and recondite. . . . His thought knows no simple stage—at the very moment of its birth it is a terribly complicated affair."[4]

If the form and style of *The Inn Album* were of small concern to James, a clue to what did intrigue him is provided in his offhand remark that "the whole picture indefinably appeals to the imagination." After this confession James hastens to regain his scornful posture. But the admission is telling. What he means by the "whole picture" is, doubtless, the basic situation of the work. Browning's poem is about sexual manipulation and the ambiguities of the master-disciple relationship. An elder man (never named by Browning), a "cynic" and a "man of ideas," as James describes him, seeks to control a passive, wealthy, naive young man. Manipulation, particularly of a sexual kind, was a theme that fascinated both writers, and this aspect of the master-disciple relation was of particular interest to James in "The Lesson of the Master" (1888). Like Browning's drama, "The Lesson of the Master" concerns the master's betrayal of the disciple; in both works the two men desire the same woman and, for different reasons, the disciple loses his beloved. In each ending the disciple avenges himself (or plans to) on his treacherous master—"a mocking fiend" (James's phrase). Both masters (Browning and James each use this term) are essentially ambiguous figures—at once wise and paternal, sinister and scheming. They are highly theatrical, as they relish playing the role of mentor to admiring followers who are too naive to discern their artful behavior.

In 1888 James rewrites what he calls Browning's "rough notes for a poem," transforming the poet's crudities into an ingeniously constructed tale. But the relation between *The Inn Album* and "The Lesson of the Master" is more complex and intimate than the mere fact that Browning's work served as a literary source. The model of James's master, Henry St. George, was none other than Robert Browning himself.[5] James's fictive portrait of Browning will be analyzed later, when I discuss how the tale dramatizes James's response to the double bind that the poet presents. "The Lesson of the Master" portrays not only the three stages of the double bind—the identification of the disciple with the model, which triggers the disciple's desire to possess the model's object (a woman) and creates the ensuing rivalry—but depicts, at its climax, the James surrogate's resolution to the master's challenge. We will see that the means by which Paul Overt neutralizes Henry St. George strikingly supports Girard's hypothesis that a division of the model into "two different domains" is required.

The double bind will be discussed after examining the other type of ambiguity implicit in *The Inn Album* and pervasive in James's tale—theatricality. That theatricality is related in these works to textuality reminds us that neither writer is untouched by the fin de siècle cult of style.

In these texts by Browning and James theatricality is part of the larger cultural movement of aestheticism, a mode of perception and being which blurs the boundaries of life and art. *The Inn Album* and "The Lesson of the Master" express this merging of the fictive and the actual through a conspicuous use of the metaphor of reality as a text. Both works are dramas of interpretation in which the characters' principal activity is reading people and events. While this metaphor of perception is familiar in the nineteenth century, in Browning and particularly in James it is more explicit and extensive. An unnamed character in Browning's work calls herself a "locked" volume "shut on the shelf"; in an attempt at intimacy she allows her friend to "profit by the title page."[6] Browning's characters implore one another to "scan and scrutinize" people. "Have I read the stare aright?" is a typical query. In James's story the disciple Paul Overt perceives Henry St. George as a "text" written in a "style considerably involved, a language not easy to translate at sight."[7] Although both conceive of experience as a vast text to be interpreted, for each writer this metaphor has significantly different implications.

For James, as is well known, the act of interpretation is the most characteristic activity of his centers of consciousness. James's "lucid reflectors" serve the dual purpose of being the basis of his compositional technique and providing the novelist's central subject. These "thoroughly interested and intelligent" witnesses, as James describes them in the preface to *The Golden Bowl*, are specifically charged with the responsibility of "contributing" a "certain amount of criticism and interpretation" of their "respective predicaments."[8] Clearly James's characters and readers are engaged in the same activity: constructing readings of experience.[9] Both must possess "the power to be finely aware and richly responsible," a power founded on an ability to read the "crabbed page of life" with maximum perceptiveness. And the "teller of a story" is "the reader of it too," insists James, who conceives artistic activity as the effort to "disengage" meaning from the "Gothic text" of experience.[10]

James's characters and readers scrutinize enigmatic texts. The former confront the social text: the code of conventions, manners, and roles that mediates public behavior and furnishes the means of self-representation. Thus James's readers, to be precise, are faced with the text of a text, a representation of representation. The pervasive textual metaphors in his novels and criticism suggest the analogies between social and literary sign systems, both of which must be interpreted rather than spontaneously perceived. Astute interpretation involves dissolving polarities and recognizing relations, for, like the light in Strether's Paris, James's work reveals "what things resemble," illuminating with the refractions of analogy as it continually subverts conventional dichotomies: appearance and reality, theatricality and sincerity, reading and writing, form and content, and inevitably, life and art.

If textuality is the foundation of James's world, for Browning, reality becomes a text when human relations are bereft of immediacy and naturalness. Whereas James conceives of textuality as an existential fact from which his fiction proceeds, in Browning the necessity of reading experience announces man's fall from a God-centered world. The catastrophe of textuality, the debasement of reality it brings, is alluded to in *Sordello* and is fully confronted in the darkest work of his career—*The Inn Album*. This bleak drama depicting a godless world is perhaps the poet's least understood, most undervalued work, and in its own peculiar way one of his most interesting later texts.

We can gauge how extreme the poet's vision has become in this late work when we place it beside the early poetic drama *Pippa Passes*. Whereas *Pippa Passes* celebrates the oral, *The Inn Album* laments the written. What is most significant about *Pippa Passes* for our present purposes is that it never becomes a drama of textuality. The meaning of Pippa's songs is transparent to her hearers and therefore immediately accessible. Characters do occasionally interpret her songs; in fact they misinterpret them in ways appropriate to their sensibilities and situation. But this misinterpretation never creates a morass of subjectivity, because God's ordering presence restores moral and epistemological harmony to potentially chaotic and violent situations. As God's messenger, Pippa four times in the course of her wanderings reveals His word to various troubled citizens of Asolo. It is thoroughly apposite that one of the genuine villains in this world is consistently associated with the written word; Bluphocks, the immoral vagabond, favors writing over speech (we first see him tracing letters) and is a brilliant interpreter. At this point in Browning's career, the figure of Bluphocks occupies the periphery. But his disturbing presence will become more conspicuous in later works, until by *The Inn Album* his descendant—the elder man—will occupy the foreground.

Thirty years after *Pippa Passes* the living voice of God's messenger has been stilled, replaced by a volume of dead language containing clichés, doggerel, trivia, and misquotations. Such distortions are, of course, found in *Pippa Passes*, but in *The Inn Album* the degraded condition of language emerges as a central preoccupation. The repository of linguistic debris is the inn album, a musty book that is this work's dominant symbol. The world of the work is as debased as the language in the album, the book of wisdom in this forsaken universe where the namelessness of characters testifies to their depleted selfhood. Two men and two women, having been abandoned by God, lack any means of transcendence and hence of redemption. Exiled from immediacy and spontaneity, they survive by feeding on the detritus of literature. Perceiving the world through a web of literary allusions, these characters reduce each other to aesthetic objects and can do nothing but play various roles derived from literary stereotypes.

Clyde Ryals believes that "art for these characters is something to ease the individual burden of seeing life on its own terms."[11] In fact, "life on its own terms" is unavailable to these people, since experience in *The Inn Album* is mediated by the products of a crass urban culture that have drained vitality from human relations. This reified condition, familiar to analysts of contemporary culture, aroused Browning to indict the vulgar, commercial values of his day. *The Inn Album* is, among other things, a work of implicit cultural criticism that reveals the corrosive effects of a degenerate milieu. Browning's strategy is to import a sampling of the ephemeral cultural "dreck" of the times into the pages of *The Inn Album*. His text is replete with contemporary slang, allusions to "commercial products, sporting events, well-known contemporary gossip, religious questions of the day, and all sorts of things and people everywhere seen in the columns of *The Times* and other newspapers."[12] To anchor his drama further to the popular events of the time, Browning based his plot upon the scandalous career of a well-known London roué. Quite appropriately this "record of 1875" was first published in America in a newspaper.

The nameless characters are designated as the young man, a sinister rogue called the elder man, a girlish cousin of the youth who is also engaged to him, and the elder woman, a friend of the cousin. The young man, not knowing of the friendship between the elder woman and his cousin, had a few years earlier fallen in love with the elder woman, whom the rogue had seduced and abandoned four years prior to the present action. Each bit of this past history is known only to those who have taken part in it. The entire drama is enacted in the parlor of an inn where an open album is spread out on a table and is continually read and annotated. Indeed the three major events in the plot are acts of annotation: the rogue calculates his gambling debts in the margins and decides on a plan of repayment; he pens a blackmail scheme in the album's pages; and at the end of the poem the woman writes a statement in the album testifying to the youth's innocence just before she commits suicide.

As the elder woman dies, there "begins outside a voice that sounds like a song." It is the voice of the cousin, who has come looking for her friend. The innocent voice of Pippa is surely meant to be recalled here, and Browning's allusion to that earlier work is sharply ironic. For Pippa always arrived at precisely the crucial moment; her timely voice made a difference. The girlish cousin, a debased, aestheticized Pippa, arrives too late to change anything. Browning's implication is unmistakable; there is no place for the pure, immediate word of God in a universe that has lost all touch with any transcendent force and has only the dusty album to commemorate its lost presence. The album, which is a memorial to what is past, is representative of writing itself, since writing is "never transparently present but must be interpreted or 'read' into being."[13]

Browning does not explicitly lament the lost world of Pippa; in *The Inn Album* he seems wearily to accept the fall of man and language. In large part the weariness derives from the slackness of the poetry; far too much of the verse is as lifeless as the characters. But this obvious fact was for too long all that critics saw in the work. What they did not note is that in *The Inn Album* Browning confronts an important phenomenon in the late nineteenth century: the rise of the culture philistine, to use Nietzsche's phrase. "The peculiar inauthenticity which comes from basing a life on the very best cultural objects" (as Lionel Trilling defines Nietzsche's term)[14] infects Browning's characters, who feed not solely on cultural ephemera but, more insidiously, use and degrade the tradition of high culture, as their allusions to Dante, Shakespeare, Milton, and others indicate. To Browning's credit he possessed the awareness to recognize and address this cultural crisis. But, in a sense, Browning is a victim of the crisis he portrays, for *The Inn Album* does not wholly transcend the degeneration it dramatizes. Its poetry, characterization, and formal coherence are deficient; in this work Browning lacks the artistic strength to master fully his subject.

The denatured, reified universe of Browning's work is an extreme version of the crass London world that oppresses the characters in "The Lesson of the Master." Like the poet, James explores the effects of philistinism, the pressure of an increasingly vulgar and materialistic society upon human relations, and the theatricality that pervades social behavior. The tale poses the question: is it possible to create genuine art amid such circumstances? This issue is of explicit concern to the two major characters, St. George and Overt, and to their mutual friend Marian Fancourt.

All three characters, St. George most firmly, maintain an opposition between the "pure spirit" (p. 67) achieved through the "decent perfection" (p. 66) of art, and the dangerously corrupting force of the "bright rich world of bribes and rewards" (p. 41). The battle between art and the "world" is a frequent, even inevitable, topic of conversation; on the afternoon when Overt falls in love with Marian, they earnestly discuss "the high theme of perfection" and "how one ought to go in for it" (p. 53). The conflict between art and the world is at the heart of the master's "lesson" to Overt, as St. George seeks to make his own surrender to the commercial world a "warning" to his gifted disciple. The master's alleged intention is to "save" Overt from any compromise of his talents. The lesson is nothing if not severe: "perfection" is attainable only if the artist withdraws into solitude to become, in effect, a "disfranchised monk" (p. 77), as Overt says at one point. When Overt is faced with this bleak equation—that the writer "can produce his effect only by giving up personal happiness"—the "trembling" young man protests St. George's extremism. "What a condemnation of the artist . . . what an arraignment of art" (p. 77). The master is careful to specify that Overt must renounce Marian, the woman he loves: "give up" your beloved or give up "the idea of a decent perfection." Overt is reconciled to surrendering Marian because "she's for the world . . . she's not for a dingy little man of letters . . . the world will take hold of her—it will carry her away" (p. 41). Clearly, Overt is under the sway of the dichotomy the master so relentlessly preaches. Convinced of the truth of St. George's harsh lesson, Overt goes abroad to write for two years.

Overt leaves London with the knowledge that the master's path of compromise could also have been his road, on the condition that he had forfeited any claim to be considered a writer of genius. St. George has long since renounced "genius"; he explains to his disciple that he was seduced by the "mercenary muse" whom he "led to the altar of literature" (p. 67). This unholy marriage was founded on "the worship of false gods . . . the idols of the market; money and luxury and the world" (p. 36). Later in their private conversation in the master's study, St. George eloquently describes his immersion in the cultural marketplace and the rewards he has reaped: "I've led the life of the world, with my wife and my progeny; the clumsy conventional expensive materialized vulgarized brutalized life of

London. We've got everything handsome . . . we're perfect Philistines" (p. 72).

Surely St. George would be at home in the world of *The Inn Album*. In both works artifice governs social relations to the point where even the unconventional becomes a convention. But self-fashioning in James's tale is more creative and playful, as St. George's example declares. The master wears a "measured mask" (p. 18) that, owing to his "impersonal lucidity," he artfully manipulates. This "lucidity," which is "practically cruel" in its rigorous self-scrutiny, allows St. George to manage precisely the impressions he projects. Whether his mask reveals the "convulsive smile" of "social agitation," the calm of "inscrutable rest," or the "quiet face" of sincerity he so often turns to Overt, the master is a most poised performer (p. 18). Perhaps the most skillful effect of his performance is his creation of the illusion that he is not performing, that he is perfectly natural.

From the first time Overt gazes upon St. George's face, the young man is struck by the formidable challenge the master presents to his efforts at interpretation. Overt (using, says the narrator, "somewhat professional" "analogies") likens St. George's face to a "text" that does not easily surrender its meaning. In fact, Overt likes it "better for its not having told its whole story in the first three minutes . . . the text was a style considerably involved, a language not easy to translate at sight. There were shades of meaning in it" (p. 18). Although this analogy seems to indicate Overt's acute awareness of the master's subtlety, one could say that Overt feels betrayed by St. George at the end of the tale precisely because he fails to probe fully the implications of his metaphor. Although "text" emphasizes the master's artfulness, Overt's egregious misreading of St. George disregards the master's ambiguity and reduces his "shades of meaning" to a simplistic interpretation. Instead of keeping

in mind St. George's "considerably involved" style, Overt
believes the master means what he says.

How does one account for the sensitivity to the master's
complexity implied in Overt's metaphor and his subsequent
blindness to St. George's manipulations? The disparity can
be explained by the effect of the master's presence and his
flattering attentions to Overt. The disciple is disarmed by
his personal contact with the great man and seems to fall
under his spell; "I'll do whatever you tell me," says the
mystified Overt (p. 39). The master's imposing authority
reduces Overt to a childlike passivity. He surrenders to St.
George's will, fully confident of his elder's wisdom and be-
nevolence. His worship of the master—"I'm prostrate before
him," he tells Marian—paralyzes Overt's powers of critical
evaluation, and he naively accepts the validity of the lesson
(p. 23).

Only in the last part of the story is Overt roused from
his lethargy, as he at last recognizes the master's duplic-
ity, the "bottomless ambiguity" (p. 51) of his lesson, and
the possibility that the "doctrine of renunciation" was a
"mistake" (p. 83). Overt revises his interpretation when,
upon returning from his sojourn abroad, he discovers that
his beloved Marian is engaged to the recently widowed St.
George. "What trick has been played . . . what treachery
practiced . . . was it a plan. . . . Have I been duped, sold,
swindled," the agonized Overt wonders (p. 88). Overt
never fathoms the precise intentions of the master; we
last see the young author "questioning himself" alone in
the dark street.

Overt's "bewilderment," his "mystification" at St.
George's behavior is shared by the reader of "The Lesson of
the Master." James's disconcerting strategy is to encourage
the reader to at first believe (along with Overt) in the good
sense of St. George's lesson; later James forces us to revise

our opinion. Faced with the master's impending remarriage, we judge the lesson a clever ruse designed to give St. George a clear field in wooing Marian. But we are not permitted certainty. Our judgment oscillates again, nudged by the tale's teasing final sentence, which suggests the possibility of the ultimate pertinence for Overt of the master's lesson: "perhaps . . . the master was essentially right and that Nature had dedicated him [Overt] to intellectual, not to personal passion." Finally we are left with no definitive interpretation of the tale because we cannot know whether St. George sincerely believed his lesson, or if his doctrine was a plan, or even if both cases are true. We shall see that James fully intends this ambiguity.

Significantly, the content of the master's lesson—its insistence upon opposing life and art so that the world will not contaminate the artist's pursuit of "perfection"—never arouses suspicion or disagreement in the story's other characters. Marian and Overt both accept the master's premises; even when Paul returns to London he questions St. George's intentions ("was it a plan?") rather than the "doctrine of renunciation" itself (p. 83). Only by examining the lesson in the context of James's own beliefs does its problematic content become evident. An excursion into James's relation to his character's lesson provides essential clues to understanding more fully St. George's supersubtle behavior, and illuminates a crucial but obscure speech he makes to Overt concerning the relation of art to "corruption."

Most critics assume that the relation of James to the master is obvious: St. George is the novelist's mouthpiece; the master's lesson expresses James's own beliefs. Given the fact of James's celibacy and his well-known insistence upon renunciation, there seems much to corroborate this critical view. Although the master's lesson is one with which James would have great sympathy, closer scrutiny reveals that St. George vulgarizes and simplifies his creator's beliefs. What

James would take issue with is the master's key term—
"perfection." James believed perfection to be a spurious
goal, for the artistic process is, in essence, a "troubled
effort—ever the sum, for the most part, of so many lapses
and compromises, simplifications and surrenders."[15] This
somber note is sounded even more strongly in his preface to
The Wings of the Dove where James "mourns" the "absent
values, the palpable voids, the missing links, the mocking
shadows" that pervade the finished creation.[16] He then extracts a general law regarding imperfection in the artistic
process: these flaws "are of course far from abnormal." Indeed, "some acute mind ought surely to have worked out by
this time the 'law' of the degree in which the artist's energy
fairly depends on his fallibility."[17] The artist must be content to erect a "substitute" rather than his "prime object"—
his original conception.

Thus James does not equate, as his master does, the doctrine of renunciation with the pursuit of perfection. For
James, renunciation satisfied a temperamental need, and he
then extended this personal belief into an axiom. But renunciation is not in the service of achieving artistic perfection.
Only a superficial view of James depicts him as believing in
a realm of pure aesthetic perfection exempt from the pressures of reality. The "compromises" and "surrenders" he
speaks of as characterizing the artistic process mirror the
conventions and "vulgarities" of life, which the artist transforms (but does not eradicate) by an act of imagination. That
the artist must seek refuge from experience, as St. George
suggests, is finally impossible for James, since art is hopelessly involved with life, though in indirect and paradoxical
ways. The truest literary realism for James is "the real most
finely mixed with life," as he writes of Browning's art in *The
Ring and the Book;* only this reciprocity produces "in the
last analysis the ideal."[18]

The conditions and product of artistic creation are as impure, as flawed, as the world of which they are inextricably a part. Ironically, St. George expresses this genuinely Jamesian insight to the uncomprehending Overt when the master responds to his disciple's protests that the lesson is an "arraignment" of the artist. St. George says: "Ah you don't imagine by chance that I'm defending art? 'Arraignment'—I should think so! Happy the societies in which it hasn't made its appearance, for from the moment it comes they have a consuming ache, they have an incurable corruption in their breast. Most assuredly is the artist in a false position!" (p. 77). The "incurable corruption" that art brings abides in the very nature of the creative act. As James's final preface makes clear, the artistic process is founded on the exploitation not only of the artist's raw materials but of his characters, whom he imagines as "more or less bleeding participants" in the "great game" the novelist contrives. No wonder that James was never very confident about the place of morality in art: "we are by no means sure that art is very intimately connected with a moral mission."[19]

St. George's cryptic but suggestive statement quoted above recalls *The Inn Album;* the master in effect broadens the operative myth of Browning's work to include all "art." The fall into textuality and the loss of the "happy" society of *Pippa Passes* are matters that James implicitly confronts in his master's speech. St. George's statement anticipates a modern version—Claude Lévi-Strauss's "writing lesson" in *Tristes Tropiques.* According to the anthropologist, the first appearance of writing among the Nambikwara "had allied itself with falsehood" and with the desire for domination. A condition of "social inauthenticity" appeared with the advent of writing (in this case literally handwriting, not literature) and corrupted what had been a "happy" society innocent of the ability to write.[20] In their various fables James, Browning, and Lévi-Strauss imply a state of original purity inevitably corrupted. But each has a different attitude to this myth of lost unity. Whereas the anthropologist nostalgically laments the loss of the Edenic world, and Browning in *The Inn Album* gloomily accepts man's corruption, James sees the expressive, creative possibilities of the modern, denatured age. His theatrical view of experience conceives of the conventions and masks of social performance as generating the intricate texture of the "canvas of life." And James remains committed to theatricality as a mode of being while recognizing that it is constantly threatened with a loss of expressive energy and congealment into an alienated condition not unlike the pervasive inertia of *The Inn Album. The Golden Bowl,* as chapter 5 will show, registers such a loss, as theatricality ossifies into the "coldness of conscious perjury."

The master's speech concerning the "incurable corruption" of art can be seen as his counterlesson, for it contradicts and empties of meaning his ostensible lesson to Overt. By insisting on the connection between art and corruption St. George gives the lie to his often-repeated assertion that a realm of absolute "perfection" exists uncontaminated. If Overt had grasped the implications of St. George's counterlesson he would have been equipped to call the master's simplistic dichotomy into question. More important, St. George's parable should have armed Overt well in his confrontation with the master's complex social style and richly ambiguous talk, which are founded on the disjunction between St. George's words and actions. However, the counterlesson is lost on Overt, and he must wander alone into the master's den: an innocent in the "bright rich world." The master's strategy in dealing face to face with Overt is to appeal to his naiveté, and thus St. George affects an artless sincerity.

Overt's ingenuousness, his openness (as his name suggests), is conspicuous in his first meeting with St. George. "He was conscious that he knew him now, conscious of his handshake and of the very quality of his hand; of his face, seen nearer and consequently seen better" (p. 28). The master's physical proximity gives Overt the illusion that he now knows his mentor. But St. George's elusiveness is soon evident, as James dramatizes the gap between the master's words and deeds. After proposing a general walk of the company around the park, the genial master tells Paul: "we must have a tremendous lot of talk." He immediately leaves Overt with Mrs. St. George; "her husband had taken the advance with Miss Fancourt, and this pair were quite out of sight" (p. 28). Although this bit of manipulation goes unnoticed by Overt, a similar incident occurs a week later, and at that time Paul perceives the first contradictions in the master's behavior. Overt accidentally meets Marian at an art gallery; she is waiting for the master, who has arranged to see her. When St. George arrives he tells Overt with his usual hearty conviviality "we don't meet often enough" and almost at once sweeps Marian away into a hansom. At this point Overt is jarred by the fact that a week before St. George had confided to him: "she's not for me." When left alone in the street, Overt reflects on the master's avowal: "his [St. George's] manner of conducting himself toward her appeared not quite in harmony with such a conviction."

Soon the long-promised intimate conversation between the writers finally occurs in the master's cloistered study. This occasion, when Overt fully accepts the doctrine of renunciation, constitutes the master's most accomplished performance, a triumph of his "personal art." St. George orchestrates all aspects of the meeting, including the scene and props. Everything is calculated to emphasize both the magisterial authority of the master and the impression that on this special evening he will at last lower his "measured mask" and confide his intimate feelings.

The master carefully sets the scene for this confession in his private writing study, which is set off from the rest of the house by a "long passage . . . in the rear." Because ordinary guests are not permitted into this sanctuary the choice of location announces the unusualness of the meeting. Standing in the "middle of a large high room," as if on stage, St. George is "in his shirt sleeves." To emphasize further his unbuttoned mood, "the servant gave him a coat, an old jacket with a hang of experience" (p. 62). This last prop heightens the enthralled Overt's excitement to a new pitch: "Paul Overt welcomed the coat; it was a coat for talk, it promised confidences . . . and had tragic literary elbows . . . it was as if he were going to let his young votary see him all now" (p. 63). Overt's absurdly romanticized perception of the coat is tempered, however, by the nagging skepticism about the master noted in the art gallery episode. In the early minutes of his talk with St. George, Overt feels the "torment of being able neither clearly to esteem nor distinctly to renounce him" (p. 63).

But by evening's end Overt's qualms give way to a conviction of St. George's sincerity and the rightness of his lesson. Overt's conflicting feelings—"bewilderment and recognition and alarm, enjoyment and protest and assent"—resolve themselves when he reflects on why the master has become so very personal (p. 73). "The idea of *his*, Paul Overt's becoming the occasion of such an act of humility made him flush and pant . . . it had been his odd fortune to blow upon the deep waters, to make them surge and break in waves of strange eloquence" (p. 73). St. George's "act of humility" is indeed an act, but not necessarily an insincere one, for his self-representation collapses the polarity between sincerity and performance. Overt's belief that he is "going" to "see him all now" rests upon the naive premise that intimacy means the dropping of the "measured mask." But the "measured mask" is never removed in social interaction, which is founded on the creative capacities of role playing. And if masks express they also shield. As social beings we exist, says James, in an "exposed and entangled state." Being in potentially vulnerable relation to others, we rely on the merciful disguises that roles provide.

The "affectation" of a "personal manner" "must have begun, long ago, with the first act of reflective expression" explains a character in *The Tragic Muse*, who states a central belief of his creator. For James, then, "manner" is inextricable from man's identity as a user of language; "manner" and "affectation" are not obstacles to but forms of expression. James would agree with Stanley Fish's assertion that "in a fundamental sense, all communications are mediated . . . characterized by exactly the same conditions—the necessity of interpretive work, the unavoidability of perspective." "All utterances are stage utterances," Fish says in his account of speech-act theory quoted above, an account deeply Jamesian in its recognition that human behavior is a performance whose intentions and meanings can only be "inferred or constructed" "at a remove."[21]

One reason the Jamesian social text is inherently ambiguous is that the self seeks expression by adopting the improvisational fluidity of a manner. The self is not static but engaged in a continual process of response and adjustment to others; thus it possesses a certain mobility and has no intrinsic bias toward consistency or stability. But in James's fiction only a few characters gain an awareness of the self's provisional status; his more naive characters, Overt included, believe in a single "true" self, a belief based on an implicit opposition between theatricality and sincerity.[22] Strether, for one, begins his journey maintaining such a polarity, which serves as the foundation for the Woollett view that the self is stable and consistent. But, of course, Strether's "double consciousness" eventually recognizes the egregious inadequacy of such a conception, a realization that is born in his initial encounter with Chad's "sharp rupture of an identity." What Strether, unlike Overt, discovers

88

is that consistency is not a privileged standard and that discontinuity may also characterize the self. Strether's acceptance of the self's instability and the plurality of the social text, his gradual understanding that in social experience deception and manipulation interact with sincerity and love, help make him one of the truly civilized figures in James's fiction.

Because Overt implicitly relies on a conception of the self as stable and sincere, uncontaminated by poses or masks, he fails to understand the essential ambiguity of the master's performance. Overt narrowly interprets St. George's "act of humility," which the disciple proudly thinks he has inspired. Viewing the master's talk solely as an expression of intimacy, Overt ignores its performed aspect—"the act." Overt misses the fact that the master in his midnight chat is at once performing (as he exaggerates his self-contempt for his artistic compromises), speaking intimately and sincerely of his views about the artist, and attempting to persuade Overt to go abroad so that Marian will be available for himself. Because these various motives are present simultaneously, Overt's focus upon intimacy as the sole element of St. George's behavior reduces and thus misinterprets the master's meaning. Overt's understanding of social behavior closely resembles what the social psychologist Richard Sennett calls "the tyranny of intimacy": "the arousing of a belief in one standard of truth to measure the complexities of social reality," the mistaken insistence that the closer one gets to people emotionally, the better one will know them and the more authentic the relation will be. Sennett explains: "Intimacy . . . is the localizing of human experience, . . . the more this localizing rules, the more people seek out or put pressure on each other to strip away the barriers of custom, manners, and gesture which stand in the way of frankness and mutual openness."[23]

To privilege frankness and openness, as Overt does, is to

deprive man the "actor" of the "art of acting." In contrast, theatricality, which originates in the child's pleasure in play, celebrates the "expressivity of impersonal behavior."[24] Thus for Sennett and James, theatricality and the conventions and impersonality it rests upon are sources of self-awareness and civilized intelligence. "To strip away the barriers of custom, manners, and gesture," to "localize" human experience, in Sennett's words, not only reduces man's creativity in social life, but deprives the novelist of the "very stuff his work is made of," as James remarks in a famous letter to Howells. Vigorously denying that "manners, customs, usages, habits, forms" are merely "dreary . . . paraphernalia," as Howells claimed, James insists that it is "upon all these things matured and established, that a novelist lives." "I think they represent an enormous quantity" of human life, declares James, who reiterates here his contention, earlier expressed in his study of Hawthorne (1879), that "it takes an old civilization to set a novelist in motion."[25]

Overt's implicit view that truth in social relations lies only in the disclosure of "deep," that is, intimately personal feelings, blinds him to the value of a more objective perspective which would enable him to see the contradictory whole of the master's behavior. In contrast to his disciple, the master's "impersonal lucidity" has the virtue of granting him the distance to survey himself and others with a measure of ironic detachment. One person St. George analyzes with considerable detachment is Marian Fancourt. In a conversation with Overt concerning their mutual admirer, the master's praise is tempered with a subtly expressed recognition of her immaturity. "I've never seen anyone like her. Her interest in literature's touching . . . she takes it all so seriously. . . . How can anything be as fine as she supposes it?" The master continues: "She's a provincial—a provincial of genius . . . her blunders are charming, her mistakes are interesting. . . . Above all she exaggerates . . . she exaggerates you and me!" In short, Miss Fancourt (as the double pun in her name suggests) is a fan, whose role is to pay court, to be uncritically effusive. Concludes St. George: "She expends herself on the second rate . . . she mixes all things up." This acute judgment is, however, lost on Overt, who finds Marian "an angel." In direct contrast to Marian's rather giddy, naive reverence for writers is Mrs. St. George's rigorously professional attitude toward her husband. One of the "really great administrators and disciplinarians," as the master describes her, this unsentimental woman efficiently managed her husband's career for twenty years, locking him up each day in his windowless study.

After his wife's death, St. George salutes her in a letter to Overt: "She took everything off my hands—off my mind . . . I was free, as few man can have been, . . . to shut myself up with my trade." This confession of gratitude startles Overt, who finds it a "contradiction, a retraction" of the master's "doctrine of renunciation" and its disparagement of women as "millstones" around the artist's neck. And Overt's bewilderment is the beginning of his disenchantment with St. George, whose professed intention to "save" his disciple seems increasingly duplicitous. One way that we might resolve the apparent "contradiction" in St. George's attitude toward his wife and reveal the possibility of the master's sincerity is to recall his mixed assessment of Marian.

In marrying the young woman, St. George could be saving his disciple from the slightly fatuous idolatry of Marian, who, according to the master, is "life herself" with all its interfering conventional needs (children, expense accounts, luxury). St. George can afford to marry her precisely because he has retired as a writer and requires in his late years only an attractive, adoring fan. While Mrs. St. George, the embodiment of discipline, was a writer's ideal mate, "few men" were as lucky as the master to have had such a wife. Thus Overt's discipline must come from within; he has to "see it through" alone. St. George drives home this point in his midnight talk by theatrically exaggerating his insistence on "independence," even to the point of impugning his wife, who, ironically, was the exception proving the rule that women intrude. From the point of view sketched above, St. George's rescue of Overt from the "conventionally unconventional" Marian can be seen as sincere and the master's estimate of her character just, especially in light of her final appearance. Here she strikes Overt as full of "mere mechanical charity" and smug happiness; at last recognizing Marian's shallowness, Overt turns "from her with a strange irritation . . . a sort of disinterested disappointment." Perhaps he has finally gained some of his master's detachment, but if Overt has, his attainment of lucidity is too meager and too late.

Overt's misreading of St. George persists, even when he radically revises his judgment of the master in the tale's final scenes. The inadequacy of his "measurement" of the master becomes vividly, even comically, evident when he arrives at the engagement party and is bewildered by a series of jarringly contradictory impressions. As he talks to Marian his mind is full of images of St. George as embodying "failure," "abdication," and "superannuation" (p. 90). But when Overt confronts him the master seems "handsome, he was young" and full of life (p. 91). After St. George tells Overt "You're very strong," the young writer reflects that "the strange thing was that he seemed sincere—not a mocking fiend" (p. 94). This judgment, however, must be as quickly revised as his impression of the master's appearance, for St. George's parting words to his disciple are maddeningly ambiguous: "Consider at any rate the warning I am at present." To Overt this is "too much—he *was* the mocking fiend"; the harried disciple is left dispirited by the impenetrable master (p. 95). For even at this late date Overt fails to understand St. George's playful, teasing multifariousness and insists on seeing him as only one thing or the other. Overt is unaware that St. George is at once a "mocking fiend" and a "sincere" mentor. The master's personal "style" is indeed "considerably involved," as Overt observed early on, for it is composed of conflicting elements that defy reduction to a single meaning.

The master's undecidability accounts for the ultimate ambiguity of the tale as a whole. In her study of ambiguity Shlomith Rimmon has said that "The Lesson of the Master" presents a "deadlock of opposites" in that "there is no way of choosing between mutually exclusive interpretations": St. George as deceiver or savior of Overt.[26] But unlike Rimmon who views this deadlock as an end in itself, an "intention" to withhold resolution entirely, I think ambiguity is James's means of enacting a central theme of the tale: the heterogeneity of social reality. The coexistence of two opposite meanings forces the reader to become actively engaged in deciphering the text of St. George. In a larger context, by making the reader struggle, James initiates him into an experience of the obliquities of social life, its resistance to univocal, stable categorization. If the reader simply extracts, like Overt, a single meaning from the master's "involved style," then the experience of the refractory density of the "bright rich world" will be lost.[27] Thus the ultimate subject of the story is "social art" (a phrase from *The Ambassadors*), which characters and readers practice with varying degrees of skill. Those readers and characters who possess the most "social art" will recognize and explore the instability of the social text as it is represented in James's text.

The tale's concern with the theatricality of social life inevitably recalls Browning's own theatricality. And James's strategy wherein we experience the tale's ambiguity as social suggests a parallel in his own confrontations with Browning's puzzling performance in the highly mannered world of London society, the milieu, of course, where St.

93

George plays the role of master. What these analogies imply is that the social text, St. George, and Browning are, in a sense, equivalent, all exhibiting that "genius for mystification" that Overt attributes to his master. There are, then, three struggles occurring simultaneously in "The Lesson of the Master": the reader's, Overt's, and James's. While the first two contend with the indeterminacy of social art as embodied in St. George, James's struggle is with St. George's model Browning. And James must cope with the public, social manifestation of Browning's ambiguity, his theatricality, but also with the more private and primal mystification the poet presents—the double bind. Before exploring how James's surrogate Overt resolves the master's contradictory imperatives, it is necessary to examine the novelist's appropriation of Browning in the tale.

James's use of Browning has gone unnoticed despite the clues he left that seem to point to the poet. At the outset of the tale Overt's opinion of the master's literary stature is mixed: "for the young aspirant he had remained a high literary figure, in spite of the lower production to which he had fallen . . . the comparative absence of quality in his later work" (p. 5). This recalls the opening of James's review of *The Inn Album* where he laments the decline of the venerable poet into "barely comprehensible" verse. Overt feels "inwardly solicited to make" his opinion of the master's falling off "public" (p. 12), an impulse that James gave in to in his review, as he declared the poet's latest work to be "really too hopeless." Browning's identity with St. George is suggested in Overt's description of the "ill-matched parts" of the master's "genius": St. George, like Browning, does not look like an author; he "might have passed for a lucky stockbroker" (pp. 7, 15). But the major allusion to Browning in "The Lesson of the Master" is the name James gives the master. Browning's well-known personal myth was Perseus rescuing Andromeda, which symbolized for the poet his

94

elopement with Elizabeth Barrett. The anglicized version of this myth is of course St. George and the dragon, and, as William DeVane says, Browning used them interchangeably.[28] The legend is also operative in both *The Inn Album* and "The Lesson of the Master." James explicitly mentions the parallel: "St. George and the dragon is what the anecdote suggests!" remarks Overt after hearing that the master once failed to stop his wife from impulsively burning one of his unpublished novels (p. 27). Interestingly, in both works, as in Overt's remark quoted above, Browning and James parody the myth; St. George in James's version is not the knight but the dragon, the "mocking fiend" who carries off the princess and defeats the would-be savior. Similarly, in *The Inn Album* the St. George figure fails to save his beloved from the fiendish rogue, although the dragon is finally slain.

Browning's presence, moreover, extends beyond James's tale itself and figures in the circumstances of the work's composition. "The Lesson of the Master" was composed in 1888 when the poet was on James's mind. Writing to his friend Daniel Curtis in October 1888 (the story had been completed about three months before) James remarks that "I have lately been reading him over a good deal."[29] And Browning (at this date) was also the novelist's London neighbor; the poet had moved into 29 DeVere Gardens in 1887, while James had settled at number 34 a year before. Browning would see James "occasionally, and . . . had lunched with him, chatting as always about mundane things in a mundane way."[30]

That James was dissatisfied with this state of affairs is powerfully evident in "The Private Life." The anxiety James expresses there derives in part from Vawdrey-Browning's rejection of the younger writer's attempt to be more than a dining companion, to become intimate and finally know the poet's private self rather than his glib social persona. Only with difficulty does the narrator accept Vawdrey's indifference to his entreaties, and he is left frustrated and embittered at the great man's elusiveness. In all his tormenting ambiguity that so baffles and infuriates Overt, St. George is an earlier, though significantly different, version of Clare Vawdrey. The climax of "The Private Life" looks back to the end of "The Lesson of the Master" written three years before. Both young writers wander away into an emptiness that mirrors their inner desolation. We leave Overt perplexed, in the same disoriented, frustrated state as the narrator of "The Private Life" after his uncanny experience.

Overt and the narrator have not only failed to become their masters' intimates, but have been literally barred at the door to the private life of sexual experience. The image of the closed door that was prominent in "The Private Life" is also crucial in the earlier tale. Twice in two pages James uses this image to express Overt's isolation from Marian Fancourt. Upon hearing that she is not at home, Overt "turned rather dejectedly from the door." He pictures his loss of Marian in this way: "he had renounced her, yes; but that was quite another affair—that was a closed but not a locked door" (p. 88). But on hearing of her engagement "he seemed to see the door quite slammed in his face" (p. 88).

Although both tales register a similar range of emotions as they dramatize James's distressed personal response to the poet, the stories employ different aesthetic strategies in confronting Browning. In "The Private Life," as we have seen, James made no attempt to hide the fact that he was writing about the poet, and this created an artistic problem, for James was unable to gain the necessary aesthetic distance. Yet earlier, in "The Lesson of the Master," he had dealt with Browning in a less direct but aesthetically more successful manner. In writing this tale James turned his back on the actualities of his relation to Browning to escape the "fatal futility of fact." Knowing that he could not "depend on the resources and discipline of the 'real' to see him through,"[31]

96

James allowed his imagination free rein to explore his ambivalence about the poet. Instead of surrendering to the facts of his relation to Browning—his frustrating remoteness from the poet—as he would do four years later in "The Private Life," James probed the "possible other case." What if Browning, instead of ignoring James, welcomed the novelist into his private writing room for a confidential talk? This hypothetical situation is, of course, dramatized in "The Lesson of the Master," as James "projects" the "rich case" of the "might be," "the case rich and edifying."[32]

"The Lesson of the Master" reveals, I think, more about James's relation to Browning than does "The Private Life." In the earlier tale James, to use words from his preface, distills the "essence" of his feelings about the "observed reality" of the poet in the very act of "destroying" Browning's "prime identity." Thus James's indirect approach grants him license to confront his deepest fears. "The Lesson of the Master" brings to the foreground the latent anxieties—betrayal, anger, rivalry, envy, inadequacy—suggested in "The Private Life." Although the earlier work is more psychologically probing and aesthetically superior to "The Private Life," the writing of "The Lesson of the Master" evidently did not end James's problem with Browning. James's anxiety lingered, so that he was compelled to confront Browning again in fiction. The effort to attain "relief" and the search for resolution were crucial not only in James's relation to Browning but also formed part of what he called "the religion of doing." To recall one of his watchwords (to Adams in 1914): "It all takes doing—and I do. I believe I shall do yet again—it is still an act of life." It remains to discuss the psychological structure of his intimately personal act of life in "The Lesson of the Master."

James's fictive representation of his struggle with the double bind of Browning begins with Overt's first glimpse of the master, as he basks in all his literary and social glory. On

the "immense lawn" of his estate, Summersoft, he is surrounded by a group of fervent admirers, including a beautiful
young woman. "Seeing him for the first time this way is a
great event for me," says Overt, whose blatant need for a
model ("I need incentives . . . *you* are an incentive," he tells
St. George) is fulfilled by the master. "I love him," gushes the
adoring Overt, who is dazzled by St. George's embodiment of
the ideal that "art" is "but an intense life," as Marian phrases
it. This enviable balance of art and life is, however, precisely
what St. George implores Overt not to imitate. Take me as a
warning of what to avoid, asserts the master, who professes to
be ashamed of his failure to achieve literary "perfection." St.
George's emphatic warning seems strangely at odds with
Overt's awed impression of his "intense life," and the disciple's sense of contradiction is expressed in his reply to the
master's pleas: "you don't affect me in the way you'd apparently like to." Overt's remark implies that St. George has
come to embody for him the "contradictory double imperative": "act like your model—don't act like your model."
These are the conflicting "signals" the master "transmits" to
his disciple.

According to Girard, the "inexplicable counterorder":
" 'Don't imitate me!' . . . really means 'Do not appropriate
my object!' "[33] Marian Fancourt is the "object" that com-
pletes the triangle of mimetic desire, igniting the rivalry of
master and disciple, as St. George seeks to protect his object
from Overt's attempted possession. Significantly, James
structures the scene in which Overt gains his initial impression of St. George as a triangle of subject, object, and model-
rival. Overt sees the great man identified as the "fellow
talking to Marian . . . he is making up to her—they're going
off for another walk." Overt takes in the couple with a "certain surprise" because of the differences in their ages and his
sense that St. George "didn't look like an artist." Later in
this recognition scene Overt perceives that St. George's

mastery extends to the sexual. As Marian, St. George, and other guests sit down to dine, Overt observes that the master has placed himself in "familiar contact" with Marian, and that "pretty women were a clear need to this genius, and for the hour it was Miss Fancourt who supplied the want." His hourly "need" and "want" of women implies that the master possesses a voracious sexual appetite.

During a later conversation with Marian, Overt's impression of St. George's sexual authority becomes even sharper. In the scene at the art gallery examined earlier, where Paul and Marian accidentally meet, Miss Fancourt tells Overt that she has arrived with St. George. Overt at once senses he is in competition with the master: "Ah that gives him a pull over me—I couldn't have 'brought' you, could I?" "Why not you as well as he," answers Marian. Paul explains: "why he's a *père de famille*. They've privileges" (p. 46). This revealing remark makes explicit that the ambiguous master's most stable identity is as *père de famille*, the hoarding father whose "privileges" are sexual. Despite his recognition of the master's special advantages, Overt nonetheless decides to pursue Marian. To be more precise, Overt really has no choice but to pursue her, for he is imitating the desires of his model rather than expressing his own sexual impulses. "You excite my envy," admits Overt to Marian after she tells him that the master has disclosed "such wonderful things" during their private strolls. Only at this point, when she has revealed her intimacy with St. George, does Overt's estimation of her rise and his attraction to her become strong; before this Overt had coldly and accurately concluded that Marian is "after all but an immature girl." Clearly, Overt's desire for Marian is mediated: the rivalry it sparks between master and disciple "does not arise because of the fortuitous convergence of two desires on a single object; rather the subject desires the object because the rival desires it."[34]

Although Overt obeys his master's advice and severs his ties with Marian before he departs for Europe, he still feels he possesses her. But when he confronts the couple at their engagement party he realizes he has lost Marian. His rivalry with St. George ends and Overt's resolution to the double bind occurs. In the extraordinary penultimate scene of the tale, as the befuddled and bitter Overt watches the "hunted herdlike movement of London society at night," the disciple explicitly divides the master's double imperative into "two different domains of application": St. George as artist and St. George as sexual being. The master has "definitely ceased to count . . . as a writer," although he is still sexually masterful. The "ripeness of his successful manhood" is founded on "a great fund of life." By breaking apart St. George's double mastery, Overt neutralizes the double bind and is able to create an identity.

In vowing to devote himself solely to art, Overt, ironically, obeys the master's "lesson" that the creation of literature requires the sacrifice of a sexual life. But Overt's failure to attain the unity St. George had achieved in his exemplification of art as "an intense life" is also lost (at least temporarily) to the master himself, since Overt has condemned him as artistically bankrupt. However, this unity haunts Overt as a possibility which still remains within St. George's reach. Should the distinguished writer, having been revitalized by his new wife, one day regain his literary powers and publish "something of prime quality," the double mastery would again be his. Overt, at the end of the tale, views this prospect with horror; it is something "that he shouldn't be able to bear," because the master's union of life and art would dissolve the young writer's solution to the double bind, which is founded on Overt's relegation of St. George into two separate domains.

Inextricable from Overt's process of adjustment is the hatred which grips him upon hearing of Marian's engagement.

This hatred, directed at St. George for having "made a fool of" him, spreads to a general disgust at the "herdlike" character of London society..In his isolation in the midst of the crowded party—"people passed him on the staircase"— Overt feels ressentiment (which is Nietzsche's concept and, according to Girard, Nietzsche's disease). Unlike Nietzsche, who suffered "irrepressible ressentiment" and could not neutralize the double bind, Overt channels this emotion and makes it sustain his decision to become what St. George had called him—a "wonderfully strong" writer, a phrase that rings in Overt's mind as he stands alone in the cold night air at the tale's end. Pondering his future in the "moonless blackness," Overt silently swears to fulfill St. George's prediction. To become a great writer "might a little serve for revenge." In this primal moment, in which his identity is formed and his motives revealed, the word *revenge* exposes the hidden violence involved in the process of adjustment to the double bind. "At the origin of any individual or collective adjustment lies concealed a certain arbitrary violence." The well-adjusted person, says Girard, is the one who "conceals his violent impulses."[35] In artistic creation Overt will conceal the violence of ressentiment which, to Girard, resembles "the consequences of the mimetic process." And I have noted that for James the act of creation is violent, requiring assault on a "quantity of stated matter."

Overt's decision to seek "revenge" by writing recalls his creator's method of achieving mastery over Browning. James's "revenge" by rewriting turns the poet's sexual threat into a creative spur. The harsh review of *The Inn Album* is in itself an act of revenge, as it demolishes Browning's work only to build upon its ruins the basis for a more creative act of revenge—a rewriting of the play as "The Lesson of the Master." This dialectic of destruction and creation reemerges when James confronts *The Ring and the Book*, which "must suffer disintegration" to be transformed into a Jamesian novel. What links revenge and writing at the conclusion of "The Lesson of the Master" is their mediated, secondary status; both are born in the shadow of a prior act. Relevant here are not only the fables of belatedness offered by Bloom and Girard but also James's claim quoted earlier, that in the artistic process the writer must surrender his "original design" for a "substitute."

Directly after this statement James makes a remark that is apt concerning himself and Overt: the artist "must be a dupe . . . to be at all measurably a master." Overt has been a "dupe" (he uses the word to describe himself); he has forfeited his "original design" of marrying Marian and has accepted art as a "substitute." One way James accepts his inability to participate sexually is to generalize his individual case as representative of the inescapable cost of art. In enduring the artist's deprivation he becomes the "dupe" of his inadequacy and thereby its master. "Master" of course was James's sobriquet, and the word links him to St. George and thus to Browning. Like his fictional master, James baffles us with his ambiguity, a quality which also connects him to Browning. James's biographical relation to "The Lesson of the Master" is, finally, double in nature: he is St. George (whose first name is after all Henry) and Overt, master and disciple.[36]

James's mastery over Browning is gained at the expense of his being, in a sense, the poet's dupe. In his two short stories about the poet James depicts himself (through his surrogate) as deceived, rejected, humiliated, manipulated, and betrayed by Vawdrey and St. George, Browning's counterparts. This pattern strongly suggests that James portrays himself with a large measure of self-abasement, which takes particular expression in parody, both of himself and of the typical Jamesian character—"that frivolous thing an observer" as the narrator is disparagingly called in "The Private Life." In that tale, James's self-representation as a myopic young writer absorbed in spinning fantastic theories about the two Vawdreys ridicules his own mystification with Browning. But the subject of James's boldest parody in "The Lesson of the Master" is not directly himself, rather it is one of his deepest beliefs—the "doctrine of renunciation." James not only simplifies his personal creed, but he turns it into a ruse used to deceive himself. To compound bitterly the irony, the perpetrator of the trick, the man who preaches the doctrine, is a surrogate of the writer whose own life seemed to mock most James's belief.

By depicting himself as humiliated by the Browning figure James reaches the most extreme and personal dimension of his self-abasement. In confronting in his imagination his deepest, almost nightmare fears of Browning as a "mocking fiend," James provokes himself to form his sexual identity. He uses Browning as a blocking agent, a contrived obstacle to the private life of sexual relations, who pressures James into defining his sexual selfhood in reaction to this menacing figure. Although James had settled upon his sexual choice long before writing the tale (in his famous 1881 letter to Grace Norton, James had ruled out marriage for himself), "The Lesson of the Master" can be read as a fable in which James re-presents and defends his decision. While this self-defense is fictive, the conclusion Overt reaches is identical with his creator's: celibacy, the submergence of physical passion in the vicarious realm of art, is his choice. By dramatizing his decision in a scenario of humiliation and betrayal, James reveals considerable anxiety about his lack of an actively sexual life. Indeed, in this context, his choice seems more a result of resentment and a sense of victimization than an active assertion of will.[37] This defensive, reactive quality links celibacy with the earlier equation of writing with revenge. Writing and celibacy, then, are acts of compromise and substitution that accept loss as the condition of their existence.

To be Browning's "dupe," to subject himself and his most personal creed to mockery, was, in all its painful self-exposure, part of the price James had to pay to resolve, if only tentatively, his problem with Browning. James transforms the poet from a figure causing sexual anxiety to a model of artistic inspiration not by simply confronting all his fears about Browning, but by exaggerating and magnifying them to parodic extremes. Then the purgation of his anxieties could occur and free him to master Browning. Ultimately, then, James's mastery "consists in the denial and in the deconstruction of his own mastery," as Shoshana Felman has written about "The Turn of the Screw."[38]

We witness in "The Private Life" and in "The Lesson of the Master" a remarkably creative and healing act of self-renewal: James in the traumatic process of coming to terms with Browning. Only the most unflinching self-knowledge can galvanize such a process. And only great artists can acknowledge the difficult and unflattering truth that "fallibility" and mastery are inextricable. Throughout James's career his profound self-awareness proved a continual source of creative energy, and never more so than in his darkest times. As he wrote in a famous and moving notebook entry during his depression over the *Guy Domville* debacle:

> Large and full and high the future still opens.
> It is now indeed that I may do the work of my life.
> And I will. I have only to *face* my problems.[39]

CHAPTER IV

JAMES, BROWNING, AND THE THEATRICAL SELF

James himself explicitly declares that rewriting is his characteristic response when he confronts interesting work. Writing in 1913 to H. G. Wells to report his less than enthusiastic reaction to the younger writer's latest work, James explains: "I am of my nature . . . a critical, a non-naif, questioning, worrying reader."[1] With this warning James hopes to justify his remarkable reading habits, which he describes: "To read a novel at all I perform afresh, to my sense, the act of writing it, that is of re-handling the subject according to my own lights and overscoring the author's form and pressure with my own vision and understanding of the way." James hastens to add that his attitude, rather than a result of restless boredom with the text at hand, is "the very measure of my attention and interest." Only on those rare occasions when James "sees a subject" in what the author has done and "feels its appeal" is he stimulated to rewrite. A year before his letter to Wells James had performed his best known rewriting—in homage to Browning's centenary.

Because Browning's poetry "has touched *everything*,"[2] the poet creates a "complexity of suggestion" hardly to be exhausted by James's sketch of how he would redo *The Ring and the Book*. James tacitly notes this near the conclusion of his homage: "I have wanted, alas, to say such still other fine, fond things—it being our poet's great nature to prompt them at every step."[3] This chapter concerns one of the things James leaves unsaid: that his impulse to redo the poet's works is not confined to *The Ring and the Book* or *The Inn Album*. While in 1912 James merely spins his "dream of the matter," in *The Wings of the Dove* ten years before, he accomplished his most creative use of Browning by rewriting *In a Balcony*, the poet's verse play of 1855.

The disarmingly personal opening of the preface to *The Wings of the Dove* has had the happy effect, from James's viewpoint, of diverting readers from investigating the work's literary sources. When James speaks of the germinal "idea" of the novel as "that of a young person . . . early stricken and doomed,"[4] critics have rightly inferred that James is alluding to the death of Minny Temple. It is with her death that discussions of the novel's sources usually begin and end.[5] But James's admission that *The Wings of the Dove* represents "to my memory a very old—if I shouldn't perhaps rather say a very young motive"—directs us back not only to his tragic cousin but to other momentous experiences of his youth. Among them is his reading of *Men and Women*, where James doubtless found *In a Balcony*. Although he waited some forty years to use the play, James's preface stresses the novel's youthful origins: "I can scarce remember the time when the situation on which this long-drawn fiction mainly rests was not vividly present to me." While he makes no specific reference to *In a Balcony*, the novelist almost certainly knew the play, since he was a life-long reader of Browning, who always remained to James "the author of *Men and Women*."

The plot of *In a Balcony*, consisting as it does of a single scene and only three characters, is easily summarized. The

play concerns the efforts of the lovers Constance and Norbert to find a way to marry without
offending the Queen. Among the obstacles to their marriage is Constance's conviction that the Queen, whom she believes is jealously possessive, will refuse to surrender her prime minister, the trusted and beloved Norbert, to her poor cousin Constance. Constance's uncertainty about the depth of Norbert's commitment to her is another barrier to their marriage. After dismissing Norbert's insistent demand that they simply ask the Queen for immediate permission, the scheming Constance creates a plot, a masquerade that will involve Norbert's false declaration of love for the Queen. According to Constance, "since none love Queens directly," she will refuse Norbert and will give Constance to him as a substitute. The plot backfires because, after a series of complications, the Queen is discovered to have fully believed Norbert's declaration; the sheltered, lonely ruler has fallen in love with her prime minister. When the forthright Norbert declares the truth to the Queen—that it is Constance he really loves—she furiously stalks off. Left alone on the balcony, their plan shattered, the lovers are convinced that the Queen plans to punish, even execute, them. Faced with the prospect of death, the lovers passionately declare their love. The play ends with the Queen's guard approaching and the fate of Constance and Norbert left unknown.

Parallels with *The Wings of the Dove* are strikingly obvious. Both works dramatize the relations among a triangle consisting of a young couple and a lonely, deprived woman, who possesses enormous power and who can remove the obstacles that prevent the lovers from marrying. The Queen and Milly, the "princess," are a peculiar combination of potency and the powerlessness—heirs to vast fortunes and emotionally and sexually deprived, vulnerable to the declarations of an attractive "suitor." Cast as suitors in their lovers' schemes, Norbert and Densher are essentially pas-

sive, subservient to dynamic, ambitious, shrewdly manipulative women. Because they suffer from a lack of will and
the obsessions of unrequited sexual passion, both men are
easily entangled in the immoral designs of their partners.
The main action in both works is the formation and enacting of a plot—a deliberately fictive stratagem that consists
of the man confessing his love to the lonely woman. But the
scheme goes awry in both cases when one member of the
triangle falls unexpectedly in love: the Queen with Norbert,
Densher with Milly's memory. There is a notable congru-
ence in the final movements of both works, as the main
characters—Densher and Constance—engage in acts of self-
purgation that leave them engulfed in stillness. The marriages that have been impending from the start end in ruin.

We can clarify our understanding of what James took from
In a Balcony by considering Blackmur's distinction between
"real" and "mechanical" plot. The latter is "what the action
is about as anecdote," while the "real plot" "reveals the
being of the people to whom the action happens and thus
reveals the action of the soul in its poetic drama."[6] James, I
think, borrows the "mechanical plot" of Browning's play as
the scaffolding for his "real plot"—the exploration of his
main characters' "inward drama," to use James's phrase
about Densher. In effect, James rewrites *In a Balcony* by
transforming "the guarded objectivity" characteristic of the
dramatic genre into the drama of consciousness. Juxtaposing
these texts makes particularly clear the novelist's attempt
at a fusion of the "scenic method" he had discovered as he
began work on *The Wings of the Dove* in 1895, with the
explanations and "amplifications" of narration. This syn-
thesis James calls "dramatic analysis," which defines the
representational technique of the three late masterpieces.

But *In a Balcony* provides James with more than a scaffolding; its characterization, formal strategy, and the complicity of author and character make Browning's play a re-

markable prefiguration in miniature (as would befit a play of one short scene) of *The Wings of the Dove*. However, the above aspects must be inscribed within the master theme that links these works—their exploration of the theatrical self. Given James's fascination with Browning's own theatricality, it is not surprising that he would find *In a Balcony* absorbing. And theatricality partly accounts for the fact that *In a Balcony* is one of Browning's personal favorites among his works.[7] Before we pursue James's "rehandling," with his "own vision and understanding" of the subject, brief consideration should be given to the irony implicit in any discussion of Browning, James, and theatricality: as playwrights both men were embarrassing failures. Indeed, it is fair to say that their vain and repeated attempts to conquer the London stage account for "no sadder or less creditable" phases in their careers.[8] This is Betty Miller's assessment of what she calls Browning's "long history of frustration and exacerbated vanity" in writing unsuccessful plays for seven years beginning in 1836. But Miller's words apply with equal force to James's own deluded hopes for theatrical glory and commercial success, hopes which were definitively dashed by the *Guy Domville* fiasco of 1895.

The infatuation of Browning and James with the theater confirms a larger cultural pattern—the post-Romantic change in attitudes toward theatricality. Jonas Barish has described this transition from Romanticism's belief "in an absolute sincerity" to, "as the century advances," "not only a tolerance for the theater, and an enthusiasm for the theater, but a cult of the theater."[9] Barish makes a crucial distinction concerning this waning of the "antitheatrical prejudice." The post-Romantic cult of the theater is "if not for the theater as an institution, at least for theatricality as a mode of existence." No two oeuvres exemplify this distinction more vividly than those of Browning and James. Yet confusion between theatrical behavior and the theater can explain, at least partially, their calamitous relations with the English stage. Writing days before the *Guy Domville* disaster, James presciently remarks: "I may have been meant for the Drama . . . but I certainly wasn't meant for the Theatre."[10] James realizes here that he has confounded one with the other; perhaps his profound understanding of the drama of human behavior, of its inherent theatricality, misled him to believe that the theater was his proper métier.

Conflict and confusion between the theater, acting, and dramatic form are evident at the very start of Browning's career in an incident that his biographers usually consider a kind of epiphany of vocation. So enthralled was the twenty-year-old Browning by Edmund Kean's performance of Richard III that he left the theater with a double vow: "to act as well as to make verses."[11] Clearly, Browning intuits a link between the two activities but he proceeds to compartmentalize them early in his career. He writes two long poetic works—*Pauline* and *Paracelsus*—and then, still stirred by the memory of Kean (and initial encouragement from the impresario and actor Macready), Browning turns to the stage—if not to act, at least to give actors words. But not until his playwriting career ended in failure did Browning discover his true genius. He channeled his love of acting and of the theater into the perfecting of a dramatic poetic form that took as its subject what Kean had displayed so memorably—man's histrionic self.

Both Browning and James had to contend with "the abysmal vulgarity and brutality of the theatre," particularly with what James called the "vast English Philistine mob"[12] of playgoers. Though both met rejection from this audience, their plays suffered from nearly opposite defects. Whereas James, in an effort to pander to popular taste, forced himself to "be as broad, as simple, as clear, as British, in a word, as possible,"[13] Browning's plays tended to be obscure, to "occur in the chambers of the mind," as one contemporary critic complained.[14] This inwardness was wholly consonant with Browning's avowed intention to portray "Action in Character rather than Character in Action," as he writes in his preface to *Strafford*. His aesthetic aim informs *In a Balcony* and also anticipates James's own description of Ibsen's innovations in his admiring 1891 essay on the playwright. James applauds *Hedda Gabler* for presenting "the picture not of an action but of a condition . . . a portrait of a nature."[15] But it would be in his late fiction, particularly *The Wings of the Dove,* and not in his rigidly conventional plays where James would most profit from Ibsen's and Browning's experiments in dramatizing what he had once supposed undramatic—the "occult psychology of a single soul," to use Swinburne's description of Browning's "sole object of interest."[16] In his farewell to playwriting, *In a Balcony,* Browning creates one of his most intriguing psychological portraits in the radically theatrical Constance, whose kinship with one of James's most seductive performers—Kate Croy—will be explored below.

As unabashedly performing selves, Constance and Kate masterfully act on the social stage, revealing a prodigious energy and skill. But they are not merely gifted dissemblers adept at playing roles; they are creators, for they author plots and fabricate fictions. In so doing, Constance and Kate literally enact Browning's and James's plots and align themselves with their creators as "delegates"—functions James explicitly sought for his figures.

Constance celebrates indirection as the essential mode of human behavior; pretense and role playing are for her the groundwork of social interaction. In an effort to instruct Norbert in her view of reality Constance offers an "example":

> I let you kiss me, hold my hands
> Why? do you know why? . . . the kiss, because you have
>   a name at court;

> This hand and this, that you may shut in each
> A jewel, if you please to pick up such.[17]

This hypothetical instance is supplemented by another:

> You love a rose; no harm in that:
> But was it for the rose's sake or mine
> You put it in your bosom? mine, you said—
> Then, mine you still must say or else be false.
>
> (lines 96–99)

For Constance sincerity seems to have been replaced by the careful management of impressions for the sake of exploiting others. The theatricality of her view of experience is implicit at this point, but comes to the fore in her passionate outpouring to Norbert quoted below, where she urges him to keep their love secret:

> Where are you now? immersed in cares of state—
> Where am I now? intent on festal robes—
>
> . . . .
>
> What was this thought for . . .
> Which broke the council up?—to bring about
> One minute's meeting in the corridor!
> And then the sudden sleights, strange secrecies,
> Complots inscrutable, deep telegraphs,
> Long-planned chance-meetings, hazards of a look,
> "Does she know? does she not know? saved or lost?"
> A year of this compression's ecstasy
> All goes for nothing! you would give this up
> For the old way, the open way, the world's.
>
> (lines 185–97)

This speech, which constitutes a summation of her perception of reality, reveals that Constance lives her life as if she is an actress in a romantic drama or, more precisely, melodrama. Moreover, the artfully composed style of her illicit love affair makes her the author of the melodrama that is her life. Constance seems to relish the intricate scheming and the "ecstasy" of "compression" it affords at least as much as her love of Norbert. It is a measure of her theatricality that what so disturbs Constance is the prospect that the clandestine plotting she cherishes must come to an end if she submits to the "old way, the open way" of marriage. Instead of being eager to marry her lover and escape the agitations of a secret romance, Constance seeks only to continue her skilled dissembling in even more ingenious plots. Given her delight in intrigue, it is hardly surprising that Constance dismisses Norbert's forthright demand for an "open, easy" love founded on the "truth" of his passion for her. His simple trust in "ourselves being true" causes him to reject Constance's insistence that they must trick the Queen: "The Queen's the Queen, / I am myself—no picture, but alive / In every nerve and every muscle, here / At the palace window . . ." (lines 148–51). Norbert's tautologies imply a view of the self as stable and substantial, anchored to the immediate by a commitment to "being true"; such a conception is precisely the opposite of his lover's theatrical self.

Like James, Erving Goffman believes that "social intercourse is itself put together as a scene is put together, by the exchange of dramatically inflated actions, counteractions and terminating replics . . . life itself is a dramatically enacted thing."[18] That Constance reveals a similar conception of life as a performance is evident in the language Browning has created for her. His energetically compressed verse, in its almost breathless pace and pungent images and phrases, mirrors his heroine's own dramatic flair. Therefore it is particularly apt that her memorable phrase "compression's ecstasy" refers to both her thrill in subtle plotting and the very manner of her speech. Constance's consciously stylized speech is an instance of that rare achievement in the drama: what James calls "really constructive dialogue"—"organic and dramatic, speaking for itself, representing and embodying substance and form."[19]

Compression characterizes not only Constance's speech but also the structure of the play; it is rigorously economical, limited to a single scene of three characters, and enacted in the austere and narrow confines of a balcony. In subtitling *In a Balcony* a "scene" in later editions Browning further emphasized the play's compression. Within this taut form an intense drama of aroused and barely manageable passion unfolds; clearly substance and form are one in this work as it achieves the "deep breathing economy and an organic form" that James believed the hallmark of successful literature. Critics of *In a Balcony* have commented on the play's tightly controlled plot, its relentless movement to a tragic climax; Stoll goes so far as to say that in this play "Browning achieved his greatest situation . . . a superbly ironical contretemps."[20]

If *In a Balcony* qualifies, in James's terms, as a "really wrought work of art" in that the "grave distinction between substance and form" "signally breaks down,"[21] Browning's play also satisfies James's conception of the drama as a literary genre. In his preface to *The Awkward Age*, one of his most important statements concerning the "fine rigor" of dramatic form, James speaks of the "coercive charm" of the genre as it challenges its creator "to make the presented occasion tell all its story itself, remain shut up in its own presence." In direct contrast, the novel "as largely practiced in English is the perfect paradise of the loose end; the play consents to the logic of but one way, mathematically right, and with the loose end as gross an impertinence on its sur-

face . . . as the dangle of a slipper. . . . We are shut up wholly
to cross-relations, relations all within the action itself; no
part of which is related to anything but some other part."²²
This is as precise a description of the achieved "compression" of *In a Balcony* as one can find.

In elaborating Densher's ambivalences, James's artistic intentions at first glance would seem to be opposed to Browning's (and Constance's) insistence on "compression." This
compression is part of what James calls the "guarded objectivity" of the drama (most apparent in one-act plays), which
comes from the "imposed absence of that 'going behind' to
compass explanations and amplifications."²³ The refusal of
the drama to explore the inner life is not a fault or limitation, emphasizes James, but rather its "divine distinction"
as a literary genre. The novel obeys a different "law of its
kind," one subtly yet importantly related to the drama. The
novel represents an "inward drama," and in its efforts to
explore interior life the novel, or at least the late Jamesian
kind, insists on going behind, as the representation of consciousness becomes its central preoccupation. In "going behind," which entails analytical "explanations," James hopes
not to sacrifice the economy or vividness of drama but to
create a fusion of the presentational (the dramatic) with the
"amplifications" of the narrator. "In the high interest of
economy" James sought, if not always successfully, to structure the novel of consciousness on "selected" and "fixed"
"centers"; "there is no economy of treatment without an
adopted, a related point of view." Although these centers are
often displaced in the inevitable compromises of creation,
James's ideal is to adhere rigorously to a character's viewpoint in order to achieve "the dramatist's greatest goal"—
"intensity."

With witty understatement James remarks that "I myself
have scarcely to plead the cause of 'going behind' which is

right and beautiful and fruitful in its place."²⁴ Such a "place" was, of course, *The Wings of the Dove*, where, instead of "compression" and the tightly ordered unfolding of event, a technique of expansion is operative: the dramatization of the intricate movements—the tortuous rationalizations, self-deceptions, hesitations, and conversion—of Densher's consciousness. The reader is permitted to experience Densher's mental life and to grasp "the rhythm of his inward drama"²⁵ as he struggles to hold fast to his commitment to "being true." James is most interested in exploring the process of "fusion and fermentation" that constitutes Densher's development.

What preoccupies Densher is his conflict with Kate, which is akin to the struggle between Norbert and Constance. Densher, like Norbert, seeks to be "true" but eventually becomes enmeshed in his lover's design. Because of a sincere wish not to deceive Milly and to maintain his moral equilibrium, Densher tentatively adopts a posture of inaction. But "the inevitabilities of the abjection of love," particularly his acute sense of sexual frustration, finally impel Densher to act in both senses of the word. As in *In a Balcony*, the refusal of sexual union is the means by which the woman coerces her lover into surrendering to her plot. Norbert's impassioned "Love has been so long / Subdued in me / Eating me through and through" is echoed in Densher's intense feeling of deprivation. Sounding like an introspective Norbert, Densher feels a "kind of rage at what he wasn't having; an exasperation, a resentment, begotten truly by the very impatience of desire, in respect of his postponed and relegated, his so extremely manipulated state" (2:175–76). Realizing that he has been "perpetually bent to her will," Densher is struck by a "sense almost of shame"; he wonders whether he has "really no will left. How could he know . . . without putting the matter to the test?" He tests his will, of course, by demanding that Kate sleep with him as payment for performing in her scheme. By linking desire and theatricality Browning and James expose their homologous structure: both are activities constituted by a lack or absence. If desire by definition implies some absent thing, theatricality also depends on a "postponed . . . state," a perpetual deferral of the fully present, stable self implicit in Norbert's phrase "ourselves being true" and Densher's plea to Kate—"take me just as I am." Constance's reply—"Not now!" (her very first words)—and Kate's response—"Let us wait"—signify the deferment these women embody; their identities are founded on the gap which creates, indeed constitutes, desire and the theatrical self. An absence of self makes possible the role playing of Constance and Kate.

Although Densher only grudgingly consents to Kate's plot, he fully recognizes "the heroic ring" of her audacity, which has its source in what Densher admiringly calls "her pure talent for life." Kate's "talent," which belittles "his own incapacity for action," is never more impressive to Densher than when he observes her "beautiful entrance" onto the social stage of Lancaster Gate in book 6, chapter 3. This scene gives rise to Densher's most awed and ambivalent response to Kate, as he defines her talent as essentially theatrical. And in glimpsing the complexity of her role playing, he finds that her theatrical self has created a distance between them.

Kate's entrance onto the "social scene" of Lancaster Gate, where Aunt Maud presides, strikes Densher as the arrival of a "distinguished actress." "As such a person was to dress the part, to walk, to look, to speak, in every way to express, the part, so all this was what Kate was to do for the character she had undertaken, under her aunt's roof, to represent" (2:34). Because Maud disapproves of the impoverished journalist as a suitor for her niece, Kate fabricates a Kate indifferent to Densher; this is the "character" she has "undertaken" to "represent." As Densher watches Kate's performance in "the glare of the footlights," he explores the theatrical metaphor that her behavior inevitably brings to mind. With characteristic passivity Densher sees himself "as in his purchased stall at the play" observing the "faultless soldier on parade." He perceives that under Aunt Maud's intense scrutiny Kate's face is "disciplined," her "expression impeccable"; and Densher has the sharp sense that "the drama . . . was between *them*, them quite preponderantly; with Merton Densher relegated to mere spectatorship" (2:35). But Densher, far from feeling comfortable in the audience, is acutely uneasy; instead of joining in the "proper round of applause" for Kate, he is "almost too scared to take part in the ovation" and can only stare in silence. Densher feels "the least bit sick . . . his appreciation had turned for the instant to fear— had just turned, as we have said, to sickness" (2:35).

Densher's "sickness" has a deeper cause than his disgust at Maud's "managerial appreciation" of her niece's "tangible value," and dissatisfaction with the minor role he has been assigned. The crucial reason for Densher's unease is that the "game" must be played at all. In his conversation with Kate before the "drama," Densher, as he had done earlier in the novel, makes his hatred of the plot explicit and reiterates his plea to marry Kate and end their scheme. What Densher craves is simply to be alone with his lover; he savors their rare and precious privacy: "They were alone—it *was* all right: he took in anew the shut doors and the permitted privacy, the solid stillness of the great house . . . What it amounted to was that he couldn't have her . . . evasive . . . He didn't want her deeper than himself, fine as it might be as wit or as character; he wanted to keep her where their communication would be straight and easy and their intercourse independent" (2:19).

Densher's anguish stems from his suspicion that he will never be able to "keep" Kate from performing; "she was made for great social uses," as Milly observes in one of the novel's shrewdest assessments of Kate. Milly's insight expresses an essential truth about Kate: in spite of her genuine love of Densher, her theatrical self not only rebels against his pleas but is at odds with the very assumptions that form the basis of his thought. Her insistence on a performing self conflicts with Densher's desire to be taken "just as I am." Social performance creates a "represented" self (as Kate is described as representing a character to Maud) in distinct contrast to the private, "natural" self Densher's language implies. For Kate, a space where "their communication would be straight and easy and their intercourse independent" is at best only temporary; she prefers the mobility of the public stage rather than the entanglements of intimacy. Thus it is strikingly apt that Kate's sexual surrender to Densher is represented only in terms of his intense memory of it. The most private act of the theatrical self is one of the gaps in James's text, which suggests that her private self is an absence and therefore not representable in literary form.

Kate's performing self, like Constance's, depends on the lack of a solid, centered self, which enables her to be perpetually "evasive," to move easily from role to role on the "plane of mere elegant representation"(1:171) in a sort of theatricalized version of the Keatsian "chameleon poet." Milly notes Kate's absence of self: "Kate had for her new friend's eyes the extraordinary and attaching property of appearing at a given moment to show as a beautiful stranger, to cut her connexions and lose her identity" (1:223). In appearing to Milly as a "stranger," "more objective," and "other," Kate reveals that her free floating, detached self is characterized by an essential blankness. James makes this conception of the theatrical self explicit in *The Tragic Muse*, where Peter Sherringham defines the source of Miriam's histrionic genius: "What's rare in you is that you have . . . no nature of your own . . . you are always playing something; there are no intervals. It's the absence of intervals, of a *fond* or background."[26] Kate's need to be "always playing something" finds satisfaction in prolonging her clandestine romance; she, like Constance, is exhilarated by the sheer activity of artful dissembling. Kate tells Densher: "there's fun in it too. We must get our fun where we can . . . our relation's quite beautiful. It's not a bit vulgar. I cling to some saving romance in things" (1:72). Clearly what constitute the largest part of "romance" for Kate are secret rendezvous with Densher and hoodwinking Maud and Milly.

Despite Kate's obstinacy about marriage, Densher remains enthralled not only by her theatrical panache, but by her talents as a dramatist. When, early in the novel, she describes Maud as having "fixed upon me herself, settled on me with her wonderful gilded claws . . . an eagle—with a gilded beak as well, and with wings for great flights" (1:73), her flow of images makes a great impression on Densher: "it had really, her sketch of the affair, a high color and a great style; at all of which he gazed a minute as at a picture by a master" (1:74). The "great style" of Kate's "sketch" is founded on her capacity for image making, which is evident in her effortless transformation of Maud into a wealth of evocative and witty guises. Whether depicting herself as a "trembling kid" about to be "introduced into the cage of the lioness Maud," or calling her aunt "a great seamed silk balloon," and, most notoriously, dubbing Milly Theale a "dove," Kate's fertile metaphoric imagination defines reality as aesthetic. Active in Kate's sensibility is the artistic (and human) propensity for imposing fictive constructs on reality by recasting experience into symbols. Inevitably her symbol making diminishes and distances the human actuality of those she perceives by imprisoning them in imagery. But the aestheticizing of reality is not confined to Kate; indeed, it is the most characteristic and frequent mode of perception in *The Wings of the Dove*, affecting all the major figures and significantly James himself.[27]

The scene in which Milly receives Kate's benediction re-verberates in a number of directions. The word *dove* makes Milly feel "herself so delicately, so considerately embraced; not with familiarity or as a liberty taken, but almost cere-monially and in the manner of an *accolade;* partly as if, though a dove who could perch on a finger, one were also a princess with whom forms were to be observed" (1:283). Milly's train of thought here is significant: she feels like a "princess," for Kate's image inevitably recalls to her mind another accolade—Susie's often-repeated image of Milly, which is, of course, "princess." "Mrs. Stringham was a woman of the world, but Milly Theale was a princess, the only one she had yet to deal with" (1:120). Susie's princess embodies the "romantic life itself" to her rather saccharine imagination, and Milly is aware of her friend "always suspi-ciously sparing her"; "to treat her as a princess was a posi-tive need of her companion's mind" (1:255). But if Milly is Susie's "princess," she is first of all James's "Princess," as he makes explicit in the final section of the preface. James ad-mits to approaching Milly "circuitously," "at second hand, as an unspotted princess is ever dealt with; the pressure all round her kept easy for her, the sounds, the movements regulated." The congruity between James's and Susie's atti-tudes toward Milly results from the novelist's effort to es-tablish an intimacy between himself and his character, whom he conceives of as the "impersonal author's concrete deputy or delegate, a convenient substitute or apologist for the creative power."[28] Susie's profession as a writer makes even clearer her kinship with James.

Apart from their wish to spare and protect Milly, Mrs. Stringham's and her creator's solicitude is simultaneously insidious, for in treating Milly as a princess they muffle her particularity, specifically her imminent doom. To be "mer-ciful" to the vulnerable Milly, and to express this feeling in imagery—"princess," "dove," "American girl"—is to transform her into a fictive construct. Once her symbolic identity eclipses her personal identity, one is free to manipulate the symbol and weave it into a plot. This process of dehumanization describes the activity of the novel's central figures, as their compulsion to use Milly is nearly inextricable from their sympathy for her. James himself is not exempt from aestheticizing Milly, for in his method of "merciful indirection"—which also describes the behavior of his characters toward Milly—James enacts an aesthetic attitude as he dramatizes it.

A passage in *A Small Boy and Others* provides further insight into the indirection and distance characteristic of the aesthetic disposition that James shares with his characters. Describing an early and momentous visit to the theater, James discovers that his "great initiation" into the "thrill of an aesthetic adventure" is constituted less by the actual play he witnesses than by his discovery of "ironic detachment" and the "first glimpse of that possibility of a 'free play of mind.' "[29] Since the theatrical self has a marked predilection for these very qualities, the autobiographical motive in James's lifelong attraction to theatricality suggests itself. Supporting this suggestion is the self-characterization made near the start of his first volume of autobiography: "I . . . hung inveterately and woefully back, . . . this relation . . . seemed proper and prcappointed." Although this famous confession concerns James's ineradicable sense of belatedness concerning William James, the distance James notes here expresses his essential stance toward experience. "Wondering and dawdling and gaping" are what he "was to enjoy more than anything," James tells us, and while this recalls Densher's "mere spectatorship," James's inclination to hang back also grants him some of the pleasures of freely circulating enjoyed by the theatrical self. And the curious blankness that propels this unmoored self, a Kate or a Constance, is not wholly absent from James, whose cultivation of distance when young provided "so little . . . to 'show' " others that he appeared to the world a "dunce." Later, after shedding this particular persona, he maintained his strategic detachment and refusal of commitment by embracing the "positive saving virtue of vagueness," which he distinguished from "mere inaction."

A curious moment at the end of the preface reveals in miniature James's intimate relation to the aestheticizing process. After disclosing that he has dealt with Milly as an "unspotted princess," James savors the word, and his mind seems to play with it, as if lost in reverie: "so if we talk of princesses, do the balconies opposite the palace gates, do the coigns of vantage and respect enjoyed for a fee, rake from afar the mystic figure in the gilded coach as it comes forth into the great *place*." Here we witness James's aesthetic attitude in the very process of smothering Milly by encasing her in romantic fantasy. At this point Milly has become even less earthbound than a princess; she has vanished in the haze of James's fancy—a "mystic figure." This last glimpse of Milly (which significantly parallels Densher's mythologizing of her late in the novel) marks her total imprisonment in romantic imagery, which reaches fairy tale proportions with the reference to a "gilded coach." The preface's portrayal of Milly's steadily diminishing actuality prefigures her fate in the novel. After this aesthetic "reverie," James seems to become aware that he has overindulged his fancy and offers a sort of apology: "But my use of windows and balconies is doubtless at best an extravagance by itself."

The set of associations sparked in James's mind by his use of the word "princess" yields other significances apart from making vivid his attitude toward Milly. No sooner does James talk of princesses than he uses the word "balconies." Besides having a logical relation to princesses, balconies can be seen as a nod at Browning's play. This conclusion be-

comes more plausible when we note the clear affinities between James's princess and Browning's Queen. In many respects the Queen is an older Milly: ethereal, love-starved,
aestheticized, controlling the destiny of the scheming lovers
who have ensnared her.

Susie's view of Milly as "effete and overtutored . . . infinitely refined" could serve as a summation of Constance's
image of the Queen. Both Susie and Constance see them in
rather cliché terms as stage princesses, a stereotype Susie
makes explicit when she calls Milly a "princess in a conventional tragedy" (1:120). Constance's romanticized perception
of reality leads her to dismiss Norbert's view that the Queen
is "just" and "generous" because it is far too prosaic. In casting her in a grander role, Constance portrays the Queen as
leading a "life / Better than life, and yet no life at all. / Conceive her born in such a magic dome, / Pictures all round
her!" (lines 104–7). Cloistered in her fabulous palace, the
"sole spectator" of the works of art that surround her, the
lonely ruler gains all her knowledge of life from the "silent
gallery," never daring to venture outside. Constance's vision
of the Queen's rarefied existence, "more grandiose than life,"
is pointedly ironic since it is most apt as a self-portrait; the
blight of aestheticism which she thinks has infected the
Queen has in fact victimized Constance.

Once the Queen comes on stage it becomes obvious that
Constance's conception of her is distorted; rather than
wholly aestheticized, the Queen is also forthright and com-
passionate, eager to convince Constance of the morally redemptive power of love. Her belief is founded on absolute
trust in God, to whom she has committed her "will and
power." In remaining "mute, passive and acquiescent," as
she describes herself (line 563), the Queen is nearly the opposite of Constance, whose mobile self depends on performing and plotting as a means of deferring the consummation
of desire and insuring the "compression's ecstasy" of subtle

masquerades. Whereas Constance refuses to come to rest in the stasis of marriage, the Queen submits to God's will, which has granted her serenity: "I will not play . . . deceive," she tells Constance, as if deliberately distinguishing herself from her cousin.

Stillness, mental and physical, is as foreign to Constance as it is to Kate, the "panther" who stalks Milly. The famous tableau in which James freezes his two heroines echoes the tense confrontation of Constance and the Queen: ". . . figures so associated and yet so opposed, so mutually watchful; that of the angular pale princess . . . mainly seated, mainly still, and that of the upright restless slow-circling lady of the court . . ." (2:139).[30] James's allusion here to "some dim scene in a Maeterlinck play" is not the only relevant dramatic analogue, for James's scene frames the essential agon of *In a Balcony.*

If "life in these four walls" has left the Queen deprived, as she confesses it has, Milly seeks to make the best of her imprisonment within her palace. In talking to Densher, her description of life within the Palazzo Leporelli recalls the Queen's existence: "She insisted that her palace—with all its romance and art and history—had set up round her a whirlwind of suggestion that never dropped for an hour. It wasn't therefore, within such walls, confinement, it was the freedom of all the centuries" (2:174). In this passage Milly's image and her reality coincide; in Venice she becomes "a princess in a palace," as she describes herself at one point. Milly enacts the role of the "dove" and joins Kate, Susie, Densher, and James in the aestheticizing process. After receiving Kate's accolade, Milly muses: "she would have to be clear on how a dove would act." Milly, then, cannot be seen simply as a passive victim; not only does she participate in the activity of transforming herself into the images people create for her, but she proves skillful in her role playing.[31] In her Venetian palace Milly gives her triumphant social performance in which she eclipses even the beautiful Kate, who seems "somehow—for Kate—wanting in lustre." Awed by Milly's luminous presence, Densher realizes she is "acquitting herself tonight as a hostess . . . under some supreme idea"—namely of portraying the role of the "American girl as he had originally found her" (2:216, 203). Milly's involvement in the novel's pervasive activity of image making is seen most blatantly in her early reaction to Kate, whom Susie and Milly imagine as "the handsome English girl from the heavy English house," "as a figure in a picture stepping by magic out of its frame" (1:171). If Milly embodies the "American girl" in the minds of the Europeans, Kate is the embodiment for Milly of "the wondrous London girl," a type derived from Milly's reading of "tales of travellers and the anecdotes of New York . . . and a liberal acquaintance with the fiction of the day" (1:171).

As our discussion of Milly should suggest, there are no characters in the novel free of roles, manners, and reliance on conventions. Indeed, the need of these forms is partly what defines us as distinctively human. As James explains, theatricality (or what in *The Tragic Muse* is named the "affectation" of a "personal manner") "must have begun, long ago, with the first act of reflective expression—the substitution of the few placed articulate words for the cry or the thump or the hug."[32] This remarkable passage, inserted into the New York edition of *The Tragic Muse*, depicts man's entry into what Lacan calls the Symbolic Order—the code of language and custom—which is simultaneous, according to James, with his adoption of a "personal manner." Language and theatricality originate as the primal "substitution"— the imposition of an alien, impersonal sign system in place of the unmediated "cry or thump." This "substitution," which permanently defers direct communication, forcing it to be expressed through the mediation of language, convention, and "manner," violates the autonomy of the self. Paradoxically, the self experiences a sense of loss or absence as it is transformed into a representation of itself in social reality.[33] This absence or lack in the self is most acute, as we have seen, in the flamboyantly theatrical self, be it Browning's self-representation in public or some of his and James's characters. Thus, for James, all self-representation creates a gap in the subject, which widens in proportion to the elaborateness and calculation of the representation. Only with the renunciation of theatricality and language is the lack in being filled; but, as the endings of both works make clear, such fulfillment is inseparable from death.

The Queen of *In a Balcony* also discovers the inevitability of role playing, and we see in Browning's character the same complex merging of fiction and reality that defines Milly's experience. Like Milly, she not only passively accepts the images of herself created by others but gives these imposed fictions credence. By her own admission the Queen exists upon a "pedestal" where she leads an exquisitely dehumanized existence, forced to "stand and see men come and go." Abandoned on this pedestal, the Queen has felt herself "grow marble"; what "young man" would be attracted to "my marble stateliness?" she asks Constance. The Queen is acutely aware that as a living artwork she has hardened into the cold beauty of a "marble statue . . . / They praise and point at as preferred to life, / Yet leave for the first breathing woman's smile" (lines 409–11). The implicit meaning in the Queen's speech—that to be perceived as a human work of art is ultimately to be dead—reveals the most extreme dimension of the aestheticizing process, which Milly painfully grasps in her famous encounter with the Bronzino portrait. Seeing the "face of a young woman," "splendidly dressed," Milly thinks she is a "very great personage—only unaccompanied by a joy." In her shock of recognition at her physical likeness to this young woman, Milly realizes, through tears, that the Bronzino woman is "dead, dead,

dead. Milly recognized her exactly in words that had nothing to do with her" (1:231). She utters: "I shall never be
better than this," revealing in her moment of tormented
communion with the portrait her acknowledgment of the
deathly "apotheosis" of her imprisonment in art.

My insistence on the aestheticizing of reality, and the essential theatricality of James's and Browning's heroines,
seeks to clarify these complex and elusive women, who have
at times been described too broadly. Critics have been con-
tented with bland remarks about Kate's "self-command"[34]
or Constance's "peculiarly wily" character.[35] Sallie Sears
correctly observes that James's novel has "manipulation" as
its "real subject," but her sense of manipulation as the regarding of a "fellow human being not as a person but as an
object for use" should be enlarged.[36] For James, like Browning, is also interested in another aspect of manipulation—
the aesthetic manipulation of reality into fictive patterns.
Significantly, James names this phenomenon in a crucial
passage in which he reflects on its implications. James confronts the aestheticizing process through his delegate
Densher, who has been left in Venice with Milly and Susie
to enact his role in Kate's plot. Alone in his rooms, waiting
in anxious anticipation for the latest word on Milly's health,
Densher at last faces "the truth about Milly," "the facts of
her condition":

> He hadn't only never been near the facts of her condition . . .
> he hadn't only, with all the world, hovered outside an impene-
> trable ring fence, within which there reigned a kind of expen-
> sive vagueness made up of smiles and silences and beautiful
> fictions and priceless arrangements, all strained to breaking;
> but he had also, with every one else, as he now felt, actively
> fostered suppressions which were in the direct interest of
> every one's good manner, every one's pity, every one's really
> quite generous ideal. It was a conspiracy of silence, as the
> cliché went, to which no one had made an exception, the great

smudge of mortality across the picture, the shadow of pain and horror, finding in no quarter a surface of spirit or of speech that consented to reflect it. "The mere aesthetic instinct of mankind—!" our young man had more than once . . . said to himself; letting the rest of the proposition drop.

(2:298–99)

In this passage James lets no one off; "every one" is indicted in the "conspiracy" against Milly. Not only does Densher, having exhausted his rationalizations, confront the facts of his entanglement, but James reveals his own complicity as he charges his "beautiful fiction" with responsibility for Milly's imprisonment inside the "impenetrable" fence of silence. For in speaking of "vagueness," "silences," "suppressions" James describes his formal strategies, especially in the novel's "false and deformed" second half, which "bristles with dodges," as he admits.[37]

Densher's acknowledgment that he has deliberately avoided the "facts" of Milly's "condition," that the "specified had been chased like a dangerous animal," seems to him a momentous breakthrough; for now "the facts of physical suffering, of incurable pain . . . had been made at a stroke intense, and this was to be the way he was now to feel them" (2:299). But this unmediated view of the "facts," a "vision" Densher now thinks "not only possible but inevitable," is compromised by the persistence of the "aesthetic instinct," which will come to dominate Densher as he moves toward an increasing isolation. As he confronts, when back in London, "*the* horrible thing to know, the fact of their young friend's unapproachable terror of the end," Densher realizes that he cannot look straight at the "terror." He can perceive Milly's agony only after cloaking it in a "vividness" of imagery; he allows himself this indulgence of his "aesthetic instinct" by rationalizing that he is preserving "the principle of his not at least spiritually shrinking." He thinks of Milly as "grimly, awfully silent, as one might imagine some noble young victim of the scaffold, in the French Revolution, separated at the prison-door from some object clutched for resistance" (2:341–42). Densher's melodramatic scenario obliterates Milly's particularity; he distances his guilt and her suffering in an image remote from Milly in time, nationality, and circumstance.

After he returns from Venice, where Milly has died, Densher repudiates his role playing—"We've played our dreadful game and we've lost," he tells Kate. He yearns to "escape everything" by seeking refuge in a purely inward life where he can think of Milly; he becomes a "man haunted with a memory." Like Susanna's music in Stevens's poem, in remembering Milly Densher's imagination "plays on the clear viol of her memory, / And makes a constant sacrament of praise." On the Christmas morning when Milly's letter arrives, Densher's "intelligence and his imagination, his soul and his sense had never been so intensely engaged," as he sits alone in the dark contemplating the possible "turns" Milly "would have given her act" of "splendid generosity." Thus Densher's rejection of theatricality ironically results in his absorption in an aestheticizing process of the most rarefied kind, since the subject of his musings is dead (2:251–52). Instead of feeling the "facts," Densher indulges in an endless process of refining the "might have been" of Milly's memory. In his indifference to reality, his imagination is liberated from the constraints of the referential, and Densher becomes the *reductio ad absurdum* of the Jamesian center of consciousness, a parody of the "supersubtle" reflector.[38]

Densher's withdrawal from Kate, whose prodigious "talent" for life ceases to matter in the "deepened," "sacred hush" of his rooms (2:396), amounts to a refusal to act—to represent himself on the social stage. But he is not only socially unrepresentable; his retreat into a purely contempla-

tive existence makes him no longer representable novel-
istically. Because "something had happened to him too beautiful and sacred to describe," Densher becomes as illegible as
Milly in James's form. As there is no "surface of spirit or of
speech that consented to reflect" the sheer actuality of
Milly's dying agony, Densher's inner allegiance to her, which
grows steadily throughout book 10, goes beyond representation and becomes another gap in James's text. The "conspiracy of silence" that betrays Milly finally victimizes
Densher; they both end engulfed by an "expensive vagueness." In a less direct sense Kate is betrayed by the novel's
form, for in the last book we are shut up wholly within
Densher's consciousness and can only glimpse her as she is
refracted through his mind.

The final movement of *In a Balcony* is remarkably con-
gruent with *The Wings of the Dove:* both works conclude in
an uneasy stillness engendered by the renunciation of theatricality. Constance, like Densher, abandons performance;
"Enough, my part is played," she says, putting an end to her
scheme (line 766). The marriages that have loomed from the
start are left "hanging unfinished"; they dissolve in the silence of "no words nor any notes at all," as Kate early in the
novel described the "ravaged" history of her "house" in
terms of a dying musical phrase (1:4). Densher's refusal to
perform coincides with the apparent extinction of his desire
for Kate, who tells him: Milly's memory is "your love. You
want no other." But Constance's rejection of theatricality
creates a moment of pure if fleeting harmony with her lover,
for they reach "the center of the labyrinth," as Norbert describes their attainment of communion. "The world fades;
only you stand there!" says Norbert to his beloved (line 896).
With the collapse of their plotting Norbert recognizes that
they are finally free of social reality and its pressure to perform roles. When "to-night's wild whirl of things" (Norbert's phrase) grinds to a halt in the final minute of the play,

the lovers face each other in all their helpless passion (line 897). "Feel my heart; let it die against your own!" cries Constance (line 904). Although Constance had earlier chosen to plot her own life, to be the sole author of her experience, in the final minute she throws herself "on the Breast of God." When the door of the balcony opens and Norbert says, "T'is the guard comes," Constance utters the play's final word: "Kiss!" With this concluding command she requests that they move beyond language to union in silence. At last permitting the fulfillment of desire in her lover's embrace, Constance reaches the still point of her passion. In closing the gap which constitutes desire, theatricality, and language, Constance reveals her authentic self; but her discovery of the center of the labyrinth of her being is simultaneous with her acceptance of "death," which "will run its sudden finger round" the lovers, shattering their transcendent moment of unity (line 917).

Only by recognizing God's authority does Constance gain authenticity; He sanctions the lovers' privileged moment.[39] If Browning dramatizes an experience of absolute presence, James depicts in Densher's silent worship of Milly a pseudo-religious devotion. Densher's isolation by the end of book 10 has often been regarded as a genuine spiritual conversion; one critic, expressing a popular viewpoint, argues that Densher's meditations "partake of the religious," providing "a glimpse of the divine."[40] Although there are legitimate grounds for a religious interpretation of James's text, such a reading must ignore what is most crucial: the tenacity of the "aesthetic instinct." Densher does indeed undergo a conversion, but we have seen that his absorption in Milly is as aesthetic as it is religious, as much a product of an "intensely engaged" imagination as a kenotic act of religious surrender.

One consequence of James's belief in the "aesthetic instinct of mankind" is that human behavior never entirely escapes the "rich, ambiguous aesthetic air" in which "impressions could mutually conflict—which was exactly the interest of them."[41] What this air nourishes is the irony with which James regards efforts, like Densher's, to transcend the aesthetic. Motivating such efforts is the lure of authentic or unmediated experience, which proves frustratingly elusive and delusive for many Jamesian characters; not only Densher, but Isabel Archer and Overt, for instance, believe in the comforting fiction of an absolute—be it self or sincerity. James both honors and mocks these deeply human yearnings for a stable ground of value, yearnings which are at once aroused and doomed by the fact that "experience is never limited and it is never complete," for "relations stop nowhere."[42] The perpetual onrush of experience creates, for the "candid consciousness," "rash multiplications" which assault every attempt at "neat and complacent conclusions."[43]

The endings of *The Wings of the Dove* and *In a Balcony* could not be less "neat and complacent," for they deliberately resist a unified form and the stability of fixed meaning. Both works conclude with a failure of a plot, which is left "hanging unfinished."[44] James confesses to this problem in closure when he speaks of the "palpable voids," "missing links," and "dodges" in his text, and Browning's play dodges a resolution, as the fate of the lovers is left suspended. These gaps arouse in the reader (as they did in Norbert and Densher) a desire to participate, to make an imaginative commitment to the text.[45] As the fates of Constance and Densher attest, the cessation of desire, the closing of gaps, creates a deathly inertness. Thus by avoiding the stasis of full representation Browning and James prolong their plots in the play of the reader's imagination. But to leave texts open, flaunting their "deformities," to use James's word, is morally risky for both writer and reader. In denying the comforts of a more stable, closed form, *In a Balcony* and *The*

Wings of the Dove solicit the reader's active engagement, which leads inevitably to his implication in the characters' moral dilemmas. Like Densher, the reader is left pondering the "might-have-been" of Milly and is thus susceptible to becoming lost in aesthetic reverie. And Browning's open ending forces the reader to participate in Constance's attempt to read the Queen and to risk adopting Constance's aestheticizing vision. But the moral hazards involved in the relation of reader and character are minor when compared to the more intimate and complex complicity between Browning, James, and their delegates. The endings of both works witness the writers, in effect, forcing their main characters to atone by leaving them in a state of passivity. As one would expect when the complicity between such characters as Constance and Densher and their authors is so marked, these acts of atonement reverberate beyond the text to involve personal motives of Browning and James.

So entangled are both authors in their characters' acts of purgation that the endings are dictated in part by the psychological needs of Browning and James. In other words, the delegates' atonement indirectly redeems their creators, who share an impulse to purge themselves. The relation of Constance's renunciation to Browning's own needs can be illuminated by briefly returning to the play's last scene. Constance's purification recalls the "ceremonies of expulsion" Leo Bersani has identified as the fate of many of the major figures of nineteenth-century fiction. These characters' lack of a "coherent wholeness of personality" threatens the central foundation of bourgeois realism, namely an "ideology of the self as a fundamentally intelligible structure unaffected by a history of fragmented, discontinuous desires."[46] The pattern Bersani notes informs Constance's final moments, where she is forced to surrender her mobile self. But the question remains: why is Browning compelled to purify the theatrical self? Apart from the conflict between theatricality and a belief in a God-centered world, another, more significant reason is connected to what Hillis Miller calls Browning's "failure to have any one definite self." To be an unstable self "was, in Victorian England, a shameful and reprehensible thing."[47] The bourgeois ideology that insisted that the novel portray the self as, in Bersani's words, "fundamentally intelligible," also demanded that writers possess a coherent self.

That Browning felt this demand concretely is suggested in a remark he made late in life concerning "the enforced habit of self-denial which is the condition of men's receiving culture."[48] Insisting on multiplicity, the theatrical self challenges the demand for "self-denial," thus raising disconcerting and subversive questions, such as the one posed by a monologist of a late poem: " 'Who's who?' was aptly asked, / Since certainly I am not I!"[49] Browning's character echoes his creator's own refusal of a single self, a refusal Browning grandly announced at twenty. He had devised a plan to write, under different names, poems, operas, novels, so that "the world was never to guess that . . . the respective authors . . . were no other than one and the same individual."[50] Browning describes the premiere work concocted under his scheme: "The present abortion [he is speaking of *Pauline*] was the first work of the *Poet* of the batch, who would have been more legitimately *myself* than most of the others" (Browning's emphases). "Abortion," "poet," "myself": what this cluster suggests is that when Browning is most himself his art is an "abortion" because it reflects and is a product of his aborted self. Evidently his abortion of selfhood, his identity that amounts to a refusal of a fixed identity, becomes the very condition of his creativity.[51] Here we reach a more extreme version of the condition of blankness or absence seen in James's own deliberate "vagueness." Both conditions are scandalous in late nineteenth-century England, for the vague or aborted self possesses a freedom from the social coercions of unitary identity. However, this freedom is deeply paradoxical, for on one level the attenuated selves Browning and James fashion accept with ironic literalness the "enforced habit of self-denial" inflicted by society. And yet this self-denial is, as it were, dialectically reversed to become the very source both of artistic liberation and the mobility of the theatrical self.

In the case of *In a Balcony* one can locate with some precision the relation of Browning's selfhood to his art. In this play the poet has created a "deputy" in Constance, who shares his theatrical self and enacts his plot. By converting her into a passive and God-loving person, Browning is able to experience vicariously his heroine's conversion. In other words, Browning forces Constance to undergo the purification he feels he needs because of his sense of "shame" at his "failure" to have a stable self. Perhaps the fact that Browning called *In a Balcony* his personal favorite among his works can be explained in that it allowed him this vicarious, mediated purgation of his "failure" and thereby liberated his imagination to enter, with renewed vitality, the lives of a great array of men and women.

If Constance is, in a sense, purified for Browning's sake, this pattern of sacrifice is explicit in *The Wings of the Dove.* In their final conversation Kate insists that Milly "died for" Densher; he, in turn, leads a death-in-life existence "for" Milly—an expression of worship and an act of expiation for having manipulated the "dove." But, like Constance in relation to Browning, Densher must also be purified "for" James. Because of James's intimate involvement in the betrayal of Milly, he forces his deputy to enact a sacrificial homage to her, an atonement that soothes the creator as much as Densher. And James's need for purgation, like Browning's, is prompted not only by what has occurred in his text; he is impelled by guilt of a more personal nature. I am alluding to his "use" of his cousin Minny as a model for Milly.

Although James speaks reverentially of "wrapping" Minny's "tragedy" in the "beauty and dignity of art," for James art is profoundly impure, as dependent on manipulation as the life it represents. Art's inevitable violation of experience entangles the artist in a "cruel crisis" requiring "courage to brace oneself," James stresses in his first preface. But in his remarks about Minny quoted above he avoids any suggestion of the moral complications involved in artistic creation. He displaces a sense of his own responsibility onto his description of what "life" did to her: "Life claimed her and used her and beset her."[52] Yet James discovers that it is inevitable that he too will "claim" and "use" and "beset" her as a stimulus to his imagination. In short, his aesthetic use of the "tragically compromised conditions"[53] of Minny's life entraps James in a moral compromise, one that attends any effort to represent extreme suffering. When depicting "the sheer physical pain of people," writes Adorno, "the aesthetic principle of stylization . . . contains, however remotely, the power to elicit enjoyment out of it . . . it is transfigured, something of its horror is removed. This alone does an injustice to the victims."[54] While Adorno is speaking of portrayals of the holocaust in art, his insight into the "injustice" inflicted by "turning suffering into images" defines James's "cruel crisis" wherein his attempt to do justice to Minny is inextricable from his injustice to her. So inescapable is the fact of the artist's aesthetic exploitations that the novel which will commemorate his beloved cousin will be about the uses made of a doomed American girl.

In *The Wings of the Dove* James makes use of another hero of his youth, as his splendidly creative "rehandling" of *In a Balcony* reveals. In the conclusion of his centenary tribute James links Browning to Minny and Milly as a muse of the imagination: "I feel that Browning's great generous wings are over us still and . . . that they shake down on us his blessing." This is a remarkable echo of Kate's final image of Milly, who in her "stupendous" bequest has "stretched out her wings" until "they cover" the lovers. In these last words of James's homage Browning takes his place with the other sacrificial doves whose fate is to inspire and bless those who plot. (Densher in book 10 describes himself as "blessed" by Milly.) And James's 1912 tribute to Browning constitutes, in part, his attempt to atone for his "irreverent" use of *In a Balcony*. It is the privilege and the burden of the "man of imagination" to both celebrate and "work over" Browning's play, Minny's life, and Milly's memory with the transforming power of the "aesthetic instinct."[55]

❧ CHAPTER V ❧

THE PRECIOUS EFFECT
OF PERSPECTIVE

Browning's sudden and startling appearance on the novelists' side of the street, which precipitates a near collision with James, is the most dramatic expression of a widespread reaction to the poet in the late nineteenth century. The wittiest and best-known perception of Browning's generic ambiguity is Wilde's remark that "Meredith is a prose Browning and so is Browning."[1] G. M. Hopkins echoed this reaction when he declared, upon reading *The Ring and the Book:* "Browning is not really a poet," and said he preferred Balzac, a response identical to Robert Louis Stevenson's concerning *The Inn Album.*[2] To Swinburne, a Browning monologue was "a model of intense and punctilious realism . . . so triumphant a thing that on its own ground it can be matched by no poet."[3] While all these writers insist on the unpoetical character of Browning's poetry, only James and Swinburne refrain from glibly ridiculing his prosiness. Although he finds Browning's generic doubleness disconcerting, James believes that the poet's crossing of literary boundaries is a bold move that provides the very basis of his unique literary achievement: the creation of a novelistic intimacy in verse.

Repeatedly in his descriptions of Browning's art James relies on certain key terms: "intensity," "intimacy," "familiarity." The immediacy of a typical Browning monologue derives from a character speaking under the pressure of the moment and addressing the reader with an "intensity of communication," in James's phrase. This "intensity" is part of what makes Browning "the intimate, almost the confidential poet," whose "bold familiarity" is "straighter upon us . . . than anyone else of his race." One reason James emphasizes intensity and intimacy is their crucial place in his own poetics. The novelist admires Browning's artistry because it is rich in qualities essential for the successful representation of consciousness.

James's appreciation of these aspects of Browning's art is part of the novelist's profound, if indirectly confessed, recognition that the poet's project anticipates and helps inspire James's own. Their shared literary intentions can be summarized as a commitment to representing a fictive mind reacting under crisis, a "single throbbing consciousness" "burnished" by the "passion, the force of the moment," to quote the preface to *The Wings of the Dove*. Two years after publishing this novel James turns again to Browning for guidance. In his last complete novel late James is inspired by late Browning, a far more innovative poet than the author of *In a Balcony*. Influenced by the interior monologue form of *Fifine at the Fair*, *The Golden Bowl* brings Browning's aesthetic of "magnification" to its fullest novelistic development. After exploring James's ambiguous 1912 homage, which contains his tribute to Browning's poetry of intimacy, and comparing their experiments with perspectivist representation, this chapter will discuss briefly how works devoted to depicting interior life remain rooted in social reality, a paradox that reveals the historicity of even the most seemingly private texts.

The complicity of author and character examined in chapter 4, the latter serving as the deputy of the creator, is an important aspect of the intimacy James and Browning create. James surmises that the source of the poet's unprecedented closeness to his characters is Browning's conviction that "to be poetic" is "to express" the "inner self . . . utterly." The poet's "method" is to "ladle out . . . from his own great reservoir of spiritual health" an "iridescent wash of personality, of temper and faculty" upon his "figures."[4] This expression of Browning's "own intimate, essential states and feelings" reveals the "preponderantly lyrical" origins of his art, which recalls James's earlier sense of Browning's ambiguous artistic identity. James's "bewildered" view of "the poet without a lyre" persists in 1912. Browning's art is founded on a "perpetual anomaly": what emerges somehow from an immersion in the "wash" of the poet's "inner self" is *The Ring and the Book*—"a great objective mass," "a living thing" of "truth and beauty," containing complex characters worthy of a novelist (p. 398). That so close an involvement with one's creations grants them an "air of reality" compels James's attention and admiration because his own "art of representation" is informed by a similar emphasis—the necessity of an author becoming intimate with his figures in order to "dramatically and objectively" render them.

James's 1912 remarks on Browning are prefigured in his preface to *The Princess Casamassima* where, in his discussion of his relation to his characters, "intimacy" emerges as a pivotal term. The preface traces the process whereby the novelist's conventional role of "story teller," which involves "his report of people's experience," gives way to a more interior art—the representation of the vision of a "vessel of consciousness"—that "person capable of feeling in the given case more than another of what is to be felt for it."[5] What allows James to create these "intense perceivers" is, first of all, his "appreciation" of what his hero or heroine does. And because he conceives their "doing" as "their feeling, their feeling as their doing," his "appreciation" must be active so as to enable James to move as close as possible to his characters: "I can have none of the conveyed sense and taste of their situation without becoming intimate with them. I can't be intimate without that sense and taste, and I can't appreciate save by intimacy."[6] Only this "intimacy" between the novelist and his fictional "agent" is certain to "make us see" "a man's specific behavior . . . as a whole." Thus intimacy with one's characters is the necessary condition for attaining intimacy with one's reader.

James insists that the individual vision of the central reflector, rather than being purely subjective, is capable of achieving objectivity. Stephen Donadio describes this paradox well: "For James . . . the most comprehensive and objective vision is achieved . . . through the most profound commitment to one's own distinctive subjectivity: the 'full measure of truth' . . . far from revealing itself to detached and disinterested observation, can only be achieved through a profoundly interested relation."[7] The aesthetic of intimacy James and Browning share is based on a "profound commitment" to revealing a character's "distinctive subjectivity"; their artistic project implies a belief in point of view, or the epistemological doctrine of perspectivism, a succinct definition of which James offers in his final preface. He speaks of the "marked inveteracy," the "accepted habit" of his representational technique, which portrays "not my own impersonal account of the affair in hand," but rather "my account of somebody's impression of it." Implicit in this statement, which could easily have been spoken by Browning, is the ambition to portray consciousness—an individual's "impression" of reality rather than a "rounded objectivity," to use James's phrase. "What I hold most dear," James states in a late letter, is the "precious effect of *perspective*, indispensable, by my fond measure, to beauty and authenticity."[8] To represent "the world of appearances" "present to a particular consciousness under particular conditions" is the aim of perspectivist art—a celebration of human limitation rather than omniscience.[9]

To clarify the relation of subjectivity, objectivity, and perspectivism, Jose Ortega y Gasset's seminal account of "the doctrine of the point of view" is useful. Although Ortega does not mention James, as the major exponent of point of view in the novel the novelist enunciates the essential "modern theme," which Ortega defines as perspectivism. The heart of his argument is an important distinction between perspectivism and "subjectivism" made in the course of a discussion of Einstein's theory of relativity. According to Ortega, Einstein's discovery is wrongly perceived as "one more step on the road of subjectivism," the revelation of "the subjectivity of time and space."[10] Ortega's point is that the individual's perceptions of time and space are "forms of the real" rather than a "deformation imposed by the subject upon reality" (which defines subjectivism for the philosopher) because "perspective is the order and the form reality takes for him who contemplates it."[11] "One of the qualities proper to reality is that of possessing perspective, that is, of organizing itself in different ways so as to be visible from different points."[12]

Seen in these terms, James's effort to depict "the world of appearances" is not a retreat from reality, a surrender to subjectivism, but rather a confrontation with reality, for, as Ortega says, "appearance is an objective quality of the real, its response to a subject."[13] Like time and space, appearance is a response that differs "according to the condition of the observer," but this difference has an "objective value" as a form of the real. Analogous to Ortega's insistence that "it is reality that is relative" is James's view that manners, theatricality, and convention are forms of the real and not "deformations" of it. While the late Browning (post–*The Ring and the Book*) might concur with Ortega and James, the early and middle Browning believes that "the relative is our index to the absolute"; "*knowable* reality . . . *human* institutions and judgments are relative" and "their fallibility" sharpens our sense of "an absolute reality that can be felt though not known," to quote Langbaum's important clarification of perspectivism in *The Ring and the Book*.[14]

The often-discussed breakdown in the nineteenth century of belief in a knowable absolute includes, in Ortega's words, a gradual rejection of the "supposition that reality possesses in itself, independently of the point of view from which it is observed, a physiognomy of its own." Browning's and James's literary responses to the collapse of this "supposition" involve an acceptance of perspective "as one of the component parts of reality" rather than a "disturbance of its fabric."[15] In the movement toward a literature of perspectivism Browning occupies a crucial place, for the dramatic monologue is the literary form that most rigorously insists that only a single perspective—a speaker's idiosyncratic perceptions—is available. And Browning's status as a forerunner of modernism's preoccupation with subjectivity has long been acknowledged by critics, who find his influence not only in Pound and Eliot but in the perspectivist novels of Proust, Ford, Conrad, and James.[16]

Usually the text mentioned in reference to the influence of Browning's perspectivism on James is *The Ring and the Book* because, in the words of Chesterton, "it is the expression of the belief, it might also be said, of the discovery that no man ever lived upon the earth without possessing a point of view."[17] Browning's verse novel, composed of a dozen dramatic monologues, is dubbed by Chesterton "the great epic of the age" because of its "discovery," which makes Browning "beyond all question the founder of the most modern school of poetry." Despite his hyperbole, Chesterton points to the grounds for James's profound interest in the poem. As Barbara Melchiori has stated, "With *The Ring and the Book* Browning suggests to the novelists to what lengths the trend toward interiorization of the narrative could be taken. Henry James was right in considering *The Ring and the Book* as a novel, but this recognition came half a century later, when indeed the novel had taken the road pointed by Browning's poem."[18]

Puzzlingly, those critics seeking to establish the connection of Browning to James and the modern novel have neglected James's own mapping of the "road" linking the two authors.[19] In his centenary address James indirectly reveals what Browning's poem offers one intent on "appropriating" the poet's "favorite system"—"point of view"—(James's words) for prose fiction. The eccentricity of James's treatment of Browning's epic—his "irreverent" urge to redo the poem as a Jamesian novel—has distracted critics from analyzing the novelist's tribute to and exploration of Browning's poetry of intimacy, which is founded, says James, on his ability to "magnify" consciousness.

"The Novel in *The Ring and the Book*" has gained notoriety for its startling premise that Browning's most ambitious and, to many, his culminating poetic achievement would have been much improved had James rewritten it as a novel.[20] What critics find most annoying in James's elaboration of his belief that the poem "might have yielded up its best essence . . . under some fine economy of *prose* treatment" (p. 386), is his casual dismissal of the poem's remarkable structure composed of twelve dramatic monologues and ten speakers all concerned with a single set of events. James "destroys at a stroke the grand design of Browning's poem,"[21] complains Philip Drew; John Killham argues that "James calmly repudiates the whole method of the poem."[22] Drew finds James most at fault in his refusal to "accept the poem on the poet's terms."

This charge is correct but beside the point, for it does not take into account the peculiar donnée stated at the essay's outset. While Drew's response implicitly assumes that James is attempting literary criticism, the novelist is careful to insist otherwise. He "hastens to add" that he is well aware of the "scant degree in which such a fresh start from our author's documents . . . may claim a critical basis. Conceive me as simply astride of my different fancy, my other dream of the matter" (p. 387). In disclosing his donnée James implicitly admits that he must rely on "fancy" to cope with the poet's suggestive artistry. "Astride" his "irreverent" "dream" James distances himself from Browning's poem and avoids a genuinely critical engagement with the text. He deliberately refuses to deal with *The Ring and the Book* "on the poet's terms" because those terms are strikingly akin to James's own.

Like the poem which is its ostensible subject, James's homage is itself marked by "convulsions" in the "mingled tissue" of its prose. Producing this texture is James's "restless," combative grappling with Browning's poem, an encounter imaged in intensely physical terms. James gradually asserts authority after his initial caution when he meekly approaches the "so vast and so essentially gothic structure." In the first paragraph James confesses to walking "vaguely and slowly, rather bewilderedly, round and round it, wondering at what point we had best attempt such entrance" (p. 385). This imagery recalls the opening of the second half of *The Golden Bowl*; like Maggie, James tentatively explores the threatening yet enticing structure that looms before him. Again like Maggie, James's initial hesitancy is soon replaced by a bold assertion of authority—his vision of the "latent prose fiction" embedded in the intricate "monument" (p. 403). But James's fanciful assimilation of the "spreading and soaring" "hugeness" of his imaginative "dream of the matter" is only one instance of his assertiveness. As his description of reading *The Ring and the Book* reveals, James conceives his encounter with

146

Browning's text as a virtual tug-of-war between reader and poet.

In describing the effect of Browning's "matchless" evocation of Renaissance Italy, James states that the reader "plunges" into the poetic atmosphere: "I confess we surrender" (p. 401). But no sooner has he surrendered than James claims: "I so desire and need" the rich impressions of "old Florence" that "by imaginative collaboration . . . I contribute to them" (p. 402). The struggle continues: "He takes his willful way with me, but I make it my own" (p. 402). Despite "Browning himself moving about . . . at his mighty ease," James, "the infatuated reader," asserts: "I make to my hand . . . my Italy" (p. 402). James's seizing of authority from the poet reflects his vivid sense of the poet's own original grasp of the "Book [the Old Yellow Book of documents concerning the Franceschini case] in the litter of a market stall in Florence, and the swoop of practiced perception with which he caught up in it a treasure." "No page of his long story is more vivid and splendid" than this inaugurating act of possession (p. 387). So compelling to James is the poet's discovery that he states: "I doubt if we have a precedent for this energy of appropriation of a deposit of stated matter" (p. 388).

For James, Browning's act of "appropriation" inspires and justifies both his combative reading of the poem and his own energetic "appropriation" of it for fanciful purposes. James makes explicit that his stance mimics Browning's own: "Browning works the whole thing over—the whole thing as originally given him—and we work him" over (p. 406). As the poet takes the Old Yellow Book and imaginatively transforms it, James seizes The Ring and the Book and seeks to redo it. In both cases, what follows this seizure is an assault on the material of "stated matter," which must "suffer disintegration, be pulled apart, melted down, hammered" (p. 388). In declaring his intention to "work over"

Browning, James, in effect, will submit him to the violence of the creative process; the novelist must destroy the "prime identity" of the poem in order to transform its latent prose possibilities into an "achieved form."

Among the oddities of James's homage is his blithe neglect of the fact that long before his "pang" of recognition of the novel *The Ring and the Book* "might have constituted," the work's novelistic possibilities had been acknowledged by none other than Browning himself in book 1. At the conclusion of that section the poet asks what the novel as a genre offers an artist whose aim is less unity than the portrayal of process. Browning plays with the idea of casting his subject in the form of a novel, as he musingly puns: "a novel country: I might make it mine."[23] But Browning rejects the temptation of that genre because of its demand for "unity" and "selection"—precisely the poem's two major formal deficiencies according to James. A novel would require, in Browning's words, "choosing which one aspect of the year / Suited mood best, and putting solely that / On panel somewhere in the House of Fame, / Landscaping what I saved, not what I saw."[24] In other words, Browning would be obligated to portray "what he remembered from observation, not what he derived from poetic meditation."[25]

Instead of novelistic unity Browning sought amplitude— an array of perspectives which would embody his belief in the relativity of perception. In lines that can serve as an *ars poetica*, the poet exhorts the reader near the end of book 1:

> Rather learn and love
> Each facet-flash of the revolving year!
> Red, green and blue that whirl into a white,
> The variance now, the eventual unity
>
> . . . .
>
> See it for yourselves,
> This man's act, changeable because alive![26]

Browning intends the "eventual unity" of his poetic form to force the reader to experience a diversity of viewpoints; a fully coherent view of the events is gained only after reading all perspectives. "The ultimate judgment" is "yours," the poet tells his reader. Because each book contains a particular individual's vision, in each there are different emphases, suppressions, and distortions, which result from various sources: sophistry, passion, sentimentality, evil. These human foibles are partly responsible for "the deviations and disparities . . . the monstrosities in the mingled tissue of the work" (p. 398). Browning seeks a raw, unfinished texture to reflect the evolving thought and feeling of human beings in the very "act" of making sense of experience. The "convulsions of soul and sense" (p. 398) involved in the "changeable" process of mental life are conspicuous too in James's art.

For both writers "the prize is in the process," as Browning says in a late poem. Browning reveals the exploratory form of his art in his famous response to Ruskin's complaint about the difficulty of reading the poet. "You would have me paint it all plain out," says Browning, "which can't be . . . you ought to keep pace with the thought tripping from ledge to ledge."[27] In such an art, meaning "is what poetry does and keeps doing," as Herbert Tucker aptly describes what he calls Browning's "principled evasiveness." That other notoriously evasive writer, James, also insists on an activist conception of literary form which, in its "demonstration" of a "process of vision," seeks to prevent "a priori judgement" on the part of writer, reader, and character.[28] James describes his act of creation as the unrehearsed exploration of the "field for dramatic analysis, no such fine quantities being ever determinable till they have with due intelligence been 'gone into.'" " 'Dramatize, dramatize!' . . . then, and not sooner, would one see." Thus the artist, "heroically improvising" like Maggie, depends on resourcefulness and resiliency to cope with the contingencies of process. Such qualities are also needed of James's reader, who must avoid the premature foreclosure of meaning when he confronts bewildering texts.[29] And Browning's reader "must be a highly imaginative one, whose pursuit of meaning retraces and in effect recreates the poet's prior pursuit."[30]

Art as an activity of "pursuit" is a conception that governs the opening pages of James's first preface to the New York edition. James's initial preface can be read as a summary of his belief, sustained through thirty years, that the novel represents a process of growth in subject and form and in the author's experience of creation. And James's oeuvre, with its own dynamic movement, reflects this belief on a larger scale. The creative process is a "wondrous adventure" precisely because it is an activity that knows no predictable end and thus is "led on by 'developments.' " Indeed the novelist is so "unduly tempted" that the "ache of fear" of "losing" one's "way" is not an exception but "the very essence" of the process.[31] In "unfolding" his "process of production" in the preface to *Roderick Hudson*, his first attempt at "a long fiction with a 'complicated' subject," James narrates "the growth" of his own "operative consciousness" in its awkward and tentative search for a "subject." His search is complicated by his initial (and thus mistaken) assumption that his "subject" would simply be his title character. But James came upon his real "subject" only when he "tried . . . with such art" as he "could command" to achieve "intensity." He realized that his original subject—"my young sculptor's adventure"—could not be retained, for intensity could be gained only by making the "subject" Rowland Mallet's "view and experience" of Hudson. To have at last "felt one's subject right" was to have discovered that a novel, to be intense and intimate, must represent a particular consciousness, a distinct point of view. Thus "the center of interest throughout" the novel is in Mallet's consciousness, and "the drama is the very drama of that consciousness."[32]

James's avoidance in "The Novel in *The Ring and the Book*" of Browning's summary of his aesthetic of process implies an awareness that the poet's intentions are uncomfortably close to the novelist's own. But James's neglect of Browning's carefully considered formal strategies in book 1 is not the only matter he evades. Another evasion occurs when James confronts the formal feature of the poem that would seem most obviously congenial to him—Browning's perspectivism, his point of view "method." James goes so far as to say that in this work the poet employs "his favorite system—that of looking at his subject from the point of view of a curiosity almost sublime in its freedom . . . on a scale on which even he had never before applied it" (p. 388). But instead of explicitly noting this "system's" affinities with his own preference for point of view narration, he forges this link covertly, by discussing the "effect" of point of view in terms derived from his own prefaces. This effect James calls "magnification," which "remains with us all the time" (p. 397). He defines "the magnified state in this work" as the "note of the intelligence, of any and every faculty of thought, imputed by our poet to his creatures; and it takes a great mind, one of the greatest, we may at once say, to make these persons express and confess themselves to such an effect of intellectual splendor. He resorts primarily to *their* sense, their sense of themselves and of everything else they know, to exhibit them" (p. 395). The language of the first half of this passage resembles the preface to *The Princess Casamassima*, where James states that the "very essence" of the "teller's" "affair" "has been the imputing of intelligence" to the central consciousness.[33] Thus when James salutes Browning's portrayal of "intellectual splendor" he is also praising his own fictional method. Both authors magnify an articulate mind's "sense of . . . everything."

The "effect of magnification" is a characteristic of modern literature. Browning's achievement is akin to Proust's, as described by Ortega, who writes: "What he [Proust] gives us is a microscopic analysis of human souls."[34] For Ortega, magnified art "overcomes realism" by "merely putting too fine a point on it and discovering, lens in hand, the micro-structure of life."[35] That Browning transcends realism is a fact James acutely grasps: "nothing could be more interesting than the impunity, on our poet's part, of most of these overstretchings of proportions, these violations of the immediate appearance. Browning is deep down below the immediate with the first step of his approach" (p. 396). Among such "violations" of verisimilitude James cites: "Franceschini fighting for his life . . . with an audacity of wit . . . a variety of speculation . . . that represents well-nigh the maximum play of the human mind" (pp. 396–97). Although "we know . . . no such reality" as Guido, or the dying Pompilia holding forth with such "intelligence and expression" that "the angels may well begin to envy her," we accept these "overstretchings" because Browning's "quest" is "the very ideal of the real, the real most finely mixed with life" (p. 396). The "ideal" is "down below the immediate" in the characters' inner lives. Ortega, in an unintentional but striking echo of James, remarks of modern literature: it "may dive beneath the level marked by the natural perspective." Discovered "beneath" is "imaginary psychology"; what becomes the "material proper" of the modern novel is "the psychology of possible human minds."[36]

The depiction of consciousness is worthwhile only when based on characters who can "vibrate," says James, "to as many occasions" as possible. In this art of magnification, "constructing human souls" takes precedence over the invention of plots; "action or plot" is no longer the "substance" but merely the "scaffolding," to use Ortega's terms in his description of a modernist aesthetic. James indicates his relative indifference to external plot in this representative statement: "I confess I never see the *leading* interest of any human hazard but in a consciousness (on the part of the moved and moving creature) subject to fine intensification and wide enlargement."[37]

Browning's method of "intensification and wide enlargement" in *The Ring and the Book* also reduces plot to a relatively incidental status. From this standpoint Carlyle's famous description of the poem as "an old Bailey story that might have been told in ten lines" is less criticism than an indication of the poem's affinities to James and modernism. In his first book Browning deliberately summarizes the eleven sections that follow, thus at once dispensing with the plot of external events. By eliminating any element of surprise or suspense he makes the reader attend to the elaboration (seemingly endless at times) of the characters' "sense of themselves."

In his abolition of traditional plot Browning reveals his implicit agreement with a central Jamesian dictum: "what a man thinks and what he feels are the history and character of what he does."[38] Where they differ (at least in regard to *The Ring and the Book*) is in the number of thinking and feeling minds they wish to portray in a single work. While James concedes that Browning invented "three characters of the first importance," "of the deepest dye," in the Pope, Pompilia, and, preeminently, Caponsacchi, the novelist holds even "three a great many; I could have done it almost, I think, if there had been but one or two" (p. 403). James had "done it" eight years earlier in *The Golden Bowl*, where, as he says, "we see very few persons." Only in his later poetry, particularly *Fifine at the Fair*, would Browning represent at great length a single mind and avoid what James perceived as the most serious structural flaw in *The Ring and the Book*—the lack of an organizing, central consciousness.

To remedy the absence of a central reflector is a primary

concern of James's project to redo *The Ring and the Book*. The novelist elects the priest Caponsacchi as the "enveloping consciousness" who comes to the rescue of both Pompilia and James's sketch of a novel. In his enthusiasm for Caponsacchi as a "great" literary creation and his praise for Browning's "beautiful" vision of him, James reveals his tacit endorsement of the poet's central goal as enunciated in the famous 1863 preface to *Sordello*. The priest's passionate monologue is one of the finest products of Browning's ambition to "stress . . . the incidents in the development of a soul: little else is worth study. I, at least, always thought so." It was this statement that Thomas Hardy recalled, soon after the poet's death, as expressing the essence of Browning's art. The poet's declaration confirms once again his emphasis on a processive art focusing on evolving states of feeling. James's warm response to Browning's representation of the priest's "tried and tempered" and finally "illuminated" consciousness makes clear that the novelist's notorious proposal to rewrite *The Ring and the Book* is only part of his homage. For in addition to his impudent "appropriation" of the poem, James appropriates the lessons of the poet's art, as he reveals how stimulating is Browning's intimate poetry of "magnification."

One can move from a comparison of aesthetic intentions to an examination of their enactment in particular forms by juxtaposing two late works by Browning and James that occupy remarkably similar places in their authors' oeuvres as essentially exploratory representations of mental life. Because "the intimacy of an art . . . is the intimacy of a form, and derives not directly from an encounter with life but indirectly from an encounter mediated by the imagination and by a form," as Laurence Holland has written, a major focus of this chapter will be on the formal influence of Browning's most intimate literary work, *Fifine at the Fair*, on James's most intimate novel, *The Golden Bowl*.[39] These

154

late creations are their authors' most radical use of point of view and explore the fullest implications of perspectivism both as a form and subject.

"I can only say that were I myself capable of using the instrument of flexible verse, I should go in with great goodwill for the dramatic form," states James in a little-known letter of 1875 to the critic E. C. Stedman regarding the latter's essay on Browning.[40] James's significant admission expresses again his sense of artistic kinship with the poet, as he tacitly confesses the affinities between Browning's dramatic monologue and the "drama of consciousness." But by 1875 the dramatic monologues of *Men and Women* and *The Ring and the Book* had evolved into a form—the interior monologue—that would have been even more congenial to James. Swinburne, always one of Browning's most astute and sympathetic readers, especially of his late poetry, locates the genesis of the interior monologue in the poet's "natural and inevitable tendency to analysis, which can only explain itself . . . in the form of elaborate mental monologue,"[41] a "tendency" and "form" that James of course shares. Browning's most "elaborate mental monologue" is *Fifine at the Fair* (1872), which, like *The Golden Bowl*, is a vast and formidably difficult work; "it may be structurally the most complex and difficult long poem in the language, *Sordello* notwithstanding," Samuel Southwell has said in his recent book on the poem. In *Quest for Eros: Browning and Fifine*, Southwell demonstrates that *Fifine at the Fair* is "the climactic development of Browning's intellectual experience"; similar claims in the context of James's oeuvre and the history of the novel have been advanced for *The Golden Bowl*, which Gabriel Pearson has dubbed "the novel to end all novels."[42]

In a suggestive remark, E. D. H. Johnson says that "after reading *Fifine* . . . one cannot help thinking that had Browning seen fit to take up the writing of novels he might have foreshadowed the accomplishments of Meredith, Conrad and James." I would revise this by saying that in *Fifine at the Fair* Browning had already "foreshadowed" James's "accomplishment."[43] The heroes of both works are isolated and inward and share a predilection for creating imaginary dialogue; their mental activity becomes the central subject of their respective texts. *Fifine at the Fair* and *The Golden Bowl* are at times consciously retrospective works containing images that refer back to their authors' entire careers, while expanding to the limit techniques developed over the years.

While James makes no mention in print of having read *Fifine at the Fair*, the fact that he on more than one occasion claimed to have read all of Browning makes it very likely that he had an acquaintance with the work. As we know from James's review of *The Inn Album* in 1875 and a passing comment on *Red Cotton Nightcap Country*, written the year after *Fifine at the Fair*, James, unlike many, did not shrink from the late Browning. What would have first attracted James to *Fifine at the Fair* is its exuberant celebration of theatricality and "the value of a lie" as a liberation from the constricting Victorian self. For it is in *Fifine at the Fair* that Browning most explicitly rebels against the "enforced habit of self-denial" that burdened him. James's choice of the subject of adultery and the resemblance of two of his characters to figures in Browning's poem suggest that the novelist is possibly leaving subtle clues of his awareness of *Fifine at the Fair*. This strategy is plausible, for as our examinations of "The Lesson of the Master" and *The Wings of the Dove* have revealed, James often planted oblique hints concerning Browning's personal identity or literary influence.

Browning's monologue takes place entirely in the mind of a Victorian Don Juan as he walks arm in arm with his wife Elvire through a fair in Pornic, France. In the course of their roamings Juan is drawn to a young gypsy girl, Fifine, who is part of a group performing at the fair. Intense desire for Fifine galvanizes Juan's intricately allusive meditation upon sexuality, selfhood, and the nature of man. The poem concludes when Juan, who seems to have accepted his lot as a "householder," runs off to place a coin in the gypsy's tambourine, thus casting doubt on the sincerity of his love for Elvire. Browning's modern (which is to say Victorian) Don Juan obsessively yearns for the adulterous affair that James's "modern Roman," Prince Amerigo, actually engages in.

These two sexual adventurers comprise the most obvious connection between *Fifine at the Fair* and *The Golden Bowl.* Both men are portrayed in a restless mood at the opening of each work. On the eve of his marriage Amerigo has "strayed"· into Bond Street, where he is alive to the "possibilities in faces" as they "passed him on the pavement."[44] But instead of pursuing these faces Amerigo finds himself "too restless . . . for any concentration" (1:4). Juan also roams freely; on seeing Fifine and her fellow players Juan feels "Frenetic to be free!": "my heart makes just the same / Passionate stretch, fires up for lawlessness, lays claim to share the life they lead."[45] But, like Amerigo, the claims of marriage restrain him (albeit in Amerigo's case only temporarily). "O trip and skip Elvire! Link arm and arm with me!" the poem begins, emphasizing his wife's literal hold on Juan's body, if not his mind. Almost immediately he becomes attracted to the gypsy and her "tumbling-troops arrayed, the strollers on their stage" (sec. 1).

If Amerigo can stand as James's Don Juan, Charlotte is his Fifine, the alluring exotic temptress. Strikingly, Charlotte is described as a kind of gypsy: her great facility with languages is compared to a "conjurer at a show" who "juggled with balls or hoops or lighted brands" (1:54). While it is true that circus imagery is associated with various characters in the novel (Maggie at one point is called a "trapezist"), Charlotte is gypsylike not only in her facility but in her obscure, mysterious origins; she possesses what Browning calls "the gipsys' foreign self"—an irreducible ·otherness. As James writes, "Nothing in her definitely placed her; she was a rare, a special product" (1:53). For Browning this deracinated quality is typical of a gypsy, who lives a life of perpetual exile, never to know again "the once familiar roof / O' the kindly race their flight estranged" (sec. 8). These "misguided ones who gave society the slip" resemble Charlotte's shadowy parents, English people adrift in Italy "themselves already of a corrupt generation, demoralized, falsified, polyglot well before her" (1:55). In Browning's view, the homeless gypsy became a brilliantly improvisational performer, adept at illusion, living by the principle that to "feign, means—to have grace" (sec. 85). Thus it is apposite that Charlotte is an accomplished actress on the social stage; the key to her becoming "the 'social success' " is that "the act of representation at large . . . fell in with Charlotte's tested facility" (1:316–17).

The theatrical metaphors pervading *The Golden Bowl* are part of the symbolic texture of a work which depicts a world of exquisite and exquisitely hollow forms and manners, of consummate artifice, where self-representation is so studied that characters acquire the inertness of "human furniture," in James's words, to be bought and sold. More decisively than ever before in his fiction, the theatrical self loses some of its dialectical energy—its freedom to be both subject and object—and becomes here nearly reified, or, more precisely, commodified. As Carolyn Porter rightly observes of the novel, "commodification is not something to be overcome; it defines the state of the world in which everyone lives."[46] Not only are Charlotte and the Prince reduced to objects by the novel's end, but Maggie's growth into consciousness entails her reliance on a hard, cold mask of passivity. *The Golden Bowl* portrays the theatrical self embedded in a specific historical context—the late nineteenth-century triumph of the acquisitive spirit of American capitalism—which encodes the self in the values and language of the marketplace. The preoccupation of *Fifine at the Fair* with theatricality suggests a markedly different nexus of meanings. The histrionic in Browning's poem resides in a socially marginal group—the Gypsies—the "wild" "truants" who stand outside society and spurn "all we so prize."

What most attracts Juan to the Gypsies, apart from their blatant sexuality, is their indifference to conventional notions of truth and sincerity: they "alone of mankind make their boast / 'Frankly, we simulate!' " (sec. 85). This declaration fascinates Juan because it subverts a sacrosanct social axiom—that "Life means—leaning to abhor / The false, and love the true" (sec. 86). Gypsies expose this belief as a social myth founded on the polar opposition of false and true. In contrast, they offer guidance wherein man may "attain to read / The signs aright, and learn, by failure, truth is forced to manifest itself through falsehood" (sec. 124). This dialectical vision is celebrated in the histrionic talent of the gypsy tribe. Exclaims Juan: "Actors! We also act, but only they inscribe / Their style and title so, and preface, only they / Performance with 'A lie is all we do or say' " (sec. 85). That to be human is to act, to dissemble, is a truth a Gypsy embraces, whereas others "o'erlooked, forgot, or chose to sweep / Clean out of door" (sec. 7) this embarrassing reality. Theatricality requires suppression, for its insistence on the interplay of truth and falsehood undermines the allegedly natural and universal distinctions on which social order is founded. The Gypsy demystifying of the natural exhilarates Juan: "I prize stage play, the honest cheating, thence / The impulse pricked . . . To bid you trip and skip." He reinvokes his opening invitation, an offer addressed not only to his wife but to the reader, whom he hopes will be seduced, as he has been, by Gypsy insouciance: "How comes it, all we hold so dear they count so cheap?" But the wooing of the reader and Juan's flirting with the Gypsies remain in a teasing state of suspension. Rather than consummation, Browning, characteristically, is more interested in the process of seduction, and the ambiguity pervading the poem enacts this avoidance of resolution.

By turning to *Fifine at the Fair* itself, which evolves from the dramatic monologue into a version of the interior monologue, we can best appreciate the poet's conviction that it was his "boldest work since *Sordello*" and Clyde Ryals's belief that it is "almost totally different from anything attempted previously" by Browning.[47] Although the interior monologue is "by definition addressed to no one, a gratuitous verbal agitation without communicative aim,"[48] *Fifine at the Fair* slightly revises this convention by ambiguously suggesting that an auditor (Elvire) is present and is being addressed by the speaker. In contrast, no such ambiguity informs the dramatic monologue, which depends on a man speaking to others; there the monologist must be "put in a situation in which he will be stirred into speech to defend himself."[49] A dramatic situation, or at least the semblance of one, frames the dramatic monologue, providing the speaker the stimulus to pour forth. The monologist confronts an audience—be it the police who detain Lippo or the sons the Bishop has called to his bedside—to which he must represent himself; in other words, he performs under the pressure of a social context and manipulates a social mask for a desired effect.

Fifine at the Fair reduces this social context and almost eliminates it by portraying speech as the silent dialogue of mental life. Social reality is less insistent in *Fifine at the Fair*, for Juan's audience is the silent Elvire, whose physical presence is vivid, but whose dialogue is created solely by her husband in his relentlessly associative imagination. Although Elvire's "slow shake of head," "melancholy smile," and "pale fingers" that "press" Juan's arm seem to testify to her concrete reality, her existence may be Juan's invention. Browning's strategy is to create an ambiguity regarding the "real" and Juan's imaginative creation of it. Thus Elvire may finally be as bloodless as Fifine, whom Juan calls a "phantom . . . fancy-stuff and mere illusion . . . dream figures" (sec. 26). To make us uncertain of the reality of these characters is consonant with one of Juan's *idées fixes:* the world is "all false and fleeting too," "nowhere things abide / And everywhere we strain that things should stay" (sec. 80). Amid such chaos, all we can know, insists Juan, is that "we ourselves are true!": "I am, anyhow, a truth, although all else seem / And be not: If I dream, at least I know I dream" (sec. 80); "In the seeing soul, all worth lies" (sec. 55).[50] Browning's submission to the fact of individual human perspective as the source of truth is one reason Southwell calls *Fifine at the Fair* a work of the "most radical implications . . . keenly disturbing even for so audacious a mid-Victorian as Browning." Here the poet most nearly resisted his "proclivity to see all existence as numinous" and insisted "nowhere more emphatically . . . that we know nothing about the beyond."[51]

Juan's unabashed solipsism is the basis of the narrative form of *Fifine at the Fair,* as Browning represents the mental life of a single consciousness in all its *"fluidity* of self-revelation" (James's phrase). Instead of finding this a hazard of first-person narration (as James did), Browning seems to revel in it: he celebrates subjectivity as the only truth. All that is certain for Juan is his unappeasable "hunger both to be and know the thing I am" (sec. 103). By interiorizing the dramatic monologue, Browning, in effect, makes an intimate form even more intimate; and this self-communing is portrayed at remarkable length—over twenty-four hundred lines of rhymed alexandrines.

"Vast interior monologues" is Richard Poirier's description, not of *Fifine at the Fair,* but of "the quality of James's later novels";[52] certainly the second half of *The Golden*

Bowl bears out Poirier's description most strongly. But in juxtaposing Browning's interior monologue with James's we must be careful to avoid an often unacknowledged confusion that results, says Dorrit Cohn, from the use of the term to designate "two very different phenomena." Cohn has clarified the generic ambiguity of the interior monologue:

> 1) a narrative technique for presenting a character's consciousness by direct quotation of his thoughts in a surrounding narrative context; and 2) a narrative *genre* constituted in its entirety by the silent self-communion of a fictional mind. Though the technique and the genre share some psychological implications and stylistic features, their narrative presentations are entirely different: the first is mediated . . . by a narrating voice that refers to the monologist by a third-person pronoun in the surrounding text; the second, unmediated and apparently self-generated, constitutes an autonomous first-person form.[53]

Clearly *The Golden Bowl* employs interior monologue as a "narrative technique," whereas it is the genre of *Fifine at the Fair*. Cohn's term for the technique that portrays Maggie's inner life so closely is "narrated monologue."[54] Cohn stresses the "indeterminateness" of the method, as it is suspended between the "immediacy of quotation and the mediacy of narration."[55] "Imitating the language a character uses when he talks to himself, it casts the language into the grammar a narrator uses when talking about him, thus superimposing two voices."[56] The oscillations of these voices were a crucial concern of James's throughout his career, especially in *The Golden Bowl*.

Fifine at the Fair, as an outgrowth of the dramatic monologue, is a product of Browning's nearly inexhaustible urge for generic experimentation, which accounts for the remarkable array of formal innovations throughout his career. While the quality of his verse does indeed falter (witness *The Inn Album*), the fertility of his formal imagination is consistently impressive, particularly in his later work. James's oeuvre reveals a similar drive to explore new forms, a persistent quest that makes the artist an intrepid "explorer" pursuing his "art of representation" in the face of "obstacles" and even "terror." Impatience with traditional narrative forces the novelist to be a"rash adventurer," an image that pervades, appropriately enough, the opening of his first preface—to *Roderick Hudson*.

Like the narrative structure of many of James's novels, *Roderick Hudson* has a central reflector framed by an omniscient narrator whose vision provides clarity and scope beyond Rowland's limited perspective. In this novel (1875), Mallet's "total adventure" is less "what happened to him" than "above all to feel certain things happening to others, to Roderick, Christina, to Mary Garland."[57] In other words, Mallet as "lucid reflector" is turned outward to record the doings of those around him, rather than to record his inner life. Not until some years later would the novelist depict with sustained attention an individual's act of thought. James reached this breakthrough, most critics agree, in chapter 42 of *The Portrait of a Lady* (1881) where "what happened" in the mind of his central consciousness Isabel takes precedence over anything "happening to others." His portrayal of Isabel's act of "motionlessly seeing" as she engages in a "meditative vigil" struck James as "obviously the best thing in the book."[58] This dramatization of mental life occurs through the narrator's virtual abdication of his omniscient perspective, so as to register Isabel's thoughts in his third-person form. What results is a delicate "two-in-one" effect characteristic of "narrated monologue." To expand the technique of the narrated monologue, so effective in chapter 42 of *The Portrait of a Lady*, would be to create a more intimate "drama of consciousness" than James had ever managed; this goal he fulfilled in the second half of his last complete novel.

In *The Golden Bowl* James sought to narrow the gap between his narrator and his "central intelligence" by granting more of the novel to Maggie's point of view, although the narrator remains omniscient. This intention is on James's mind at the opening of his final preface: "anything . . . must always have seemed to me better . . . than the mere muffled majesty of irresponsible authorship."[59] The novelist "can never be responsible enough," says James, who finds irresponsibility the problem endemic in conventional third-person narration, where the narrator's omniscience makes him superior to his characters. Although the "muffled majesty of authorship" does "ostensibly reign" in *The Golden Bowl*, James gamely struggles to shake "it off" and "disavow the pretense of it." In so doing, he reaches a remarkable position of attempting to subvert the very narrative form he refuses to relinquish. Believing that art thrives on the tensions generated by the "strongest pressure we throw on it," James combats the "muffled majesty" of his omniscient narrator by "the manner in which the whole thing remains subject to the register, ever so closely kept, of the consciousness of but two of the characters."[60]

Because in his final performance James strives for maximum artistic responsibility he provides an unprecedented intensity of concentration on two characters' perspectives. In the novel's first half we see the action through the Prince, who "virtually sees and knows and makes out, virtually presents to himself everything that concerns us." Of course we are also provided other characters' points of view; at times Adam, Charlotte, and Fanny serve as reflectors. But James, in Maggie's half, tightens his focus, as the "register" of her consciousness is more closely kept than any character in James's fiction. Such limitation to a single viewpoint obviously reduces the number of characters who can be portrayed. James acknowledges his small cast, which he describes as a "group of agents who may be counted on the fingers of one hand." But this very spareness is what James seeks: "to play the small handful of values really for all they were worth" provides the "amusement of the chronicle in question."[61] James notes the experimental daring implied in his intention to circumscribe radically his fictional world, for he remarks that while "we see very few persons in *The Golden Bowl* . . . the scheme of the book, to make up for that, is that we shall really see about as much of them as a coherent literary form permits."[62]

With this statement James joins the author of *Fifine at the Fair* at the very boundary line of "coherent literary form." Their shared aesthetic of magnification deliberately expands that border; maintaining coherence while moving beyond conventional notions of it, into a world where "we are left to float . . . seemingly without solid fact." The "peculiarly fluid and unsettling reality" of these works induces in the reader "a kind of epistemological vertigo, for he is granted no secure position from which to judge the moral or even the factual truth of what is being said."[63] These quotations from Ruth Yeazell concern conversation in late James. Besides being acute about *The Golden Bowl*, her remarks are the most accurate descriptions I know of the experience of reading *Fifine at the Fair*. Disorientation is inevitable when a reader is locked inside a single consciousness, and this condition is precisely what James seeks to produce in *The Golden Bowl*: "one should, as an author, reduce one's reader . . . to such a state of hallucination by the images one has evoked as doesn't permit him to rest." His extraordinary remark aptly describes the "literary spell" that Browning seeks to "cast" in *Fifine at the Fair*.[64]

Maggie's half of the novel depicts her transformation from "the dearest little creature in the world" to a Maggie "audacious and impudent," to quote Fanny's astute prediction of what Maggie will become (1:396). Her prolonged process of awakening to the fact of adultery is enacted almost entirely within her mind, save for occasional conferences with Fanny; the reader alone is permitted entrance into her intensely private world. In "deciding to do something" to regain her husband, the once retiring Maggie—"a little dancing girl at rest"—must become a "heroically improvising" actress. As her plan proceeds with awesome effectiveness she feels "not unlike some young woman of the theatre who . . . should find herself suddenly promoted to leading lady and expected to appear in every act of the five" (2:208). What Maggie discovers, in short, is that theatricality "is one of power's essential modes."[65] Hers is the power of restraint; her role is to wait, circle, and linger.

Maggie grows to be an accomplished performer against a backdrop of nearly total solitude. She is as isolated as Juan is in his ramble through the fair, and like him she can rely only on herself in a world of pervasive illusion and deception. Early in her awakening to the "funny form" of her life, she comes to a sharp realization: "Ah! Amerigo and Charlotte were arranged together but she—to confine the matter only to herself—was arranged apart. It rushed over her, the full sense of all this . . . and as her father himself seemed not to meet the vaguely clutching hand with which, during the first shock of complete perception, she tried to steady herself, she felt very much alone" (2:45).

Strikingly, Maggie and Juan in their isolation pursue the same activity—the invention of hypothetical speech for those around them. Imaginary speech comes to pervade Maggie's mental life; "in her mind's ear" she hears the "doomed" Charlotte, in all her terrible pride, "speaking" to her stepdaughter; as well, Maggie brings to speech Amerigo's opaque silences, at one point articulating the "unspoken words" of his facial expression: "in her ear she had spiritually heard them" (2:221). The context varies in which Maggie's inventions occur. Often her hypothetical speech is born during her frequent bouts of solitary reflection; at other times Maggie is inspired by the immediate circumstances that confront her, as when she is alone with Amerigo after his adulterous weekend with Charlotte at Gloucester. In this encounter with her husband Maggie has yet to discover the true relationship of Amerigo and Charlotte, but her dawning awareness that she has become estranged from Amerigo resolves her to spend more time with him. Because Maggie wants now to share "with him, whatever the enjoyment, the interest, the experience might be" she makes his weekend with Charlotte "the subject of endless inquiry." As they rise from the dinner table where her inquiry has been conducted, Amerigo gives his wife "yet another of his kind conscious stares." "It was as if he might for a moment be going to say: 'You needn't *pretend*, dearest, quite so hard, needn't think it necessary to care quite so much!'—it was as if he stood there before her with some such easy intelligence" (2:27). Maggie's fabricated dialogue here results from her scrutiny of Amerigo's stare, but late in the novel her inventions grow considerably more complex as their basis becomes less concrete.

In the last fifty pages of *The Golden Bowl* James gives a name to Maggie's activity; he calls her constructions "translations." No longer does she translate the text of appearances (such as her husband's stare) but instead converts her intuition of Charlotte's agony into elaborate metaphor. But we cannot be sure if it is Maggie or the narrator who produces the metaphors, nor can we be certain that Charlotte is in agony. In the latter case, because we are not permitted entrance to Mrs. Verver's mind, everything is filtered to us from Maggie's perspective; we have only her perceptions to rely on. By examining an instance of Maggie's act of "translation," her complex relation to Charlotte and the narrator is set in relief.

When Maggie, near the end of the novel, watches Adam and Charlotte "making their daily round" at Fawns they strike her as "so together, yet at the same time so separate":

Charlotte hung behind, with emphasized attention; she stopped when her husband stopped . . . and the likeness of their connexion would not have been wrongly figured if he had been thought of as holding in one of his pocketed hands the end of a long silken halter looped round her beautiful neck. He didn't twitch it, yet it was there . . . and those indications that I have described the Princess as finding extraordinary in him were two or three mute facial intimations which his wife's presence didn't prevent his addressing his daughter—nor prevent his daughter, as she passed . . . from flushing a little at the receipt of. They amounted perhaps to a wordless, wordless smile, but the smile was the soft shake of the twisted silken rope, and Maggie's translation of it, held in her breast till she got well away, came out only, as if it might have been overheard, when some door was closed behind her. "Yes, you see—I lead her now by the neck, I lead her to her doom."

(2:287)

Maggie's invention of Adam's dialogue continues, but what is significant is how far we have traveled in this passage: we move from Maggie's perception of appearances ("her encountering the *sposi* as Amerigo called them"), to a metaphorical construct based on what she perceives, to Maggie's translation of this metaphor, formed as she walks away after observing her father's smile. The ambiguity occurs in James's deliberate blurring whether the narrator (who intrudes directly into the scene) or Maggie produces the metaphor expressing Charlotte and Adam's "connexion." As the metaphor is not attributed directly to Maggie, we might assume it is the narrator's. But this assumption is shaken when we find that her translation is not simply of Adam's "smile" but the smile in its transformed, metaphorical form: "the smile was the soft shake of the twisted silken rope." The dialogue Maggie invents for Adam is structured on this image: "I lead her now by the neck." Thus the metaphor now seems to have been Maggie's, but actually both have created it. There has been a fusion (or confusion) of the narrator's and Maggie's voices.

This ambiguity is characteristic of the "indeterminateness of the narrated monologue." But the blurring is not simply a technical effect; it serves an expressive purpose by enacting the collaboration that occurs between the narrator (that is to say James) and Maggie. For it is not only Maggie whose empathic imagination is stimulated into creating speech for another. The narrator performs an analogous imaginative feat as he creates a metaphor "for" Maggie. But if in saying this I seem to give the narrator credit for the metaphor, his is only the slightest priority, for the image expresses feelings arising from the most personal depths of Maggie's sensibility. Only a profound sensitivity to and intimacy with her mind allows James to translate for Maggie her perception of her father and stepmother into a metaphor connoting the eroticized torture she senses in the relation of the two.

Maggie's creation of imaginary dialogue, which occurs throughout her half of the novel, continues unabated even during the moments in which she is at the center of the novel's climax—Fanny's smashing of the golden bowl in front of her and, unknown to them, Amerigo. The stage seems to be set here, as it would be in a typical melodrama of adultery, for the long-awaited showdown between husband and wife. But at precisely this point James interiorizes the scene, placing it in Maggie's consciousness. After she silently, calmly bends to the floor for the broken pieces, Maggie imagines herself telling her husband: "Only *see, see* that I see, and make up your mind, on this new basis" (2:184). " 'Yes, look, look,' she seemed to see him hear her say even while her sounded words were other . . . 'I'm not such a fool as you supposed me . . . I *am* different, there may still be something in it for you' "(2:187).

This silent speech that Maggie comes "within an ace" of

saying to Amerigo is doubly momentous in that it is the explicit articulation (however silent) of her long-sought-for knowledge, and also adumbrates the "new basis" on which her marriage can be rebuilt. But this crucial realization of "finally . . . knowing everything" leaves her with "nothing else to add." "The least part of her desire was to make him waste words"(2:183). That Amerigo has witnessed Fanny's violent act is all that Maggie requires, for the broken bowl is "proof" that she knows. Maggie's "possession . . . of real knowledge" and her recognition of the possibility of redeeming her flawed marriage almost fulfills her "lucid little plan"; all that remains is for Charlotte and Adam to leave for America (2:201).

In the same scene, Maggie acquires what she calls (in relation to the new possibilities in her marriage) the "responsibility of freedom," which, in part, is the "responsibility" all great creators must assume, as James insists in his preface. Maggie in this confrontation becomes, in a more dramatic way than ever before, the sole source of truth, her imagination the measure of all things. Needing nothing but absolute confidence in her "conviction," she has no desire to verify matters by interrogating her husband; what she has deduced in her imagination is the only truth she requires. Proof of Maggie's authority is the very reticence of her behavior; so total is her mastery that she need never insist on it and is content to seem strangely passive.[66] "My only point now," she tells Amerigo, when their encounter moves from her mind to an actual conversation, is "your knowing that I've ceased" "not to know" (2:201–2).

Maggie's authority is founded on her acceptance of the fact that her knowledge is unverifiable; thus she becomes indifferent to any confrontations with her family that might reveal a different perspective. Her unconditional faith in herself is something the reader experiences on an intimate level because we know only what she knows; the framing narrator does not correct Maggie's restricted viewpoint or dispel ambiguities by the novel's end. The narrator's surrender of omniscience leaves us without a source of full reliability. Like Maggie, the reader must accept the condition of uncertainty and accept also the "disparities" and "monstrosities" produced in the text by this condition of extreme subjectivity. Such matters as the extent of Adam's knowledge—the intriguing possibility that "his motive and principle" may be identical with Maggie's—are never clarified. As the single maker of her world, Maggie's truth becomes the only truth.[67]

In the second half of *The Golden Bowl* we watch Maggie "express and confess" herself to "an effect of intellectual splendour," as James portrays her "extraordinarily magnified range of spirit and reach of intelligence," to borrow his words describing the dramatic monologues in *The Ring and the Book*. "Deviations" and "overstretchings of proportion" occur, of course, because James and Browning seek to imitate "not life, but a particular perspective towards life, somebody's experience of it. . . . The resulting limitation and even distortion of the physical and moral truth, being among the main pleasures of the [dramatic monologue] form."[68]

The distortions of *Fifine at the Fair* are strikingly akin to those of *The Golden Bowl*. Like Maggie's invented dialogue, Juan's "make-believe communications underscore the pervasive loneliness of the monologist, whose only true interlocutor remains the 'Imprisoned Self,' " to describe the general condition of the speaker of the interior monologue.[69] Not only does Juan create hypothetical dialogue but he also invents descriptions of people based less on observation than on his imagination. As in Maggie's world, the universe of *Fifine at the Fair* possesses no certainty, only interpretation: ". . . who knows? / Ay, who indeed! Myself know nothing, but dare guess," admits Juan (sec. 25). By "guess" work Juan creates fictive constructs to fill his empty world. His "power to guess the unseen from the seen, to trace the implications of things," as James describes the imaginative mind, is most incited by Fifine, who becomes his major creation. She is first introduced as little more than a stimulus to his meditations: "this way Fifine! / Here's she, shall make my thoughts be surer what they mean!" (sec. 15). Juan "guesses" that the "phantom" Fifine has a brutish husband because "she prefers sheer strength to ineffective grace, / Breeding and culture" (sec. 25). Juan's detailed portrait of her husband, whom he has never seen, and of whose existence he has no proof, has an even shakier epistemological status than Maggie's inventions, which are always based on known personages.

Juan's portrayal of Fifine's "husband" is only the first in a series of imaginary portraits he creates. Predictably, his infatuation with Fifine, or rather the idea of Fifine, leads him back to her, whose stance at a "happy angle" "reverberates Sunshine." "And now the mingled ray she shoots, I decompose," is Juan's striking description of his process of inventing a biography for her (sec. 31). In constructing her childhood, Juan remains fully aware that he is blithely fabricating: "Her antecedents, take for execrable! Gloze / No whit on your premise: let be, there was no worst / Of degradation spared Fifine: ordained from first / To last, in body and soul, for one life-long debauch"(sec. 31). As he concludes his guessing, his imagination takes a new turn: he has Elvire, his "sexless and bloodless sprite," respond to his description of Fifine's sordid childhood—"You comment" he implores Elvire. In giving words for Elvire to speak Juan invents an imaginary conversation. Elvire says: "Fancy us / So operated on, maltreated, mangled thus! / Such torture in our case, had we survived an hour?"(sec. 31). "Come, come," Juan chides his wife, "that's what you say, or would, were thoughts but free" (sec. 31).

In Juan's creation of dialogue for Fifine, the subject of his erotic musings, there is an underlying pathos. In his utter isolation he seems condemned to wander, never to achieve intimacy with another; his own Gypsylike status draws him to the elusive Gypsy Fifine, whom he sees (if she exists at all) only in passing through the fair. Thus Juan's inventions can be seen as a desperate attempt to communicate, an effort that can succeed nowhere but in his mind. Faced with such solitude Juan will make his inventions as lifelike as possible; in the speeches he invents for Fifine he creates a bitingly sarcastic coquette, whose "silent pose and prayer proclaimed aloud":

> Know all of me outside, the rest be emptiness
> For such as you! I call attention to my dress,
> Coiffure, outlandish features, lithe memorable limbs . . .
>   Do you seek further? Tut!
> I'm just my instrument,—sound hollow: mere smooth skin
> Stretched o'er gilt framework, I . . . naught else within—
> Always, for such as you!
>
> (sec. 32)

Juan's dialogue for Fifine in this passage is only the beginning of a torrential outburst of nearly one hundred lines which reveal his impressive powers of ventriloquism. Like Maggie's inventions, Juan's fictive creations range from the relatively simple (as in his portrait of Fifine's husband) to the dauntingly intricate. Juan is at his most ambitious when, after giving Fifine a voice, he has her mimic various other figures; she introduces each impersonation with the phrase "Do I, say like . . ." "Your Helen," "Your Queen of Egypt," "Your Saint." These female archetypes are all potential rivals of Fifine; her most obvious rival is the subject of her most elaborate impersonation: "Do I, say like Elvire . . ." (sec. 32). Before playing Elvire's part she describes "the wife's" insecure emotional state: ". . . her mixed unrest and discontent /

173

Reproachfulness and scorn, with that submission blent / So strangely, in the face, by sad smiles and gay tears." "Do I say" "As you loved me once, could you but love me now! / Years probably have graved their passage on my brow . . . / Such tribute body pays to time" (sec. 33).

As in Maggie's "translations" of observed reality into metaphor, we are faced in the above passage with a blurring of voices; here Elvire's lament can also be heard as Fifine's, Juan's, and ultimately Browning's. Both Browning and James, then, make their texts reverberate with the oscillations of overlapping voices. This "dire debate," as Juan calls his convoluted set of imaginary dialogues, achieves the kind of Chinese-box complexity found in Maggie's most abstract "translation." Juan's complicated invention derives from the number of voices he impersonates within a single act of dialogue: Juan creates for Fifine, who in turn creates for a series of archetypal figures, and finally the Gypsy mimics Elvire, who berates her husband and Fifine.

In the middle of his monologue Juan reflects on what has prompted his flow of thoughts. Although the fair "pricked" his "impulse" to philosophize, the major stimulus was a dream he had prior to his stroll. In seeking to account for the "outbreak and escape" of "intrusive fancies," Juan examines the dream. He had been lulled into sleep by Schumann's *Carnival*, and because he had anticipated visiting the fair, in his mind "the Fair expands into the Carnival / And Carnival again to . . . ah, but that's my dream!" (sec. 91). "I soon was far to fetch— / Gone off in company with Music!" (sec. 93). In his dream he finds himself in Venice, "carnival country proper," "pinnacled" above St. Mark's square. "From above I gazed, however I got there. / And what I gazed upon was a prodigious Fair. / Concourse immense of men and women . . . but masked— / Always masked" (sec. 95). From his remote vantage point the gathering of humanity below seems grotesque. He looks down on "the wrinkled brow, bald pate / And rheumy eyes of Age . . . Age reduced to simple greed and guile" (sec. 105). But even though he feels "repugnance" at what he sees, Juan is determined "to observe . . . / By shift of point of sight in me the observer" (sec. 101). Before shifting his view, Juan is struck by a "conviction to my soul, that what I took of late / For Venice was the world; its Carnival—the state / Of mankind" (sec. 108). Once he has grasped the symbolism of what he is observing, his "disgust / At the brute-pageant" becomes understandable—it results from his aloof perspective. In "my pride of place I passed the interlude / In critical review" (sec. 108).

To show his kinship with "mankind" massed below him, Juan realizes he must join them. He recounts this crucial movement of his dream in detail, for it expresses his attainment of "wisdom" and "wonder."

> . . . from such pinnacled pre-eminence, I found
> Somehow the proper goal for wisdom was the ground
> And not the sky,—so slid sagaciously betimes
> Down heaven's baluster-rope to reach the mob of mimes
> And mummers, whereby came discovery . . .
> . . . only get close enough!
> —What was all this except the lesson of a life?
>
> (sec. 108)

This "discovery" is the climax of Juan's dream; the vision it discloses expresses his understanding that only the achievement of intimacy can permit one to perceive the beauty of mankind. For when he gets "close" to the crowd they no longer look grotesque.

Juan's "discovery" can also be seen as an allegory of Browning's literary career, and particularly his achievement in the monologue form, dramatic and interior. Through Juan's dream, Browning takes a retrospective view of his career; he gathers together the "men and women" he has created through the years and reveals the aesthetic "wisdom" that allowed him to invent these figures. In Juan's "shift of point of sight" from "pinnacled pre-eminence" to "the ground," he reaches Browning's poetic stance in the monologue form—the portrayal of men and women from as intimate a perspective as possible. Browning's monologues and Juan's fabrications impersonate speakers "from the inside, marrying" their mind and sense to their monologists.[70] Juan, in short, is a Browningesque poet, indeed, Browning's alter ego. Like his creator, Juan's empathic imagination is adept at depicting the idiosyncratic sensibility and tone of voice of various individuals; witness the pungent portraits of Fifine and Elvire, among others, that emerge from Juan's mimicry. In a larger sense, of course, *Fifine at the Fair* is a single, enormous act of impersonation, with Browning playing the part of Don Juan.[71]

"Only get close enough!" is not only the "lesson" (Juan's word) of Browning's and Juan's art of intimacy, but is the very lesson James teaches in his preface to *The Golden Bowl*. To depict his relation to his characters James creates an image remarkably similar in meaning to the Carnival passage in *Fifine at the Fair*. "I get down into the arena and do my best to live and breathe and rub shoulders and converse with the persons engaged in the struggle that provides for the others in the circling tiers the entertainment of the great game."[72] This passage recalls the "descendental thrust" of Juan's discovery, as James makes the same movement from remote "majesty" to the "ground" to be with his characters in the "arena" of his fiction.[73] James's choice of "narrated monologue" as his narrational mode ideally suited his intentions to topple what he calls the "irresponsible majesty" of the third person. This technique aims at creating closeness between narrator and character; indeed, as Cohn states, it reduces "to the greatest possible degree the hiatus" between the two voices.

The difference between these two acts of descent is revealed in the connotations of the metaphors that portray the worlds in which these figures exist. James's image of the gladiator arena suggests a mood of grim struggle and symbolizes his conception of art as ineluctably sacrificial, founded on a tormented relation between author and characters. The latter are victimized regardless of how close their creator is to them; despite James's proximity, they remain "more or less bleeding participants." This disturbingly brutal image of the artistic process, which I have touched on in previous chapters, contrasts with the sanguine and affirmative resonance of Browning's image of his "men and women" in the "concourse immense." They seem horrific only from above; once Juan has "pitched into the square / A groundling like the rest," he finds "brutality encroach / Less on the human, lie the lightlier" (sec. 99). The "ugliness had withered" from the faces in the crowd. The Venetian carnival becomes a joyous occasion celebrating the communion achieved between the poet and his "men and women."

While they conceive the relationship between author and character differently, both writers share the compulsion to descend from their "pride of place" (Juan's phrase), or what James calls the "majesty of authorship" that portrays characters from an impersonal distance. Generating the movement toward proximity is a belief that the responsible author must "deprive himself of the authority of transcendent vision," as Feidelson describes one of James's "major concerns."[74] This refusal of transcendent perspective is precisely what is enacted in James's arena and Browning's dream carnival. "Bid a frank farewell" to life led on "altitudes of self-sufficiency," Juan insists, for such a stance distances one from the fictive creations one is responsible for (sec. 109). That this fulfillment of responsibility is achieved only through a surrender of authority, a deferral to fictive minds, is the central paradox structuring James's and Browning's relation to their characters.

The call sounded by Juan in his dream and James in his preface to achieve "nearness . . . close and sensitive contact" is heard by Maggie as she confronts the "wonderful, beautiful, but outlandish pagoda" (2:3). She has remained aloof from the pagoda, the "situation" that has been "occupying for months and months the very center of the garden of her life" (2:3). But like James she must become responsible by "stepping unprecedently near" it. Instead of "circling" about "quite helplessly to stare and wonder," Maggie must enter the structure and thereby "answer for what she had done." In so entering, Maggie will discover the "point of view" that will give her "most instead of least to answer for," as James describes the vantage point he sought in *The Golden Bowl*.[75] Maggie attains this stance of maximum responsibility, a perspective that embraces both her own vision and that of her three relatives: to see "for" Amerigo, Charlotte, and Adam becomes her burden. In her imagination Maggie takes upon herself "the whole complexity of their peril"; "to charge herself with it as the scapegoat of old" (2:234). She thus moves from aloofness to empathic involvement, descending into the "arena" of her grossly distorted family situation to become immersed as "a more or less bleeding participant."

The pagoda, like Juan's carnival image, casts a retrospective view, for it is a metaphor of the exotic, formidably ambiguous world of James's late fiction. "The great decorated surface . . . consistently impenetrable and inscrutable" describes both the "fair structure" and the intricate texture of the novels of the "major phase," which confront the reader with all the strangeness the pagoda possesses for Maggie (2:4). Like Maggie, the reader must be initiated into the elaborate deceptions and opacities of this fictional world; ultimately he will enter this mysterious structure and become responsible for its meaning. James's pagoda and Browning's dream carnival, which stand at the center of their respective works, both require an observer to charge them with meaning, a fact that dramatizes the perspectivism of these texts. Carnival and pagoda solicit the interpretative efforts of characters and readers, all of whom struggle to reach intimacy with what confronts them. Thus this imagery underscores Browning's and James's concern in these late works with perspectivism not simply as a matter of technique but as a central subject of their art.

James and Browning create a new depth of intimacy in literary form. Although Richardson and Austen helped shape the audience for subjective fiction, Browning in 1872 and James in 1904 were left feeling isolated from the reading public. In probing this sense of isolation, found most acutely in James, one discovers that it goes beyond mere personal frustration and is a fact of significant cultural and social import, capable of illuminating the relationship between literary form and history. Far from being a symptom of the hermetic, ahistorical decadence that Georg Lukács, for instance, finds in most modernist art, the solitude of James and Browning, Maggie and Juan, reflects the historical conditions in which modernism's radical subjectivity was born. And juxtaposing *Fifine at the Fair* and *The Golden Bowl* reveals that their decisive inward turn, a legacy of the Romantic concern with the solitary self, is accompanied by a preoccupation with modern forms of theatricality, which involve both writers in a dialectic of public and private. They are entangled in and responsive to the alienating social world in which they suffer isolation and psychic withdrawal.

The greatest English literary critic of the mid–nineteenth century stopped writing poetry partially in self-disgust at succumbing to the rampant subjectivism he deplored in the Romantics and his contemporaries. "Disinterested objectivity" has disappeared, announced Arnold in 1853, "the dialogue of the mind with itself has commenced."[76] Nowhere does this dialogue receive more sustained portrayal than in the fictive minds of Maggie and Juan, who join Arnold's Empedocles as "prisoners of . . . consciousness." Indeed, *Fifine at the Fair* and *The Golden Bowl* could serve Arnold as touchstones in his indictment of modernism. Browning's calculated indeterminacy and James's commitment to hallucinatory disorientation embody the "caprice and eccentricity," the want of "sanity," which constitute for Arnold "the great defect of the modern."[77] The lustful peregrinations of Juan and the adulterous schemes of Amerigo and Charlotte are flagrantly deficient in the "moral grandeur" Arnold thought necessary to create adequate representations of great actions.

Whereas Arnold, "amid the bewildering confusion" of his age, found the "only sure guidance, the only solid footing among the ancients," his friend Browning, according to Arnold's private opinion, surrendered to the "confused multitudinousness" of contemporary reality.[78] Predictably, the first reviewers charged *Fifine at the Fair* with confusion: "It might just as well have been written in Sanscrit," complained one critic, who found that "a perfect anthology of beauties might be culled," but the poem's constant "breaks and digressions" made reading a "positive fatigue."[79] The local brilliance of *Fifine at the Fair* would, in Arnold's view, confirm the tendency of contemporary work to rely on "exquisite bits and images" in direct contrast to the unity and wholeness of ancient literature. "They regarded the whole; we regard the parts," a condition engendered by modernism's pronounced subjectivity, which substitutes for the integrated unity of action and character a distorted emphasis on individual vision. A failure to depict a "total impression," the inability to "clasp and feel the All," as Arnold wrote of Empedocles, is also manifested in a disproportion between action (plot) and expression. "With us the expression predominates over the action," while the opposite holds true for the ancients.[80] Clearly the ratio in *Fifine at the Fair* and *The Golden Bowl* would strike Arnold as woefully unbalanced, for minimal action generates a luxuriance of expression.

Judged by Arnold's neoclassical standards of moral balance, simplicity, and wholeness, these texts are hopelessly infected with the "strange disease of modern life."[81] It is precisely this condition that grants them a historical consciousness. Ironically, four years after his staunch antimodernism has softened, Arnold provides terms useful in revealing Browning's and James's responsiveness to their times. In "On the Modern Element in Literature" Arnold writes: "The present age exhibits to the individual man who contemplates it the spectacle of a vast multitude of facts awaiting and inviting his comprehension." The man who finds "the true point of view from which to contemplate this spectacle . . . who communicates that point of view to his age . . . who interprets to it that spectacle, is one of his age's intellectual deliverers."[82]

What makes Browning and James "intellectual deliverers" is their insistence that "the true point of view" is point of view, that is, perspectivism, which denies that there is a "true point of view." Perspectivism, and its formal embodiment in the interior monologue and the novel of consciousness, constitutes a profound "comprehension" of the age, for the solitary heroes of perspectivist art reflect the socially enforced isolation of man in the late nineteenth century. As sociologists and cultural historians have observed, the ascendancy of bourgeois individualism as an ideological category occurs within a growing free-market economy governed by the principle of competition. Rapid industrial growth brings increasing economic opportunity and with it an implicit demand that men be cautious, secretive, masked, trusting only themselves. Thus in his emergence as an absolute, the individual suffers social alienation and loneliness.[83] It is in such a context that "modern subjectivistic relativism" develops, an epistemology that, as Jameson contends, "reflects an increasing atomization of middle-class society, a fragmentation and decay of the larger social units and institutions."[84] This historical context shapes James's life. His sense of theatricality registers, in its need for protective disguise, the impact of an increasingly coercive, if empty, public world. The theatrical self presses back against the pressure of reality by insisting on a saving measure of control and creativity in social life.

Within this historical reality that Jameson describes, the novelist witnesses the decay of the institution of literature. To James it is an age of "merely material expansion"; the ever growing reading public only succeeds in coarsening taste to the point where he fears "the age of letters" to be "waning,"[85] relegating the serious writer to marginal status, read by a "little community of the elect," as one contemporary reviewer scornfully described the potential audience for *The Golden Bowl*.[86]

While James's problems with the public are notorious, Browning's popularity (after years of critical disparagement), beginning with *The Ring and the Book* and continuing to his death, would seem to be in obvious contrast to James's career. But Browning's late poetry bewildered and annoyed readers, and his animus against the literary establishment continued to grow in his years of acclaim. The adulation of the Browning Societies provided more than just welcome relief from Browning's mistreatment by professional literary men. The ceaseless activity of the Societies served well the obsessively private and secretive poet for, as Park Honan has observed, "it obscured much of his past life and simplified his entire life."[87] Like his shield of inexhaustible heartiness (which permitted him to "gossip and dine by deputy," as James noted in "The Private Life"), the Victorian sage that

Browning became was one more protective mask to hide an abiding sense of distrust in his adoring public. Quite probably, Browning shared James's "singular contempt" for the " 'critical world' at large"; indeed he found a "grotesque side" to the public worship he smilingly endured.[88] Browning's most candid reaction to his insatiably prying readership is contained in a late poem: "Here's the work I hand, this scroll, / Yours to take or leave; as duly, / Mine remains the unproffered soul."[89] As they approached the ends of their careers, both men turned their backs on the public to concentrate on inventing new literary forms, regardless of the fact that, in James's words, "the last thing" the mass audience "expects of you is that you will spin things fine."[90] The intricately spun monologues James and Browning fabricate are rooted in their personal withdrawals from public life, in that loneliness, which, Adorno reminds us, is "socially mediated and so possesses a significant historical content."[91]

James dramatizes his loneliness in Maggie, who becomes an unorthodox figure of the artist. Maggie has often been identified as an authorial character since she creates a plot and dialogue; at one point James calls her a dramatist. But it is in her extreme isolation, which forces her to live an almost entirely inward life, that Maggie becomes truly emblematic of her creator, who more than once described the artist's life as one of "absolute solitude." Faced with continued public apathy, he refused to capitulate: "My work definitely insists on being independent [of the 'childish' public] and on unfolding itself wholly from its own innards." With his typical flair for self-dramatization James goes on to lament proudly: "in our conditions, doing anything decent is pure disinterested, unsupported, unrewarded heroism."[92]

The similarity of James's self-characterizations here and his portrayal of Maggie is striking. Like her indefatigable creator, Maggie unfolds in near-complete independence of those around her. In an 1890 letter when he is once again on the verge of public defeat James writes: "One must go one's way and know what one's about and have a general plan and a private religion. . . . One has always a 'public' enough if one has an audible vibration—even if it should only come from oneself."[93] This declaration suggests remarkable parallels with Maggie's strategic withdrawal from a disturbing world. The "general plan" that creator and character devise is the same: the cultivation of inwardness—James in his art, Maggie in her artful rearrangement of her life. Their "private religion" consists in a devotion to inventing words for others; these words are the "audible vibration" sounded for an audience of one—themselves. Mediating "absolute solitude," then, is a public realm, however minimal.

The link implied here between a troubling public world and the growth of a rich inward life is a connection that has recently been observed. "When the public moral world proves fragile and untrustworthy," writes Stephen Toulmin in an important essay on "The Inwardness of Mental Life," "internalization may serve . . . as a mechanism of defense."[94] His key point is that "our mental lives are not essentially inner lives. Rather, they become inner because we make them so. And we do develop inner lives . . . because we have reasons for doing so."[95] Toulmin argues that "inwardness is in many respects an *acquired* feature of our experience, a *product*, in part, of cultural history."[96] The evidence of James's fiction and career endorses such a view. Repeatedly, when the larger web of social relations—family or marriage in his fiction, or a community of colleagues in his career— begins to unravel because of deception, infidelity, philistinism, the response is an inward turn, which becomes a "refuge or asylum from the public world" (Toulmin). In the cases of Maggie and Isabel Archer refuge is short-lived. Their recognitions of a treacherous outer world prompt their inward growth, but they rejoin, even hope to repair, the public institution of marriage. When young, James, like his heroines, had

put his faith in a great public form—the brotherhood of letters. Believing that "art lives upon discussion . . . upon the
exchange of views," James sought the "stimulus of suggestion, comparison, emulation," for "every man works better
when he has companions working in the same line."[97] But
soon this vision of artistic community was disappointed.
"How barren he found the sensibility of his milieu," Matthiessen has stressed; "there was no novelist in England with
whom he could share his aims."[98] Only with foreign novelists—Balzac, Turgenev, Flaubert—did James find artistic
kinship. But public neglect was a more painful problem. In
1888 James felt himself "staggering" from the "inexplicable
injury" of commercial failure. James regained his balance in
part by eventually moving from the center of the London
multitude to a more private existence in Rye, a direction that
parallels the increasing inwardness of his fiction.

The pattern I have been tracing—the split between public
and private experience—has in recent years received much
attention, for the gap has been widening in the twentieth
century.[99] The careers and work of Browning and James re-
mind one with particular force how acute the disjunction
had grown in the second half of the nineteenth century,
when the loosening of the social bonds linking the individual and the larger world permitted fragmented, unstable,
theatrical selves to flourish. As Toulmin remarks, our cultivation of inwardness has as its obverse our learning "to wear
masks" in a public world increasingly pervaded by an "absence of mutual trust."

Refusing the Arnoldian nostalgia for wholeness and inte-
gration, Browning and James bear witness to the "spectacle" of the age and represent its fractures and disloca-
tions.[100] That their late masterpieces should be cloistered,
self-referential, and formally innovative to a startling degree, and yet responsive at the same time to historical reality, is a paradox Adorno explains well in reference to twen-

185

tieth-century modernism; his words have equal relevance here: ". . . taken to its logical conclusion, loneliness will turn into its opposite: the solitary consciousness potentially destroys and transcends itself by revealing itself in works of art as the hidden truth common to all men. This is exactly what we find in the authentic works of modern literature. They objectify themselves by immersing themselves totally, monadologically, in the laws of their own forms, laws which are aesthetically rooted in their own social content. . . . The voice of the age echoes through their monologues."[101]

Another aspect of James's isolation remains to be examined. In venting his wrath at the reading public and colleagues alike with complaints of "the ignoble state to which in this age of every cheapness I see the novel as a form reduced,"[102] James is sincere and also strategic. His embattled stance is partly exaggerated, designed to preserve a sense of originality. And this strategy is not absent from his public declarations of lavish admiration for Browning. It is not simply for aesthetic reasons that Browning is one of the very few English writers James consistently praises. As a poet he was less of a direct competitor and literary threat to James, who could far more easily maintain the enabling fiction of "priority" by using a poet rather than a fellow novelist. Ironically, Browning the poet, unlike the disturbing figure of Browning the man, proved a nourishing refuge from the anxieties of the novelists' side of the street.

As the last two chapters have shown, by the dawn of the new century, which coincided with his major phase, James had surmounted his uneasy fascination with Browning the man and had turned to the poet's work and its aesthetic premises as a "stimulus" of "suggestion" and "emulation." Whereas Browning's influence on *The Wings of the Dove* centers on the "subject" of theatricality as a theme and form, Browning's intention in *Fifine at the Fair*—to "get close enough" as possible to the point of view of a single consciousness—becomes James's in *The Golden Bowl*. By incorporating into his fictional narrative lengthy passages of "narrated monologue," James in effect makes Maggie's section a kind of prose equivalent of Browning's version of an interior monologue. Thus in his last complete work James fulfills his ambition, which had been boldly accomplished in another genre thirty-two years before by the one English writer who had "touched everything and with a breadth!"

JAMES'S
FINAL APPROPRIATION
OF BROWNING

 James's entry into the public arena in 1912 to pay tribute to Browning marks his first public appearance since the traumatic evening of the *Guy Domville* premiere in 1895, when James was booed off the stage.[1] The circumstances surrounding James's return to public view are worth mentioning because the ambivalence of his aggressive homage has its source in a psychological struggle enacted not only within the address but in its biographical context. Thus both dimensions will concern us in discussing the novelist's final declaration of esteem and anxiety. Since James had expressed his mixed admiration in print on a number of occasions, his acceptance of the Royal Society's invitation involves motives deeper than another chance to salute the poet. That Browning draws James out of the privacy of Lamb House testifies to the poet's continued exertion of psychological pressure. Perhaps by participating in Browning's centenary celebration James saw a way to relieve this pressure.[2]

A seemingly tangential fact suggests another aspect of James's decision to confront Browning in public. Both Wil-

liam James and John La Farge had very recently died. For
James these men were, like Browning, prestigious figures of
masculine authority from as far back as his adolescence. All
three shared an identity as virile men "occupying a place in
the world to which I couldn't at all aspire," as James wrote
of William at the beginning of *A Small Boy and Others.*
James's unease before two of these men has been made clear,
and his rivalry with his brother has often been noted. But in
1912 James has survived them all. At last he vanquishes his
sense of never having "in the least caught up with" these
"essentially harmonious" men.[3] Liberated from their op-
pressive weight, he is free to take over their authority,
which he accomplishes by imitating the most disturbing of
them: the poet of adult sexuality, who, being simultaneously closest (as a fellow writer) and farthest apart (as a
famed lover), has snared him most completely in a double
bind. This context suggests that the homage represents a
symbolic initiation for James; he uses the occasion to rise in
public as "master"—he will take Browning's place as the
venerable "head of the profession." Thus in 1912 James effects a reversal of his public humiliation suffered seventeen
years before.

In James's act of substitution, his usurping of the master,
the ambivalence of the Oedipal struggle inevitably emerges.
By seizing and assaulting *The Ring and the Book* James re-
venges himself on Browning. Yet James's revenge is inextricable from his veneration for his model; he pays tribute to
Browning by symbolically and literally imitating him. "My
voice *was* on that Centenary itself Centenarian," James remarked in a letter a few days after the address.[4] In his "desire
to be a model" James speaks in Browning's voice (as he
seems to acknowledge), stressing the "relation between man
and woman . . . as the relation most worthwhile in life for
either party."[5] So powerful is James on this subject that one
of his listeners, Lord Charnwood, found most memorable

the novelist's declaration (in Charnwood's words) that "the one thing that might really satisfy a man's desire of life [is] namely to love a woman."[6] This emphasis, richly ironic coming from James, seems a sincere espousal of the poet's most familiar and popular theme. In his ringing insistence on the value of love between men and women, James, in effect, becomes the author of *Men and Women*, finally taking sole possession of that sacred text from his adolescence, at last becoming a sexual man, if only verbally.

Sitting down to great applause, James, reports Edel, "had richly paid his debt to Browning . . . but now the audience paid its homage to him." Edel's implication that a double homage is occurring is apt and points to the other aspect of doubleness: James's imitation of his model. The novelist's "appropriation" memorializes his effort to make creative use of Browning to nourish his art. Summoning all the audacity and authority that his prodigious career can grant, James publicly restages the process of rewriting by which he had solved his problem with the poet, commemorating both his master and his own mastery of Browning's "monstrous magnificence." In probing a major source of this magnificence—the poet's compelling if disconcerting emphasis on adult sexuality—one uncovers the homage's psychological structure.

As James insisted on more than one occasion, Browning's "complete and splendid" portrayal of the "great human passion" possessed an authenticity nearly unmatched by any other writer, in part because it was founded on his own experience as a lover. In his Westminster tribute of 1891, James suggests another reason for the memorableness of the poet's subject matter: Browning's "eagerness" to "participate in complications and consequences—a restlessness of psychological research that might well alarm any pale company for their formal orthodoxies."[7] Chief among the "complications and consequences" which the poet was keen to represent were sexual manipulation and rivalry, both present in varying degrees of explicitness in all of the Browning works that James is drawn to. Since sexual rivalry and usage are so conspicuous in *The Ring and the Book*, when James first read the work at twenty-five he might well have included himself in the "pale company" suffering "alarm" at Browning's subject.[8] But if he felt "alarm" James was also absorbed, for his own work was to reveal a similar preoccupation. Thus it is hardly surprising that when James returns to *The Ring and the Book* in 1912 he is fascinated by the confrontation between the vicious manipulator Guido and the celibate priest Caponsacchi; James salutes their subtly depicted sexual rivalry for Pompilia as one of the finest things in the poem, throwing "across our page as portentous a shadow as we need." But there are other, less obvious reasons for James's attention to their conflict.

Guido's entrapment of Caponsacchi grips James because it grotesquely reflects his own psychological relation to Browning, who is a threatening figure blocking entry to the private life of sexuality. Caponsacchi's renunciation of the world doubtless had a strong personal relevance for James; the priest's resolve to live in the imagination makes him the kind of artist-celibate James would come to celebrate in his fiction and exemplify in his life. Caponsacchi, then, belongs in company with Overt, the narrator of "The Private Life," and the young man of *The Inn Album* as a victim of an older, manipulative character. And obviously Guido joins St. George, Vawdrey, and the rogue of *The Inn Album* as a disturbing, devious figure. What this alignment suggests is clear: Browning remains a potent symbolic figure in James's imagination nearly twenty-five years after confronting him in "The Lesson of the Master."

James is drawn to the poet one last time in 1912 to reveal that the problem of Browning still resists complete solution. In this centenary homage we witness James's effort to adjust to Browning's double bind. James declares here that he will imitate Browning the artist and enacts his identification with the poet by rewriting his masterpiece. According to Girard, identification is the disciple's "desire to be the model" and realizes itself "naturally enough, by means of appropriation, that is by taking over the things that belong" to the model. This description precisely explains James's peculiar relation to Browning in 1912; indeed, Girard's term "appropriation" is a key word in the tribute. As shown earlier, James's appropriation is an aggressive usurping of the poet's artistic authority, a violent assault whereby James enacts the revenge that Paul Overt envisioned.

James's reckless, even brutal seizure links him with those other appropriators, Guido and Browning. The poet seizes "the old yellow book," James seizes *The Ring and the Book,* and Guido seizes Pompilia from her parents. It is a measure of the psychological complexity of the address that James can be identified both with the priest and with Guido and Browning. These latter identifications result from James's elaborate mimicry of his master Browning; for in his "irreverent" redoing of the poem James successfully rivals the poet and dissolves the differences between them, as master and disciple become indistinguishable.[9]

In the homage James's relation to Browning is refracted through the novelist's absorption in the "complications and consequences" of the "great human passion" that bring Guido, Caponsacchi, and Pompilia into confrontation. Amid the moral decay of his world Caponsacchi stands nearly alone in his condemnation of society and its corrupt institutions, including the priesthood and the law. His passionate outrage at Guido's murderous animality and the judicial system that implicitly condones Guido's violence elicits James's most lavish praise: "the soul of man at its finest," the "rarest fruit of a great character" (p. 397). In the course of his monologue Caponsacchi recounts his psychic withdrawal from a world where the wholly innocent Pompilia is "bleeding out her life . . . / This minute." As she is dying the embittered priest addresses the tribunal that three months before had unjustly relegated him to a country parish for three years, as punishment for "flight and adultery" with Pompilia. Caponsacchi had finally decided to rescue Pompilia less from simple nobility than from his desire to prove to her that he is not afraid of Guido: "If she should . . . come / On the fantastic notion that I fear / The world now . . . fear perhaps / Count Guido . . . Let God see to that— / Hating lies, let not her believe a lie!"[10] Browning's ironic portrayal of Caponsacchi's character and actions in this episode uncovers the implicit sexual rivalry between the priest and Guido; James singles out Browning's indirect depiction of their relation as one of the poem's most artful touches. When Pompilia confirms Caponsacchi's suspicions—that her husband enjoys using her as "bait" to "trap" "others"—this sexual triangle is made explicit and creates a "portentous . . . shadow." Her fear that she might "become a snare" is fulfilled when Caponsacchi responds to Guido's baiting.

With obvious relish James envisions "a relation" between the two men "of strong irritated perception and restless righteous convinced instinct in the one nature, and of equally instinctive hate and envy, jealousy and latent fear, on the other" (p. 407). An aspect of the poem particularly stimulating to James is Guido's invention of love letters between Pompilia and Caponsacchi; in his "jealousy" and "fear" and "debased wit" Guido literally forges a link between them. These letters, imagined by James to be "scandalous scrawls of the last erotic intensity," constitute "the last luxury" of Guido's baseness (p. 408). James's interest in Guido's letters (letters Browning never reveals), at first glance a minor matter, is actually rich in implications. By focusing on Guido as a writer, a creator of an "imputed correspondence," as James says, the novelist makes an im-

193

plicit identification of the Count with Browning. At the same time, Guido, the writer, and his creator recall the other writer James, whose embellishment of Guido's letters imitates Browning's prior act of embellishment of the documents that furnished him with his "Roman murder story." James's description of Guido's forged letters has additional significances, which relate to the triangle involving the Count, his wife, and the priest. Guido in this context and James in his life are denied passionate intimacy with another. In his "jealousy" Guido, like James, responds by an act of writing: 'forged . . . words for me, made letters he called mine," says the priest. This phrase expresses James's sense of "the very essence" of novelistic method: the "imputing" of words, thoughts, and feelings to a character. Guido and James, then, are both barred from the private life and therefore imagine, not without titillation, an intensely erotic life denied to them except in writing. And where is Browning in all this? James must imagine what Guido imagines in his letters because Browning, by not revealing them, in effect refuses to imagine. Or, more precisely, because Browning personally *knows* sexual experience, he need not imagine. The poet's abdication of his poetic role, his lack of a need to write, aligns him with the devoted couple in flight—Caponsacchi, the heroic actor, and Pompilia, who cannot write. At this moment in his poem the poet, like his hero and heroine, has absconded. In other words, Browning is where he usually is in relation to James—beyond the novelist's grasp, on the other side of the private life.

But deeper than his relation to Guido here is James's identification with and admiration of Caponsacchi throughout the poem. In considering James's absorption in the "complications" of Caponsacchi's dilemma, inevitably we wonder what, beyond his stated reasons, accounts for his fascination with the priest. When looking for an answer in James's fiction we find that Merton Densher suffers a "keen and inter-

194

esting agitation" strikingly similar to Caponsacchi's. Not as savior or rescuer does Densher resemble the priest, but in their both being converted, by the end of their respective works, to a vision of the "might-have-been" so absorbing that they are left isolated. Although Densher's conversion is depicted to be as much the result of self-deception as love of Milly, both he and the priest are plunged into despair and disenchantment with the social world by the tragic loss of a saintly female.

Having been "blessed by the revelation of Pompilia," Caponsacchi is free to create in his imagination a private church of worship founded on her memory. Like the priest, Densher feels "that something had happened to him too beautiful and sacred to describe. He had been . . . forgiven, dedicated, blessed." In his final speech Caponsacchi confronts the most painful matter of all: what might have been had Pompilia lived. In a tone of melancholy resignation, purged of the arrogance and shrill sarcasm of much of his monologue, the priest wistfully states: "You see, we are / So very pitiable, she and I, / Who had conceivably been otherwise" (6.2069–71). The lines have grown short, as the weight of emotion makes speech an effort. Faced with the unyielding facts: "Pompilia will be presently with God . . . / She and I are mere strangers now," Caponsacchi turns from them to ponder what might have "been otherwise" (6:2074, 2078). "I do but play with an imagined life," he muses, as he dreams of their impossible life together:

> . . . unfettered by a vow, unblessed
> By the higher call . . .
> Leads it companioned by the woman there.
> To live and see her learn, and learn by her.
> . . . .
> To have to do with nothing but the true,
> The good, the eternal—and these, not alone
> In the main current of the general life,

> But small experiences of every day,
> Concerns of the particular hearth and home.
> ....
> ... All this, how far away!
> Mere delectation, meet for a minute's dream!
>
> (6:2082–85, 2089–93, 2096–97)

This "play" of the imagination, as it tenderly articulates lost possibilities, recalls Merton Densher's act of imagination as he ponders Milly's unopened letter, "extraordinarily" filling out and refining it. The priest's monologue concludes with an extended metaphor that compares his "minute's dream" to a student's absorption in contemplating life's illusory prospects:

> Just as a drudging student . . .
> Opens his Plutarch, puts him in the place
> Of Roman, Grecian; draws the patched gown close,
> Dreams, "Thus should I fight, save or rule the world!"—
> Then smilingly, contentedly, awakes
> To the old solitary nothingness.
> So I, from such communion, pass content. . . .
>
> (6:2098–2104)

Both the priest and Densher are "as good as out of it," "content" to exist in "solitary nothingness"; only in their imaginations will they find "communion." Keats's declaration, "My imagination is a monastery and I am its monk," offers an apt image of the two men's elected isolation at the conclusions of their respective works. Densher, like Caponsacchi, yearns to "escape everything," as he admits to Kate; seeking refuge in a purely inward life, he is a "man haunted with a memory," as is the priest. Unlike Browning, James invokes the ideal of renunciation and simultaneously renders it ironic, as his hero prissily prefers to reject Kate as impure, thus freeing himself to aestheticize Milly.

"I feel that Browning's great generous wings . . . shake

down on us his blessing." In these final words of the homage, his last recorded image of the poet, James acknowledges the gifts that Browning's art has bestowed. The poet's "blessing," what James calls the "all-touching, all-trying spirit of his work," does not fully reside in, in fact must exceed, the particular texts of which the novelist made use and which have concerned us in this study. The configuration imposed in these pages stabilizes what is of unresolvable tension and complexity. James is alert to the inevitably defensive motive in interpretation—the effort to contain what can never be wholly contained. And one reason that James prizes, even cultivates, this urge to appropriate is its close relation, as we have seen, to the artistic (and theatrical) impulse. He describes this root impulse of defense in the preface to *The Princess Casamassima* as a "slashing out": when confronted with bewilderment be sure "there is plenty of slashing out in the bewilderment too." Rather than repressing his sense of Browning's "bewildering modernness,"[11] James struggled with the poet and in so doing remained true to his belief that what most counts is "the very slashing, the subject-matter of any self-respecting story"[12] including the present one. Browning is important for his special power to provoke in James this slashing out—the making of intricate fictions in life and art.

No one was more aware than James himself of what he owed the poet; his sense of indebtedness informs the conclusion of the novelist's tribute to the poet upon his burial in Westminster Abbey: Browning's achievement "will seem to us to have widened the allowance, made the high abode more comfortable for some of those who are yet to enter it." The imagery is suggestive: the "abode" stands open, is now "widened" and "comfortable" thanks to Browning, who for once appears wholly benevolent, even nurturing, as he prepares for the arrival of other luminaries. Tacitly expressed here is James's yearning for intimacy, for a space where he might dwell with Browning as an equal. If only for a moment, James finds open the closed doors that appear in both short stories, signifying his anguished distance from the elusive Browning. Ironically, the beckoning comfort that James envisions is depicted as a posthumous moment, to occur when the novelist himself might stand at the threshold of interment in the Abbey. Not on earth, James realized, would Browning's threatening presence be replaced by the welcome of kinship.

❄ NOTES ❄

INTRODUCTION
A WIDENING, NOT A NARROWING CIRCLE

1. Robert Lowell, "After Enjoying Six or Seven Essays on Me,"
Salmagundi 37 (Spring 1977): 113.
2. Leon Edel, *Henry James: The Conquest of London* (Philadelphia: J. B. Lippincott, 1962), p. 330.
3. Kenneth Graham, *Henry James: The Drama of Fulfillment*
(Oxford: Oxford University Press, 1975), p. 141.
4. James's relation to Browning, Balzac, and Hawthorne has at
least one significant thing in common: onto each writer James
projects his own highly personal feelings and thereby turns them
(at least in part) into symbolic figures to which he is, in varying
degrees, opposed or in sympathy. In so doing, James partially estab-
lishes his identity as artist and man. For instance, Browning's sexual mastery is James's impression and has little to do with the
poet's actual sexual life. As Betty Miller has shown, Browning was
anything but sexually at ease. Similarly, James's cherished image
of Balzac as a monk conflicts with the fact of his famous love affair.
Since this study examines James's use of the first two writers, a
brief look at what use he makes of Hawthorne is in order. I rely
here on Richard Ruland's "Beyond Harsh Inquiry: The Hawthorne
of Henry James" (*ESQ* 25 [1979]: 95–117), an insightful assessment
of their complex relationship. Ruland emphasizes that "as early as
1879 James felt compelled to emphasize their differences and open
as wide a distance between them as he could." James employs this
strategy, suggests Ruland, because he was only too well aware of
their profound artistic affinities. And by refusing to look too
closely at Hawthorne because his art is not as rich as Balzac's or
Flaubert's (as James insists) James is able to maintain his belief that
"Europe is necessary" (p. 105). Similar strategies of avoidance and

distortion, if for different purposes, inform James's relation to Browning. Another light on these matters is provided by Harold Bloom's paradigm of anxiety between masters and disciples, as discussed in chapter 1. Note 15 below shows James's refusal to look too closely at Emerson.

5. Among the best comparative studies are: Peter Brooks, *The Melodramatic Imagination* (New Haven: Yale University Press, 1976); Stephen Donadio, *Nietzsche, Henry James, and the Artistic Will* (New York: Oxford University Press, 1978); Elsa Nettels, *James and Conrad* (Athens: University of Georgia Press, 1977); John Carlos Rowe, *Henry Adams and Henry James* (Ithaca: Cornell University Press, 1976).

6. Henry James, *The Art of the Novel: Critical Prefaces*, ed. R. P. Blackmur (New York: Scribner's, 1962), p. 348.

7. A tension between the moral and theatrical is evident throughout James's work. For instance, he finds a source of the mediocrity of the London stage in the "temperament and manners" of the English people: "These people are too highly moral to be histrionic . . . they have too stern a sense of duty." See Henry James, *The Scenic Art* (New York: Hill and Wang, 1957), p. 100.

8. Stephen J. Greenblatt, *Renaissance Self-Fashioning* (Chicago: University of Chicago Press, 1980), p. 3.

9. Henry James, *Autobiography*, ed. F. W. Dupee (New York: Criterion, 1956), pp. 59–60.

10. Ibid., p. 200.

11. Ibid., p. 107.

12. Warwick Slinn's *Browning and the Fictions of Identity* (London: Macmillan, 1982), which came to my attention after my own work was completed, provides an excellent account of the poet's emphasis on "the fictional dimension of human experience" (p. 76) and the "histrionic truth" of Browning's monologists.

13. Anthony Wilden, *System and Structure* (London: Tavistock, 1980), p. 89.

14. Fredric Jameson, "The Symbolic Inference; or Kenneth Burke and Ideological Analysis," *Critical Inquiry* 4 (Spring 1978): 520–21.

15. While rejecting Romantic sincerity, Browning embodies another Romantic impulse—impersonation. As Hillis Miller ob-

serves, Browning takes the Keatsian "chameleon poet" aesthetic "just about as far as it can go." J. Hillis Miller, *The Disappearance of God* (New York: Schocken, 1965), p. 106.

James's opposition to American Romanticism is expressed in his mocking, if affectionate, condescension to Emerson, whom he misreads solely as an apostle of "sincerity and independence and spontaneity," "and a great many other things which it would be still easier to present in a ridiculous light." Henry James, *Hawthorne* (Ithaca: Cornell University Press, 1966), p. 67.

16. James, *The Art of the Novel*, p. 64.

17. For a brief but incisive discussion of the emergence of the "discontinuous self" in the late nineteenth century, see Jackson Lears, *No Place of Grace* (New York: Pantheon, 1981), pp. 35–39. Lears, like other cultural historians, connects this phenomenon to the new social relations demanded in an increasingly urban, capitalist, consumerist culture. Lears places James, and the debate between Isabel and Madame Merle, at the center of the growing awareness that "there might be 'no clear core of self.' " (Lears is quoting David Riesman's phrase.) Another source of fragmentation—the widening gap between public and private experience—is examined in chapter 5 of the present work.

18. R. P. Blackmur, *A Primer of Ignorance* (New York: Harcourt, Brace, 1967), p. 191.

19. Studies of James and Browning have been few and, with small exception, not very suggestive. Because James explicitly named Browning as the original of his fictional character Clare Vawdrey in "The Private Life," this story is the best-known aspect of their relation. There are two studies of "The Private Life": Sidney E. Lind, "James's 'The Private Life' and Browning," *American Literature* 33 (1951): 315–22, and Earl Bargainnier, "James and Browning and 'The Private Life,' " *Studies in Short Fiction* 14 (1977): 151–58. There have been a few short essays concerning James's indebtedness to Browning in specific works. By far the best of these is George Monteiro's "Henry James and the Lessons of *Sordello*," *Western Humanities Review* 31 (Spring 1977): 69–78.

Also note: Michael Ross, "Henry James's 'Half-Man': The Legacy of Browning in 'The Madonna of the Future,' " *Browning Institute Studies* (New York: Browning Institute, 1974), 2:25–42; Mario

D'Avanzo, "James's 'Maud-Evelyn': Source, Allusion, Meaning," *Iowa English Yearbook* 13 (Fall 1968): 24–33; Karen Wadman, "W. W. Story and His Friends: Henry James's Portrait of Robert Browning," *Yearbook of English Studies* 11 (1981): 210–18. General considerations include: Philip Drew, *The Poetry of Browning: A Critical Introduction* (London: Methuen, 1970), pp. 385–96; Barbara Melchiori, *Browning's Poetry of Reticence* (New York: Barnes and Noble, 1968), pp. 190–95; Giorgio Melchiori, "Browning e Henry James," in *Friendship's Garland: Essays Presented to Mario Praz*, ed. V. Gabrieli (Rome: Edizioni di Storia e Letteratura, 1966), pp. 143–80; Hugh Sykes-Davies, *Browning and the Modern Novel* (Hull, England: University of Hull Publications, 1962), pp. 3–27.

CHAPTER I

HENRY JAMES AND THE PROBLEM OF ROBERT BROWNING

1. Harold Bloom, *The Anxiety of Influence* (New York: Oxford University Press, 1973), p. 94.

2. Ibid., p. 11.

3. Jerome McGann, "Formalism, Savagery and Care," *Critical Inquiry* 2 (Spring 1976): 607.

4. John T. Irwin, *Doubling and Incest: Repetition and Revenge* (Baltimore: Johns Hopkins University Press, 1975), p. 158.

5. Harold Bloom, *Poetry and Repression* (New Haven: Yale University Press, 1976), p. 4.

6. Wesley Morris, *Friday's Footprint* (Columbus: Ohio State University Press, 1979), p. 179.

7. Ibid.

8. Bloom, *The Anxiety of Influence*, p. 70.

9. René Girard, *Violence and the Sacred* (Baltimore: Johns Hopkins University Press, 1977), p. 146. Subsequent references are in parentheses in the text.

10. In outlining Girard's belief in the primacy of mimesis a comparison with Bloom suggests itself, since the latter's theory of poetic influence makes mimesis pivotal: "you cannot write or teach or think or even read without imitation, and what you imitate is what another person has done" (*A Map of Misreading* [New York:

Oxford University Press, 1975], p. 32). But Bloom avoids what is, for Girard, the primary mimetic relation—the relation of imitation to sexual behavior. And this relation is also the concern, of course, of the writer to whom Girard must be compared—Freud—since it is his theory of the Oedipal complex which Girard's conception of mimetic desire revises. While I cannot do justice to the subtlety of Girard's "Freud and the Oedipus Complex" (chapter 7 of *Violence and the Sacred*) I will briefly sketch his divergence from Freud. Girard admits that his reinterpretation of Oedipal rivalry "in terms of a radically mimetic situation must logically result in conse-quences that are at once similar to and quite different from those attributed by Freud to his 'complex.' " The difference hinges on the child's degree of conscious awareness of his desire to usurp his father's place with the mother. Girard's mimetic conception of the Oedipal rivalry "detaches desire from any predetermined object, whereas the Oedipus complex fixes desire on the maternal object" (Girard, p. 180). In rejecting Freud's "surely untenable assertion that the child is fully aware of the existing rivalry . . . ," Girard insists that the child's attraction to the mother is "wholly inno-cent," the product of his desire for his father's (the model's) object (Girard, p. 174). In his "unsuspecting innocence" the child, accord-ing to Girard, "fails to see the model as a rival and therefore has no desire to usurp his place." Girard sums up what he finds most objectionable in Freud: his "obstinate attachment . . . to a philoso-phy of consciousness . . . the conscious knowledge of patricidal and incestuous desire" (Girard, pp. 176–77).

11. René Girard, *"To Double Business Bound"* (Baltimore: Johns Hopkins University Press, 1978), pp. 67–68.

12. Ibid., p. 70.

13. Ibid., p. 79.

14. James, *Autobiography*, p. 292. Subsequent references are in parentheses in the text.

15. Leon Edel, *Henry James: The Untried Years* (Philadelphia: Lippincott, 1953), p. 162.

16. Ibid., p. 165.

17. Perry's remark is quoted in Louise Greer, *Browning and America* (Chapel Hill: University of North Carolina Press, 1952), p. 84.

18. In comparing James's unconscious and conscious solutions to the double bind it will be noted that he transmutes the terms in which he conceives of Browning's doubleness. His psychological resolution is based on his initial impression of Browning as a famed lover and poet. In his theory of two Brownings, first sketched in 1877, James repressed his sense of Browning's sexual identity in an effort to relieve this major source of anxiety about the older writer. This aspect of my argument is enlarged in chapter 2's discussion of "The Private Life." This tale dramatizes a return of James's repressed awareness of Browning's sexuality, which produces an uncanny moment.

19. Henry James, *Notes on Novelists* (London: J. M. Dent, 1914), p. 307.

20. Quoted in Maisie Ward, *Two Robert Brownings?* (New York: Holt, Rinehart, 1969), p. 175. Ward quotes from an unpublished James letter.

21. This notion of theatricality as a gap in the self is central to Browning's *In a Balcony* and *The Wings of the Dove*, which is the novelist's "rehandling" of the poet's drama. Chapter 4 examines how James's and Browning's view of the theatrical self has both personal and artistic meanings for them.

22. Chapter 3 concerns, in part, James's confrontation with the most private and most public manifestations of Browning's ambiguity—the double bind and theatricality. The scene of this confrontation is "The Lesson of the Master," where the "bottomless ambiguity" of the Master baffles his disciple.

23. Boyd Litzinger and Donald Smalley, eds., *Robert Browning: The Critical Heritage* (New York: Barnes and Noble, 1970), p. 532.

CHAPTER II

THE SHARP RUPTURE OF AN IDENTITY

1. Edel, *The Conquest of London*, p. 330.

2. Ward, *Two Robert Brownings?* pp. 169–70.

3. Betty Miller, *Robert Browning* (New York: Scribner's, 1953), p. 291.

4. Gosse's entry for Browning in *The Dictionary of National Biography*.

5. B. Miller, *Robert Browning*, p. 228.
6. Ward, *Two Robert Brownings?* p. 170.
7. Ibid., p. 171.
8. Ibid.
9. Erving Goffman, *The Presentation of Self in Everyday Life* (Garden City: Doubleday, 1959), p. 75. Browning was not the only literary figure who disappointed James's notion of how an artist should comport himself in public. Upon hearing Tennyson read, he remarked that the poet "was not Tennysonian." Significantly, however, Tennyson's social behavior never proved a problem to James.
10. Simon Nowell-Smith, *The Legend of the Master* (New York: Scribner's, 1948), p. 10.
11. Ezra Pound's remark is quoted by John Espey in his *Ezra Pound's Mauberly* (Berkeley and Los Angeles: University of California Press, 1955), p. 54.
12. Edel, *The Conquest of London*, p. 330.
13. Peter Keating, "Robert Browning: A Reader's Guide," *Robert Browning*, ed. I. Armstrong (Athens: Ohio University Press, 1975), p. 304.
14. Litzinger and Smalley, *Robert Browning: The Critical Heritage*, p. 530.
15. Henry James, *William Wetmore Story and His Friends*, 2 vols. (Boston: Houghton Mifflin, 1904), 2:88.
16. Ibid., p. 89.
17. Ibid., p. 285.
18. James, *Notes on Novelists*, p. 317.
19. Litzinger and Smalley, *Robert Browning: The Critical Heritage*, p. 532.
20. Ibid., p. 533.
21. Henry James, *The Future of the Novel*, ed. Leon Edel (New York: Vintage, 1956), p. 104.
22. Litzinger and Smalley, *Robert Browning: The Critical Heritage*, p. 533.
23. James, *The Art of the Novel*, p. 250.
24. Henry James, "The Private Life," in vol. 17 of *The Novels and Tales* (New York: Scribner's, 1907–9), p. 217. Subsequent references are in parentheses in the text.

25. Samuel Weber, "The Sideshow, Or: Remarks on a Canny Moment," *MLN*, 88 (1973): 1102–33.

26. Ibid., p. 1131.

27. Ibid., p. 1122.

28. If Vawdrey is not presentable in a social sense, neither is he aesthetically representable. For James believed that the novel could not encompass dramatically "the artist *in triumph.*" Seeking to explain the failure of Nick Dormer, the artist-hero of *The Tragic Muse*, to be "the best thing in the book," James concludes in the preface to the novel that "any presentation of the artist *in triumph* must be flat in proportion as it really sticks to its subject . . . to put the matter in an image, all we then—in his triumph—see of the charm compeller is the back he turns to us as he bends over his work. . . . His triumph . . . is but the triumph of what he produces." James uses the above image strikingly in "The Private Life," as Vawdrey, his back turned to the narrator, toils at his desk.

29. Weber, "The Sideshow," p. 1112. For a shrewd critique of Weber's phrase "negative perception" see Eric Sundquist, *Home as Found* (Baltimore: Johns Hopkins University Press, 1979), p. 109.

30. Leo Bersani, *A Future For Astyanax* (Boston: Little, Brown, 1976), p. 134.

31. Weber, "The Sideshow," p. 1113.

32. T. S. Eliot, *Selected Essays* (New York: Harcourt Press, 1932), p. 125.

33. Ibid.

34. Henry James, *The Notebooks of Henry James*, ed. F. O. Matthiessen and Kenneth Murdock (New York: Oxford University Press, 1947), p. 110.

35. Henry James, *The Ghostly Tales of Henry James*, ed. Leon Edel (New York: Grosset and Dunlap, 1948), p. 211.

36. James, *Notebooks*, p. 110.

37. James, *Ghostly Tales*, p. 211.

38. Blackmur, *A Primer of Ignorance*, p. 194.

39. T. Todorov, *The Poetics of Prose* (Ithaca: Cornell University Press, 1977), p. 182. Shlomith Rimmon affirms this view in *The Concept of Ambiguity—The Example of James* (Chicago: University of Chicago Press, 1977), p. 14.

40. Laurence B. Holland, *The Expense of Vision* (Princeton, 1964; reprint, Baltimore: Johns Hopkins University Press, 1982), p. 183. This phrase describes the narrator of *The Sacred Fount*. A more complex self-parody is a crucial element of "The Lesson of the Master," as discussed in chapter 3.

41. Greer, *Browning and America*, p. 30.

42. Ibid.

43. Ibid., p. 84.

44. Litzinger and Smalley, *Robert Browning: The Critical Heritage*, p. 534.

45. The discovery of the private life of sexuality, as critics have often observed, occurs throughout James's fiction; indeed one could describe the paradigmatic Jamesian plot as the attempt of two lovers to keep their affair hidden from a third person. "The Private Life" presents a variation on the pattern, since the secret affair remains hidden, but the narrator's uncanny experience has all the shock of sudden revelation found in the most famous Jamesian discovery scenes, particularly Strether's traumatic reaction to the exposure of hidden intimacy between Chad and Marie. "The violence of their having 'cut' him" is keenly felt by Strether, and the pun on "cut" reminds us that the shock of sexuality is suffered as a physical assault upon the observer. The castration anxiety bound up in the narrator's uncanny moment is more emphatically suggested in Strether's bruising experience, which begins, as does the narrator's, with a refusal of recognition—Chad and Marie first pretend not to see their friend.

46. Blackmur, *A Primer of Ignorance*, p. 199.

47. It must again be noted that James's image of Browning's sexuality does not accord with more objective views of the subject. Cf. B. Miller's *Robert Browning* for a provocative analysis.

48. James, *Notes on Novelists*, p. 103.

49. Ibid.

50. Ibid., p. 104.

51. Ibid., p. 105.

52. James, *The Future of the Novel*, p. 111.

53. Ibid., p. 124.

54. Ibid., p. 105.

55. Ibid., p. 111.

56. James, *Notes on Novelists*, p. 307.

57. It should be noted that the word "rewriting" is one James carefully avoids, both in his essay on Browning and in his prefaces when he discusses his project of rewriting earlier texts for inclusion in the New York edition. James prefers "revise," "which means in the case of a written thing neither more nor less than to re-read it," as he notes in his final preface. Thus, to be precisely Jamesian in diction, to speak of James as rewriting Browning is to say that he revises or re-reads the poet, since his argument insists that there is an "essential continuity . . . between what are understood as the almost twin processes of reading and revising," to quote Walter Michaels in his interesting discussion of James's strategic avoidance of the word "rewriting." See Walter B. Michaels, "Writers Reading: James and Eliot," *MLN* 91 (1976): 828.

CHAPTER III

THE MOCKING FIEND

1. Henry James, "On a Drama of Mr. Browning," *Views and Reviews*, ed. Leroy Phillips (Boston: Ball Publishing, 1908), p. 42.

2. Ibid.

3. James, *The Art of the Novel*, p. 119.

4. James, "On a Drama of Mr. Browning," p. 47.

5. After completing this chapter I was pleased to discover that George Monteiro also identifies St. George with Browning. See "Henry James and the Lessons of *Sordello*."

6. Robert Browning, *The Inn Album*, vol. 8 of *The Complete Works of Robert Browning*, ed. Charlotte Porter and Helen Clarke (New York: Thomas Y. Crowell, 1878), lines 261, 263.

7. Henry James, "The Lesson of the Master," in vol. 15 of *The Novels and Tales*, p. 18. Subsequent references are in parentheses in the text.

8. James, *The Art of the Novel*, p. 327.

9. See Donadio, *Nietzsche, Henry James, and the Artistic Will*, p. 125.

10. James, *The Art of the Novel*, p. 63.

11. Clyde Ryals, *Browning's Later Poetry* (Ithaca: Cornell University Press, 1975), p. 129.

12. Ashley Bland Crowder, "*The Inn Album:* A Record of 1875," *Browning Institute Studies* (New York: Browning Institute, 1974), 2:43.

13. Stanley Fish, "With the Compliments of the Author: Reflections on Austin and Derrida," *Critical Inquiry* 8 (Summer 1982): 703.

14. Lionel Trilling, *Sincerity and Authenticity* (Cambridge: Harvard University Press, 1972), p. 104.

15. James, *The Art of the Novel*, p. 126.

16. Ibid., p. 297.

17. Ibid. Browning concurs with James's dismissal of perfection; indeed one of his most famous poems concerns the sterility of perfection: "A common grayness silvers everything," says Andrea del Sarto of his painting (indicting his craft with the pun on "common"). "All is silver-gray / Placid and perfect with my art: the worse!"

18. James, "The Novel in *The Ring and the Book*," *Notes on Novelists*, p. 396. Donadio describes the relation of art and reality for James (and Nietzsche): "Art thrives by feeding on all that opposes it; it is strengthened by the opposition of the actual" (*Nietzsche, Henry James, and the Artistic Will*, p. 224).

19. James, *The Scenic Art*, p. 14.

20. Claude Lévi-Strauss, *Tristes Tropiques* (New York: Harper and Row, 1964), pp. 292–93. For a critique of Lévi-Strauss's writing lesson, see Jacques Derrida, *Of Grammatology* (Baltimore: Johns Hopkins University Press, 1976), pp. 104–40.

21. Fish, "Reflections on Austin and Derrida," pp. 700, 705. Fish claims that "face-to-face exchange" provides "no assurance that communication will be certain or even relatively trouble free" (p. 699).

22. The opposition between theatricality and sincerity is a belief shared not only by James's naive characters but by his naive critics. A moralizing devaluation of the theatrical is a misconception found too often in James criticism (see chap. 4, n. 36). To moralize about or ignore theatricality, to limit the self to a single need, be it stability or love, reduces the boldness of James's vision of social life to bland and reassuring dimensions. A recent work—Philip Sicker's *Love and the Quest for Identity in the Fiction of Henry James* (Princeton: Prince-

ton University Press, 1980)—exemplifies this naive view of the Jamesian self. Sicker compounds his misunderstanding of theatricality by his unfortunate reliance on Erik Erikson's ego psychology, with its suspicion of " 'mere roles' played interchangeably . . . mere strenuous 'postures' [which] cannot possibly be the 'real thing' " (p. 52). Although Erikson's devaluation of role playing and his positing of an a priori absolute (something called the "real thing") is blatantly un-Jamesian, Sicker somehow believes that James would have "concurred." For further discussion of the simplifications that hamper Sicker and other James critics, see my "Responsible and Irresponsible Authorship: Recent Henry James Criticism," *Review* 4 (1982): 179–205.

23. Richard Sennett, *The Fall of Public Man* (New York: Vintage, 1977), p. 338.

24. Ibid., p. 315.

25. Henry James, *The Letters of Henry James*, ed. Percy Lubbock, 2 vols. (New York: Scribner's, 1920), 1:72.

26. Rimmon, *The Concept of Ambiguity: The Example of James*, pp. 81, 94.

27. This discussion of James's ambiguity has been influenced by Rachel Salmon's revisionist reading of Rimmon in "A Marriage of Opposites: Henry James's 'The Figure in the Carpet' and the Problem of Ambiguity," *ELH* 47 (1980): 799–800.

28. William DeVane, "The Virgin and the Dragon," *Yale Review* 37 (1947): 34–46. The legend of St. George appears in several places in Browning's poetry, most prominently in *The Ring and the Book*, where St. George's heroics form part of the mythic structure of that work. Caponsacchi is a figure of the mythic rescuer, as he saves the maiden Pompilia from her monstrous husband Guido.

29. Quoted in Ward, *Two Robert Brownings?* pp. 175–76.

30. Leon Edel, *Henry James: The Middle Years, 1884–1894* (Philadelphia: J. B. Lippincott, 1962), p. 275.

31. Charles Feidelson, "Henry James and the 'Man of Imagination,' " in *Language and Structure: Essays in Honor of W. K. Wimsatt*, ed. Frank Brady, John Palmer and Martin Price (New Haven: Yale University Press, 1975), p. 341.

32. James, *The Art of the Novel*, p. 222.

33. Girard, *Violence and the Sacred*, p. 147.

34. Ibid., p. 145. Overt's deepest desire, it would appear, is for St. George. Overt desires Marian because the master does; she possesses St. George and it is he that Overt really wants to possess. Freud and Girard both see the son's desire for the father (the disciple's desire for the master) as potentially making the mother (or object) superfluous.

35. Ibid., p. 177. James indirectly suggests this arbitrary violence in his imagery of the "hunted herd," which reveals, in Overt's mind, a subconscious violence: not only is he hostile toward the herd, but herd implies a group of animals, a random crowd of scapegoats who further stimulate his desire for "revenge." The herd's indifference to him galvanizes Overt's decision to avenge himself by becoming someone to respect—"a wonderfully strong writer."

36. This dual identity of master and disciple is what James celebrates in his 1912 tribute, as he rewrites a Browning text and acknowledges his profound debt to the older writer. The psychological structure of James's ambiguous homage is explored in the Epilogue.

37. In another context, his autobiography, James's choice of celibacy is implicitly presented in a far less anxious light, as a strategic, liberating avoidance of commitment. See chapter 4 for a discussion of this self-characterization and its relation to theatricality.

38. Shoshana Felman, "Turning the Screw of Interpretation," *Yale French Studies* 55–56. (1977): 205.

39. James, *Notebooks*, p. 179.

CHAPTER IV

JAMES, BROWNING, AND THE THEATRICAL SELF

1. James, *Letters* 2:334. Additional confirmation that James often felt the urge to rewrite works he admired comes from his close friend of thirty years, Elizabeth Robins, who baldly stated: "If a book interested him he wanted to rewrite it." Because he was so aware of his susceptibility to other work, James was particularly careful to refrain from reading while his own ideas were germinating. In 1895 he told Robins that he "positively could not . . . read

anything now for the sake of the story." The oddity of James's logic should be noted. His announcement to Robins implies a desire to preserve an absolute originality for his novel; James reasons that because he refuses to read while creating he will be protected from influence. James's statement seems designed to conceal the possibility of literary influence. Robins's remarks are quoted in Michael Egan, *Henry James: The Ibsen Years* (New York: Barnes and Noble, 1972), p. 117.

    2. Ward, *Two Robert Brownings?* p. 175.

    3. James, *Notes on Novelists*, p. 411.

    4. James, *The Art of the Novel*, p. 288.

    5. There are exceptions, of course; Bewley's labored comparison of *The Marble Faun* and James's novel; more recently *Hedda Gabler* has been put forth as a source. See Marius Bewley, *The Complex Fate* (New York: Grove Press, 1954); and Egan, *The Ibsen Years*, pp. 115–48. A recent discussion of the preface's opening is admirable in its attempt to loosen the hold Minny Temple has had on the preface. In the commentary to their critical edition of the novel, Donald Crowley and Richard Hocks suggest a variety of plausible meanings in James's remarks. They correctly argue that "James's conception is indeed a matrix of things at once 'very old' and 'very young.' " Among James's "pressing old memories and associations from his youthful past," the editors cite "his sense of the beginning of his own career as a writer; the influence of Hawthorne; the development of his early literary idiom and method. . . ." Although this interpretation is commendable in its scope of reference, it neglects to probe the implications of its own findings, for Browning is a crucial figure in James's sense of his literary beginnings. See J. Donald Crowley and Richard Hocks, eds., *The Wings of the Dove* (New York: Norton, 1978), p. 439.

    6. Crowley and Hocks, *The Wings of the Dove*, p. 506.

    7. Browning's fondness for the play has not been shared by critics, most of whom have largely neglected the work, perhaps because the great monologues of *Men and Women* have overshadowed *In a Balcony*. E. E. Stoll and Morse Peckham have been among the very few modern critics to have discerned the work's importance. See E. E. Stoll, "Browning's *In a Balcony*," *Modern*

Language Quarterly 3 (1942): 407–17; and Morse Peckham, *Beyond the Tragic Vision* (New York: George Braziller, 1962), p. 275. Peckham provides only a brief assessment of the play. In his *Victorian Revolutionaries* (New York: George Braziller, 1970) Peckham makes equally brief but suggestive remarks.

8. B. Miller, *Robert Browning*, p. 54.

9. Jonas Barish, *The Antitheatrical Prejudice* (Berkeley and Los Angeles: University of California Press, 1981), p. 350.

10. James, *Letters*, 1:226.

11. B. Miller, *Robert Browning*, p. 25.

12. James, *Letters*, 1:228.

13. Ibid.

14. Litzinger and Smalley, *Robert Browning: The Critical Heritage*, p. 151.

15. James, *The Scenic Art*, p. 250.

16. Litzinger and Smalley, *Robert Browning: The Critical Heritage*, p. 394.

17. Robert Browning, *In a Balcony*, vol. 4 of *The Works of Robert Browning*, ed. F. G. Kenyon (London: Smith and Elder, 1912), lines 79–83. Subsequent references are in parentheses in the text.

18. Goffman, *The Presentation of Self in Everyday Life*, p. 72.

19. James, *The Art of the Novel*, p. 106.

20. Stoll, "Browning's *In a Balcony*," p. 416.

21. James, *The Art of the Novel*, p. 115.

22. Ibid., p. 114.

23. Ibid., p. 111.

24. Ibid., p. 111.

25. James, *The Wings of the Dove*, vols. 19–20 of *The Novels and Tales*, 2:180. Subsequent references in the text.

26. Henry James, *The Tragic Muse*, vols. 7–8 of *The Novels and Tales*, 2:210. In *The Tragic Muse*, James's most sustained exploration of the theatrical self, Peter's relation to Miriam recalls the conflicts in the two works under discussion. Like Densher and Norbert, Peter is attempting to force an inveterate performer off the stage (in this case literally so) to exist in the private realm of marriage.

27. Image making is, of course, habitual to the human mind in

its effort to order experience. In writing of Gombrich's theory of the psychology of perception, one critic has spoken of our "natural tendency to read things into what we see, to interpret any shape as an image of something else." In *The Wings of the Dove* this "natural tendency" for image making acquires moral and aesthetic significance.

28. James, *The Art of the Novel*, p. 327.

29. James, *Autobiography*, pp. 94–95.

30. The association of the theatrical with movement and the antitheatrical with immobility and stasis is a traditional dichotomy beginning with Plato and evident in Rousseau and many others. See Barish, *The Antitheatrical Prejudice*, p. 288.

31. Too often Milly's theatricality is slighted by critics in an effort to maintain a valid but superficial dichotomy between Kate the performer and Milly the doomed innocent. Even as acute a critic as Leo Bersani enforces this dichotomy when he writes of Milly (in company with Maggie Verver and Fanny Price) that she has "no talent for representing the self in the world." See *A Future for Astyanax*, p. 81.

32. James, *The Tragic Muse*, 1:173.

33. My rhetoric here is borrowed from Lacan by way of Fredric Jameson's discussion of the alienating effect of the Symbolic Order in "Imaginary and Symbolic in Lacan," *Yale French Studies* 55–56 (1977): 363. It should be noted that this primal "substitution" not only originates language and theatricality but also desire, which is a gap "introduced into being by language itself," according to Lacan. Only with language can need be translated into demand, and this act of translation or substitution is the origin of desire. Analogous to this inaugurating act of "substitution" is art itself which, for James, originates as "the artist's . . . actual substitute" for his "prime object" or "original design."

34. Dorothea Krook, *The Ordeal of Consciousness in Henry James* (Cambridge: Cambridge University Press, 1962), p. 215.

35. The remark is Arthur Symons's; quoted in Stoll, "Browning's *In a Balcony*."

36. Crowley and Hocks, *The Wings of the Dove*, p. 553. Sears's view is echoed in Nicola Bradbury's *Henry James: The Later Nov-*

els (New York: Oxford University Press, 1979). Bradbury makes correct but broad and unfocused remarks concerning Kate's "manipulative vigour" (p. 121) and the "myth-making process" and "manipulative categorization of other people" in the novel (p. 86) and ignores James's participation.

37. James, *The Art of the Novel*, p. 302. James's complicity with his characters, and the fusion of moral and formal problems this creates, figures prominently in Laurence Holland's seminal *The Expense of Vision*. The present analysis of this aspect of *The Wings of the Dove* is indebted to Holland.

38. For a view of Densher directly opposing the one argued here see Robert Caserio, *Plot, Story and the Novel* (Princeton: Princeton University Press, 1979), pp. 198–212; this is a provocative if unconvincing reading. It should be noted here that *In a Balcony* is not the only Browning text to leave a mark on *The Wings of the Dove*. As James's 1912 homage obliquely reveals, Densher is partly modeled on the priest Caponsacchi, who in *The Ring and the Book* also resolves to exile himself from worldly matters and devote himself to the silent worship of the memory of a doomed and angelic young woman. This parallel is discussed in the Epilogue.

39. The presence of God in *In a Balcony* as the absolute and original source of meaning makes his absence twenty years later in *The Inn Album* all the more conspicuous. The distinguishing mark of some of Browning's late works (post–*The Ring and the Book*) is the depiction of a decentered universe where the transcendent and redemptive love that is expressed in the final moments of *In a Balcony* (and works of the early and middle Browning) is desperately yearned for but impossible to achieve.

40. R. W. B. Lewis, *The Trials of the Word* (New Haven: Yale University Press, 1964), pp. 113, 123. More recently, John Goode has argued for a religious interpretation. See his " 'The Pervasive Mystery of Style': *The Wings of the Dove*," in *The Air of Reality: New Essays on Henry James*, ed. John Goode (London: Methuen, 1972), pp. 244–300.

41. James, *The Art of the Novel*, pp. 4, 213-14.

42. James, "The Art of Fiction" in *The Art of the Novel*, p. 5.

43. James, *The Art of the Novel*, pp. 213–14.

44. Herbert Tucker, in his penetrating study of Browning, also emphasizes Browning's incomplete and imperfect poetic forms. In his belief that "Browning's moral doctrine of incompleteness finds a clear aesthetic analogue in his poetics," Tucker stresses the poet's strategies of deferment. While agreeing with Tucker's view of the importance of deferral in Browning's art, I view deferral as also reflecting the poet's preoccupation with the theatrical self, which is necessarily unstable and deferring. See *Browning's Begin nings* (Minneapolis: University of Minnesota Press, 1980), p. 5. Chapter 5 of the present study expands on James's and Browning's conception of form as process.

My argument that the representation of the theatrical self in these texts creates gaps and "missing links" raises an issue concerning James that should be noted here. To focus on the "deformities" in James's work runs counter to the still prevalent belief that his prefaces and fiction celebrate the novel as the prc-eminently unified and centered art form, grounded in the stability of a central reflector's point of view. This familiar view presents at best a partial truth, one that ignores a crucial drama enacted throughout the prefaces and fiction: James's soliciting of conflict and "convulsions" that disrupt, even mock, his "original design" of unity. In great works, he says, we take pleasure in feeling "the surface . . . bear without cracking the strongest pressure we throw upon it" (*The Art of the Novel*, p. 304). The renowned advocate of the economy and order of organic form also insists that the novel appears "more true to its character in proportion as it strains, or tends to burst, with a latent extravagance, its mould" (*The Art of the Novel*, p. 46). Some of the pressures and strains James cultivates are embodied in the theatrical self—a mode of being that resists unity and full presence in a culture that valorizes these qualities. And as theatricality has tended to be neglected in James studies, so has the dialectical complexity of James's art of fiction. As David Carroll has recently demonstrated in an important discussion: "Formalist purifications of James . . . simplify the very concept of form in whose name they pretend to speak." Carroll shows that what makes James's prefaces interesting is the novelist's refusal to resolve contradiction and his stress, in Carroll's words, both on unity and "the complex conditions dividing, interfering with, and complicating that unity." See David Carroll, *The Subject in Question: The Languages of Theory and the Strategies of Fiction* (Chicago: University of Chicago Press, 1982), pp. 51–66.

45. A number of critics have remarked on the role of the reader in *The Wings of the Dove*. Most recent is William W. Stowe in *Balzac, James, and the Realistic Novel* (Princeton: Princeton University Press, 1983), pp. 143–70.

46. Bersani, *A Future for Astyanax*, pp. 55–56.

47. J. H. Miller, *The Disappearance of God*, p. 105.

48. Quoted in B. Miller, *Robert Browning*, p. 261.

49. Browning, *Prince Hohensteil-Schwangau, Saviour of Society*, in vol. 7 of *The Works of Robert Browning*, lines 2078–79.

50. Quoted in William Irvine and Park Honan, *The Book, The Ring, and The Poet* (New York: McGraw-Hill, 1974), p. 32.

51. James has been described in a similar way, as possessing "a kind of identity in his very lack of identity." See Daniel Schneider, *The Crystal Cage* (Lawrence: Regents Press of Kansas, 1978), p. 26.

52. James, *Autobiography*, p. 509.

53. Ibid.

54. Theodor Adorno, "Commitment," in *Aesthetics and Politics* (London: New Left, 1977), p. 189.

55. James, *The Art of the Novel*, p. 313; James, *Notes on Novelists*, p. 406.

CHAPTER V

THE PRECIOUS EFFECT OF PERSPECTIVE

1. Wilde's remark is reprinted in *Robert Browning's Poetry*, ed. J. F. Loucks (New York: W. W. Norton, 1979), p. 481.

2. Hopkins's remark is reprinted in Loucks, *Robert Browning's Poetry*, p. 480.

3. Swinburne's remark is quoted in Roy E. Gridley, *Browning* (London: Routledge and Kegan Paul, 1972), p. 62.

4. Henry James, *Notes on Novelists*, p. 398. Additional references to the homage are in parentheses in the text.

5. James, *The Art of the Novel*, p. 67.

6. Ibid., p. 66.

7. Donadio, *Nietzsche, James, and the Artistic Will*, p. 135.

8. James, *Letters*, 2:335.

9. Krook, *The Ordeal of Consciousness in Henry James*, pp. 401, 399.

10. Jose Ortega y Gasset, *The Modern Theme* (New York: W. W. Norton, 1933), pp. 141–42.

11. Ibid., p. 142.

12. Ibid., p. 141.

13. Ibid., p. 143.

14. Robert Langbaum, Preface, in *The Poetry of Experience* (New York: W. W. Norton, 1971).

15. Ortega, *The Modern Theme*, pp. 91, 90.

16. See, for instance, Langbaum, *The Poetry of Experience*, p. 226. Recently Dorrit Cohn has supplied another view of the dramatic monologue's relation to prose fiction: "The presence of a fictive speaker relates the dramatic monologue not only to the soliloquy in drama, but also to fictive narrative in the first-person. . . . All dramatic monologues are first-person narratives in verse form." Oddly enough, this sensible, even obvious connection between the genres has been, according to Cohn, "largely disregarded . . . perhaps because of the 'dramatic' emphasis of the English term." Swinburne's remark quoted at the opening of the chapter, in its insistence on the unpoetic "realism" of the dramatic monologue, suggests something of the relationship Cohn perceives. Dorrit Cohn, *Transparent Minds* (Princeton: Princeton University Press, 1978), p. 257.

17. G. K. Chesterton, *Robert Browning* (New York: Macmillan, 1903), p. 173.

18. Barbara B. Melchiori, *Browning's Poetry of Reticence*, p. 193.

19. Not only does Barbara Melchiori ignore "The Novel in *The Ring and the Book*," but so does Giorgio Melchiori in "Browning e James," in *Friendship's Garland: Essays Presented to Mario Praz*. Though Hugh Sykes-Davies in *Browning and the Modern Novel* quotes from the essay, he does little analysis of it.

20. James's charge that the poem is a "great loose and uncontrolled composition," less an "achieved form" than a "mere preparation for one," soon became an influential judgment that the poem's modern defenders are still attempting to overturn. See Donald Hair, *Browning's Experiments with Genre* (Toronto: University

of Toronto Press, 1972), and Richard Altick and James Loucks, *Browning's Roman Murder Story* (Chicago: University of Chicago Press, 1968).

21. Drew, *The Poetry of Browning*, p. 392.

22. John Killham, "Browning's Modernity: *The Ring and the Book* and Relativism," *The Major Victorian Poets*, ed. I. Armstrong (Lincoln: University of Nebraska Press, 1969), p. 169.

23. Browning, *The Ring and the Book*, vols. 5–6 of *The Works of Robert Browning*, book 1, line 1348.

24. Ibid., book 1, lines 1349–52.

25. Altick and Loucks, *Browning's Roman Murder Story*, p. 34.

26. Browning, *The Ring and the Book*, vols. 5–6 of *The Works of Robert Browning*, book 1, lines 1360–66. In his valuable essay on Browning and William James, E. D. H. Johnson states that Browning "fully subscribed" to the philosopher's pluralism, and *The Ring and the Book* "most comprehensively exhibits" the poet as Jamesian pluralist: one who replaces "the ideal demand for absolutes with a commonsense acceptance of the actual in all its multiplicity and heterogeneity." However, Browning's pluralistic universe, Johnson rightly insists, remains God-centered: "It is a world in which God relies on human assistance for the fulfillment of his intent . . . the progressive revelation of Truth." As is well known, Henry James shares his brother's (and Browning's) pluralism, but in a more secularized version. Johnson's essay "Robert Browning's Pluralistic Universe: A Reading of *The Ring and the Book*" is reprinted in *Robert Browning's Poetry*, ed. James F. Loucks (New York: Norton, 1979).

27. Published in John Ruskin, *The Works of John Ruskin*, ed. E. T. Cook and Alexander Wedderburn (London: Allen, 1909), 36:xxxiv.

28. James, *The Art of the Novel*, pp. 265, 308.

29. James, *The Art of the Novel*, p. 265. Recently Martha C. Nussbaum has situated in a new context what she calls James's emphasis on "improvisatory response" and the "adventure of the reader." In *The Golden Bowl* the density of late Jamesian style produces, she argues, a "Socratic working-through" of one's "moral intuitions" to clarify "moral aims." Thus the adventure of reading the novel "involves valuable aspects of human moral experience

that are not tapped by traditional books of moral philosophy," which seek to extricate us from the bewilderment James cultivates. See her "Flawed Crystals: James's *The Golden Bowl* and Literature as Moral Philosophy," *New Literary History* 15 (Autumn 1983): 25–47.

30. Herbert Tucker, *Browning's Beginnings*, p. 12.

31. James, *The Art of the Novel*, pp. 4–5.

32. Ibid., p. 16.

33. Ibid., p. 63.

34. Jose Ortega y Gasset, *The Dehumanization of Art* (Princeton: Princeton University Press, 1968), p. 81.

35. Ibid., pp. 35–36.

36. Ibid., p. 101.

37. James, *The Art of the Novel*, p. 67.

38. Ibid., p. 66. In this context Browning's statement in his original preface to *Paracelsus* takes on a strikingly Jamesian cast: "Instead of having recourse to an external machinery of incident to create and evolve the crisis I desire to produce, I have ventured to display somewhat minutely the mood itself in its rise and progress." In its emphasis on crisis, process, inner feeling ("mood"), and magnification, this statement encapsulates Browning's and James's shared aesthetic aims.

39. Holland, *The Expense of Vision*, p. 163.

40. James's letter to Stedman is quoted in L. Stedman and G. Gould, *The Life and Letters of E. C. Stedman*, (New York: Moffat, Yard), 2:65. I wish to thank Robert Scholnick for bringing this letter to my attention.

41. Litzinger and Smalley, *Robert Browning: The Critical Heritage*, p. 396.

42. Samuel Southwell, *Quest for Eros: Browning and Fifine* (Lexington: University of Kentucky Press, 1980), pp. 1, 3. Pearson's phrase is the title of his essay on *The Golden Bowl*, in Goode, *The Air of Reality: New Essays on Henry James.*

43. E. D. H. Johnson, *The Alien Vision* (Princeton: Princeton University Press, 1952), p. 138.

44. Henry James, *The Golden Bowl*, vols. 23–24 of *The Novels and Tales*, 1:3. References in the text are to this edition.

45. Browning, *Fifine at the Fair*, vol. 9 of *The Complete Works*

of Robert Browning, section 6. Further citations of section numbers are in the text.

46. Carolyn Porter, *Seeing and Being* (Middletown, Conn.: Wesleyan University Press, 1981), p. 148.

47. Ryals, *Browning's Later Poetry*, p. 60.

48. Cohn, *Transparent Minds*, p. 225.

49. J. H. Miller, *The Disappearance of God*, p. 127.

50. The indeterminacy of reality and character in *Fifine* frustrates efforts to designate precisely its genre. In calling it a version of an interior monologue, as compared to the dramatic monologue, I hope to preserve its more private and internal stance. Surprisingly, Southwell shows little concern to attempt a precise generic description of *Fifine*. While correctly noting that "the discursive spirit of the dramatic monologue is overwhelmed in an efflorescence of symbolism," Southwell mistakenly insists on labeling it a dramatic monologue.

51. Southwell, *Quest for Eros: Browning and Fifine*, p. 35.

52. Richard Poirier, *A World Elsewhere* (London: Chatto and Windus, 1967), p. 20.

53. Cohn, *Transparent Minds*, p. 15.

54. Cohn uses this term to replace the more familiar "free indirect style." However, on Roger Fowler's terms (in *Linguistics and the Novel*) there are stylistic criteria for free indirect style which *The Golden Bowl* doesn't meet, namely the "combination of a past-tense verb with a present-tense adverb," which Fowler calls the "distinctive feature" of the technique. Nonetheless, I find Cohn's term and her conception useful in discussing James's novel and therefore will employ it, while aware that it is perhaps less precise than Fowler's definition (Roger Fowler, *Linguistics and the Novel* [London: Methuen, 1977], p. 102). "Narrated monologue" has the additional advantage of more clearly suggesting its relation to the dramatic and interior monologue.

55. Cohn, *Transparent Minds*, p. 105.

56. Ibid. Ann Banfield offers a critique of what she calls Cohn's "dual voice" theory of narrated monologue in her concept of the "narratorless" model of "represented minds." See chapter 5 of Banfield, *Unspeakable Sentences* (Boston: Routledge, 1982), esp. p. 211.

57. James, *The Art of the Novel*, p. 16.

58. Ibid., p. 57.

59. Ibid., p. 328.

60. Ibid., p. 329.

61. Ibid., p. 331.

62. Ibid., p. 330.

63. Ruth Yeazell, *Language and Knowledge in the Late Novels of Henry James* (Chicago: University of Chicago Press, 1976), pp. 2, 71, 73.

64. James, *The Art of the Novel*, p. 332.

65. Stephen Greenblatt, "Invisible Bullets: Renaissance Authority and Its Subversion," *Glyph* 8 (1981): 56.

66. The passivity of Maggie's authority recalls the Jamesian dialectic in which master and dupe are entangled, and her stance has some resemblance also to James's characterization of himself as appearing to the world, when young, as a "fool," so absorbed was he in inwardly appropriating experience.

67. In one of the best recent discussions of the novel, Ruth Yeazell notes that though Maggie's half causes us to identify with her "intensely," "yet we may also find our very confinement [to her viewpoint] stifling." We are left, she says, "curiously like the baffled Prince" (p. 125). Yeazell also rightly insists on Maggie's hypocrisy and lies, her "impenetrably ambiguous" moral status (p. 124). See Yeazell, *Language and Knowledge in the Late Novels of Henry James*.

68. Langbaum, *The Poetry of Experience*, p. 137.

69. Cohn, *Transparent Minds*, p. 245.

70. J. H. Miller, *The Disappearance of God*, p. 103.

71. Interestingly, the critical response to *Fifine* often centers on a biographical approach that sees Browning sexually restless after the death of his wife, and suffering with guilt from his rash marriage proposal to Lady Ashburton in 1869. My statement equating Juan and Browning does not, however, imply this biographical link. Though fascinating, it is beyond my scope here.

72. James, *The Art of the Novel*, p. 328.

73. Ryals, *Browning's Later Poetry*, p. 75.

74. Feidelson, "Henry James and the 'Man of Imagination,' " p. 345.

75. James, *The Art of the Novel*, p. 328.

76. Matthew Arnold, "Preface to *Poems*, Edition of 1853," in *The Portable Matthew Arnold*, ed. Lionel Trilling (New York: Viking Press, 1949), p. 185.

77. Ibid., p. 204.

78. Ibid., p. 620.

79. Litzinger and Smalley, *Robert Browning: The Critical Heritage*, p. 377.

80. Arnold, *The Portable Matthew Arnold*, p. 190.

81. From "The Scholar Gypsy," in Arnold, *The Portable Matthew Arnold*, p. 147.

82. Matthew Arnold, *Matthew Arnold: Poetry and Prose*, ed. John Bryson (Cambridge: Harvard University Press, 1954), p. 270.

83. See, for instance, *Aspects of Sociology*, The Frankfurt Institute (Boston: Beacon Press, 1972), pp. 45–48. Chapter 3 of Engels's *The Condition of the Working Class in England* (1845) remains the locus classicus for a description of modern urban alienation: "This isolation of the individual . . . is everywhere the fundamental principle of modern society. But nowhere is this selfish egotism so blatantly evident as in the frantic bustle of the great city." It should be pointed out that this condition of bourgeois isolation is also evident in the pre-industrial commercial society of Renaissance Italy, as Alfred Von Martin has shown in *The Sociology of the Renaissance*. In short, as capitalism expands, subjectivity and isolation become more extreme and pervasive versions of trends first evident in the bourgeois humanist society of Italy and elsewhere.

84. Fredric Jameson, *Marxism and Form* (Princeton: Princeton University Press, 1974), p. 357.

85. Roger Gard, ed., *Henry James: The Critical Heritage* (New York: Barnes and Noble, 1968), p. 87. James's remarks are in an 1881 letter. My argument concerning the relation of social alienation and theatricality in James implicitly takes issue with Fredric Jameson's provocative remarks on the extent to which the Jamesian invention of point of view is also "part and parcel of a whole ideology" of the self—"the fiction of the individual subject—so-called bourgeois individualism." "As this fiction becomes ever more difficult to sustain . . . more desperate myths of the self are generated. . . . Jamesian point of view, which comes into being as a

protest and a defense against reification, ends up furnishing a powerful ideological instrument in the perpetuation of an increasingly subjectivized and psychologized world, a world whose social vision is one of a thoroughgoing relativity of monads." There are many things to quarrel with in Jameson's scenario, and space forbids a thorough discussion. Suffice it to say that by simplifying James's relation to reification Jameson ends up with the wholly unconvincing image of James the celebrant of bourgeois individualism. James defends the self against reification not, as Jameson would have it, by fleeing to the "desperate myth" of a privatized subject, but by showing the self at once accepting reification and resisting it. I have called this dialectical movement of the self theatricality and it is this mode of being, so prominent in James, as we have seen, that Jameson wholly ignores. His scenario is structured by polarities: the "fiction of the individual subject" versus the reified subject. The potent middle term between these poles, and energized by interplay with both of them, is the theatrical self—celebrating its ambiguity as neither wholly subject nor wholly object. Jameson's remarks are in *The Political Unconscious* (Ithaca: Cornell University Press, 1981), pp. 221–22.

86. Gard, p. 381.

87. Irvine and Honan, *The Book, The Ring, and The Poet*, p. 504.

88. Quoted by Irvine and Honan, *The Book, The Ring, and The Poet*, p. 502. James, in his Westminster Abbey tribute, spoke of the poet's "victimization by societies organized to talk about him."

89. From "At the 'Mermaid' " (1876), in vol. 9 of Browning, *The Complete Works*.

90. James, *The Scenic Art*, p. 232.

91. Theodor Adorno, "Reconciliation Under Duress," in *Aesthetics and Politics* (London: New Left, 1977), p. 158.

92. Gard, *Henry James: The Critical Heritage*, p. 324. James's remarks are in a 1902 letter.

93. Ibid., p. 194.

94. Stephen Toulmin, "The Inwardness of Mental Life," *Critical Inquiry* 5 (Autumn 1979): 13.

95. Ibid., p. 5.

96. Ibid.

97. James, *The Future of the Novel*, p. 4.

98. Henry James, *Stories of Writers and Artists*, edited, with an introduction, by F. O. Matthiessen (Norfolk, Conn.: New Directions, 1944), p. 7.

99. Heinz Kohut, Christopher Lasch, and Richard Sennett have all been exploring this split's contemporary manifestations in the narcissistic personality.

100. In recent years there has been a salutary effort to "break the seal of historical solipsism and idiosyncrasy surrounding James," in the words of Jean-Christophe Agnew. See, for instance, Agnew's "The Consuming Vision of Henry James," in *The Culture of Consumption*, ed. Jackson Lears and Richard Fox (New York: Pantheon, 1983), pp. 67–100; William Greenslade's "The Power of Advertising: Chad Newsome and the Meaning of Paris in *The Ambassadors*," *ELH* 49 (Spring 1982): 99–123. These essays conclusively demonstrate James's deep involvement in the social and cultural upheavals of the late nineteenth century, particularly the rise of an advertising and consumer culture. In her book *Seeing and Being*, Carolyn Porter presents an interesting reading of *The Golden Bowl* through a Marxist framework—specifically Lukács's conception of reification.

101. Adorno, "Reconciliation Under Duress," p. 166.

102. Gard, *Henry James: The Critical Heritage*, p. 318.

EPILOGUE

JAMES'S FINAL APPROPRIATION OF BROWNING

1. Leon Edel, *Henry James: The Master, 1901–1916* (Philadelphia: Lippincott, 1972), p. 465.

2. Part of this pressure, as was suggested at the end of chapter 4, may have been derived from guilt for having used the poet for his own artistic purposes. In paying tribute James atoned.

3. James, *Autobiography*, pp. 8, 291. The first phrase concerns Henry's relation to William, the second to John La Farge.

4. James, *Letters*, 2:235.

5. James, *Notes on Novelists*, p. 409. Further references to the homage are in parentheses in the text.

6. Edel, *The Master, 1901–1916*, p. 467.

7. Litzinger and Smalley, *Robert Browning: The Critical Heritage*, p. 533.

8. While Browning acquired the status of a sexual authority after James's discovery of *Men and Women* at the age of sixteen, at twenty-five James's sense of this authority was doubtless deepened by his exposure to the sexual combat depicted in *The Ring and the Book*. When the subject of sexual manipulation is again dramatized in *The Inn Album*, the poet's expertise is probably confirmed for James. Thus when the two writers first meet in the winter of 1876–77 (James reviewed *The Inn Album* in January in 1876), James's image of Browning as a sexual authority is more vivid and disturbing than ever. And this awareness may have helped prompt in James the fears and envies that we have seen characterize his relation to Browning.

9. The violence of the homage results from the loss of differences James's appropriation engenders. This blurring of distinctions, wherein James comes to resemble Browning, Guido, and Caponsacchi during the course of the homage, is analogous to what Girard calls the "sacrificial crisis." This is a "crisis of distinctions" disrupting the "cultural order," which is defined as "nothing more than a regulated system of distinctions in which differences among individuals are used to establish their 'identity' and their mutual relationships." Another instance in the homage where a loss of difference leads to violence (which always occurs in a "sacrificial crisis") or near violence, is James's metaphor depicting Browning on the novelists' side of the street. In crossing over generic boundaries Browning erases the mark of differentiation and nearly collides with the startled novelist.

10. Browning, *The Ring and the Book*, vols. 5–6 of *The Works of Robert Browning*, book 1, lines 1042–48. Further references are in parentheses in the text.

11. Litzinger and Smalley, *Robert Browning: The Critical Heritage*, pp. 531, 532.

12. James, *The Art of the Novel*, p. 64.

✤ INDEX ✤